D1536172

The Executive Guide to Improvement and Change

Also available from ASQ Quality Press:

The Quality Improvement Handbook
John E. Bauer, Grace L. Duffy, and Russell T. Westcott

The Certified Quality Manager Handbook, Second Edition
Duke Okes and Russell T. Westcott, editors

Principles of Quality Costs: Principles, Implementation, and Use, Third Edition
Jack Campanella, editor

The Change Agent's Guide to Radical Improvement
Ken Miller

From Quality to Business Excellence: A Systems Approach to Management
Charles Cobb

The Change Agents' Handbook: A Survival Guide for Quality Improvement Champions
David W. Hutton

Managing Change: Practical Strategies for Competitive Advantage
Kari Tuominen

Principles and Practices of Organizational Performance Excellence
Thomas J. Cartin

Customer Centered Six Sigma: Linking Customers, Process Improvement, and Financial Results
Earl Naumann and Steven H. Hoisington

ISO 9001:2000 for Small and Medium Sized Businesses
Herbert C. Monnich, Jr.

To request a complimentary catalog of ASQ Quality Press publications, call 800-248-1946, or visit our Web site at http://qualitypress.asq.org .

The Executive Guide to Improvement and Change

G. Dennis Beecroft, Grace L. Duffy,
and John W. Moran

ASQ Quality Press
Milwaukee, Wisconsin

The Executive Guide to Improvement and Change
G. Dennis Beecroft, Grace L. Duffy, and John W. Moran

Library of Congress Cataloging-in-Publication Data

Beecroft, G. Dennis, 1944–
   The executive guide to improvement and change / G. Dennis Beecroft,
Grace L. Duffy, and John W. Moran.
      p. cm.
   Includes bibliographical references and index.
   ISBN 0-87389-579-7 (Hard cover, case binding : alk. paper)
   1. Organizational change. I. Duffy, Grace L. II. Moran, John W.,
1944– III. Title.

   HD58.8.B433 2003
   658.4'06—dc21   2003001445

10 9 8 7 6 5 4 3 2 1

ISBN 0-87389-579-7

Publisher: William A. Tony
Acquisitions Editor: Annemieke Koudstaal
Project Editor: Paul O'Mara
Production Administrator: Gretchen Trautman
Special Marketing Representative: Robin Barry

ASQ Mission: The American Society for Quality advances individual, organizational, and
community excellence worldwide through learning,
quality improvement, and knowledge exchange.

Attention Bookstores, Wholesalers, Schools, and Corporations: ASQ Quality
Press books, videotapes, audiotapes, and software are available at quantity discounts with bulk
purchases for business, educational, or instructional use.
For information, please contact ASQ Quality Press at 800-248-1946, or write to ASQ Quality
Press, P.O. Box 3005, Milwaukee, WI 53201-3005.

To place orders or to request a free copy of the ASQ Quality Press Publications Catalog, including
ASQ membership information, call 800-248-1946. Visit our Web site at www.asq.org or
http://qualitypress.asq.org .

Printed in the United States of America

 Printed on acid-free paper

American Society for Quality

Quality Press
600 N. Plankinton Avenue
Milwaukee, Wisconsin 53203
Call toll free 800-248-1946
Fax 414-272-1734
www.asq.org
http://qualitypress.asq.org
http://standardsgroup.asq.org
E-mail: authors@asq.org

To my wife Mary Louise, and sons Michael and Douglas, who have always supported and continue to support me in all my ventures.
—G. Dennis Beecroft

To my husband, John G. Duffy, and to Dr. Mary Thornley, President of Trident Technical College, who supported my intense desire to learn.
—Grace L. Duffy

To my family, and all those improvement teams I have worked with over the years that have contributed greatly to my knowledge of how to do organizational improvement successfully.
—John W. Moran

Table of Contents

Foreword xi

Preface xiii

Introduction: Notes to the Reader xv

I Initiating Change 1

Chapter 1   The Challenge of Successful and Sustainable
Organizational Change 3
John W. Moran and Jeffry M. Mead

Chapter 2   Problem Solving and Decision Making for
Continuous Improvement 17
Grace L. Duffy

Chapter 3   Quality Costs 31
G. Dennis Beecroft

Chapter 4   Supply Chain Management 39
Mike H. Ensby

II Paths to Implementation 53

Chapter 5   Corporate Planning Models 55
G. Dennis Beecroft

Chapter 6   Core Process Redesign and Management 67
Richard A. Waks and John W. Moran

Chapter 7   Using Teams to Achieve Organizational Improvement 81
Grace L. Duffy

**Chapter 8   The Management and Utilization of External Resources
in the Workplace** **95**
Jeffry M. Mead, John W. Moran, and John W. Moran III

Chapter 9   Quality Management Systems **111**
G. Dennis Beecroft

Chapter 10   Environmental Management Systems **123**
R. J. Garrison

Chapter 11   Lean Enterprise **129**
George Alukal and Anthony Manos

III   Measuring and Evaluating Improvement **145**

**Chapter 12   Customer Satisfaction As a Driver for Improvement
and Change** **147**
Grace L. Duffy

Chapter 13   Performance Enhancement through Management Audits . . .   **161**
Terry L. Regel

Chapter 14   Measurement—The Balanced Scorecard **179**
Kevin Sharlow

Chapter 15   Six Sigma **195**
Michael D. Nichols and Richard D. Collins

Chapter 16   How to Get Results: Setting Goals and Hitting Targets **207**
Mary Thornley

IV   Appendixes **213**

Appendix A   Audit-Related Certifications **215**

Appendix B   ASQ Quality Awards Listing 2002 . . . .   **229**

About the Authors **243**

Index . . . .

Foreword

What this world needs is more "how to" books. As an executive, I would love to have a cookbook that I could open and select just the right recipe for leadership, change, problem solving, or employee motivation. As a realist, I know that isn't going to happen. *The Executive Guide to Improvement and Change* comes pretty close, however. And, it comes at a time when I am working on exactly the challenges this book addresses.

The president of ASQ gave me a mandate in May 2002 to broaden our society's appeal to executive and senior management. Some of the phrases in that mandate are:

Increase the rate of strategic progress

Shorten the change cycle

Stimulate innovation

Develop leadership

Improve relations

As a fellow of the American Society of Association Executives, I am well versed in the concepts of management and leadership. The increased focus on leadership outside the traditional bounds of ASQ is an enjoyable challenge and one that serves the future of quality and performance excellence well.

One of the major topics of business literature now is "improvement and change." How do we anticipate it? How do we plan for it? How do we implement it and get employee participation? How do we keep riding the leading wave of change? These questions are the grist of many news channel talk shows. The need for innovation is clear, as competition intensifies for new technologies, scarce resources, and broader markets.

These challenges are not new to executives. The pace with which we are bombarded by these challenges is. Managers do not have the time to sit in a quiet office and consider multiple alternatives. We must elicit ideas from those around us, generate options, and drive the best opportunity forward to success. We need executive tools to assist us in executive decisions. We need a fast and reliable source of techniques for success.

Little in the executive world is simple. The higher we go in the organization, the more complex our challenges become. Nothing comes in a box for us to add water and stir. There are those, however, who have been successful and who are willing to share their success. The messages in *The Executive Guide to Improvement and Change* are from executives and senior leaders who have successfully applied what they are sharing with us in the pages of this book.

Change happens with or without us. Improvement is something we can lead, and lead successfully.

Paul E. Borawski, CAE
Executive Director
American Society for Quality

Preface

The *Executive Guide to Improvement and Change* is designed to help managers and executives understand the many approaches available today to assist in improvement of their organizations. This is a book to assist executives and senior management in leading improvement and change initiatives within their organization and the larger business community. The book will also help educate those who aspire to senior positions of leadership.

The Quality Management Division of the American Society of Quality has sponsored the development of this book. The Quality Management Division has sponsored many books over the years to help managers and executives improve not only their organizations but their professional development as well.

This book is written by professionals with many years of direct, hands on experience in change and improvement techniques and/or many years of consulting experience. The authors have made improvements and change in many different types of organizations from healthcare, to manufacturing, to service, to telecommunications, to government, to academic institutions.

There are many techniques and tools available to improve or change an organization. These tools and techniques can be combined in different forms and shapes to provide an improvement or change process. Many of the chapters contain models that can be combined with techniques from other chapters to form such processes.

It is up to you, the manager and executive, to blend the approach that will work best for your organization and its culture. One technique that was successful at company X may be a total failure at company Y. Real improvement does not come from the model but rather from leadership commitment. You cannot substitute a change or process improvement model for leadership involvement and commitment. This book provides excellent models, processes, techniques, and tools to assist you, but you must lead the change and improvement in your organization or it will not happen.

As the principal authors of this book, we have had the privilege to work with the various chapter authors over the years, both professionally and in various volunteer efforts, and thank them for sharing their expertise in this effort.

G. Dennis Beecroft
Grace L. Duffy
John W. Moran

Introduction:
Notes to the Reader

The *Executive Guide to Improvement and Change* is written by executives for executives. The authors share with you their techniques and tools that have helped make change and improvement successful in organizations where they have worked.

STRUCTURE OF THE BOOK

The content of this book is presented in three parts: Initiating Change, Paths to Implementation, and Measuring and Evaluating Improvement. The three principal authors begin Part I with chapters on anticipating rapid change, leading the transformation through decision making, and using the cost of quality as a key driver for improvement. An additional chapter on supply chain management is included because of the holistic nature of the interactions required to accomplish this goal. Regardless of how the corporation is structured, establishing, monitoring, and modifying the various operations inherent in the total supply chain must be led from the very top of the leadership pyramid. Improvement is critical in the single organization. When organizations progress to the next level—partnership, dealing with change, decision making, problem solving, and cost allocation become increasingly difficult.

Part II, Paths to Implementation, includes a select set of approaches to organizational change and improvement. The authors explain that there is no one technique that works best for every organization, but rather that executives and managers need to develop their own strategies utilizing a combination of different methods. The authors share tools and techniques they have used to successfully make changes and improvement in their own organizations. Each chapter is self-contained, although the authors direct the reader to associated information in other parts of the text. It is important to note that the authors do not espouse only one model for improvement. For example, the chapter on corporate planning models approaches organizational improvement from the self-assessment, top-down view, while the chapters on quality and environmental management systems use the bottom-up approach of structure through application of external standards. The executive is encouraged to consider each chapter's technique as it relates to the vision and culture of their particular organization.

Part III, Measuring and Evaluating Improvement, includes a series of special chapters that focus on results. The first four chapters address techniques widely used by the most successful organizations: *customer satisfaction* is not just a goal—it is a core business feedback loop for continual improvement; the value of *auditing* is so much broader than the internal or external comparison of actual operations to a chosen standard; the chapter on *balanced scorecard* is a valuable guide to identifying, measuring and acting upon what is most crucial for organizational success; and the chapter on *Six Sigma* offers an excellent executive guidebook to the value and ultimate rewards of this most important technique. Finally, Part III ends with a true success story of improvement and change. This last chapter takes the reader through the planning, implementation, and evaluation of a major organizational rebirth that received both state and national acclaim for its risk-taking and quality of execution.

Each chapter is structured in two sections. First, the author(s) provide the latest in theory, tools, and techniques specific to their subject. Where appropriate, the authors have included either original or publicly available figures, graphs, and listings to support their topic. Second, the authors have included references and additional readings the executive can use for their own information, or pass on to others who need more implementation detail. Because the authors have extensive experience in their subject, it is anticipated that the reader may wish to communicate further with these experts. For this reason a short biographical sketch of each author, including contact information, can be found in the About the Authors section at the back of the book. The authors welcome additional questions and are pleased to share ideas or point the reader to other resources.

SELECTION OF GUEST AUTHORS

While the principal authors, G. Dennis Beecroft, Grace L. Duffy, and John W. Moran, have had significant success in their business careers, they are not experts in all fields of improvement. A series of guest authors were handpicked to write chapters based on their own leadership excellence. These authors were not picked because they already have texts available in their subject. They were picked because they have proven their leadership competence on the organizational playing field. These are the organization leaders, executives, and senior staff, most sought after for process improvement and change. Several of the guest authors are active in the establishment and documentation of international standards and have been recognized by their states and nations for leadership results. They have agreed to share their techniques for success with other executives as a way to support continual improvement.

AVAILABILITY OF REFERENCE MATERIALS

Where applicable, the authors have included additional readings and references at the end of their chapter. Most of the references are available through the indicated publisher or through traditional and Web-based book sources. Many are available from ASQ Quality Press. In a few cases the authors clearly indicate where a work is no longer in print. The reader is encouraged to contact the author for further information on these particular works.

CONTACTING THE AUTHORS

Biographical sketches along with contact information are given for each author, should the reader wish to contact the author for further dialogue. Contact is generally recommended through Internet communication. Since contact information may eventually change, or where this option is not available, the reader is encouraged to contact the editor at ASQ Quality Press for assistance.

Part I
Initiating Change

Chapter 1   The Challenge of Successful and
Sustainable Organizational Change

Chapter 2   Problem Solving and Decision Making for
Continuous Improvement

Chapter 3   Quality Costs

Chapter 4   Supply Chain Management

1

The Challenge of Successful and Sustainable Organizational Change

John W. Moran and Jeffry M. Mead

This chapter will illustrate the need for leaders to focus on change processes and mechanisms. We will also put forth a construct that leaders may find useful for drafting proactive measures to prepare people for large-scale organization changes, in planning for specific changes and for diagnosing stalled or failing change efforts.

"Our moral responsibility is not to stop the future, but to shape it. . . ."

Alvin Toffler, *Future Shock*

A common question asked by leaders and employees in organizations is "Why do we need to change our organization on a regular basis? We like the place the way it is. Why keep changing all the time?" The answer is simply that the old ways of accomplishing our organization's purpose are not effective and efficient and do not work any longer in the current market environment. For most organizations and their leadership, this is usually found out too late in today's Internet-based world of rapid change.

Change is critical to the survival of organizations, especially technical organizations. And at this point in business history, what organization is *not* technical? Increasing competition and heightened customer expectations create constant demands for creative ways to approach problems and develop solutions. Yet most organizations have internal constraints that thwart rather than encourage change and innovation.

The business landscape is littered with organizations that were unable to get out of their own way while attempting to respond to economic demands, bring new ideas to the marketplace, or grow and change in order to ensure continued profitable survival.

Some of these organizations continue to exist as the walking dead, hollow silos of work groups attempting to survive through employee attrition, ongoing cutbacks in resources, and "holding the line" of vestigial processes, procedures, and ways of doing business.

Other organizations have flamed-out for the same reasons, in public and often in spectacular fashion. Polaroid Corporation, the creator of instant photography, went from being a half-billion-dollar world leader to holding a Chapter 11 fire sale primarily because of their internal organization's inability to change far enough, fast enough, and with the least amount of friction possible. The world-renowned engineers and inventors in Polaroid's research and development group created the forerunner of digital imagery nearly ten years before its popular acceptance in the 1990s. Yet feudal power struggles between departments and a fierce allegiance to status quo legacy systems conspired to relegate a number of advances and inventions to the "Good Idea But . . ." file cabinet.

Corporations have "antibodies" that resist change and challenges to their legacy, and drive out ideas and people that are considered "renegades" or at odds with the organization's existence. One example is how Xerox was unable to change itself to embrace great ideas that came out of the company's own Palo Alto Research and Development Center. Xerox gave the concept of a computer "mouse" to Microsoft and Apple, who subsequently made millions on the idea that Xerox was unable to exploit.

The majority of organizations change because they are forced into it kicking and screaming by the aggressiveness of their competitors in their market. The minority of organizations change because they have visionary leadership that is able to foresee a shifting and sliding marketplace and position their organization for the next market momentum move. These leaders understand the "triggers of change" and the four variables of successful change. As leaders, we want to know what and how much to change and when. The *triggers of change* and the *four variables of successful change* are shown in Figure 1.1 at different levels of intensity from high to low. The intensity levels require varying levels of effort and investment of scarce resources. When making an investment

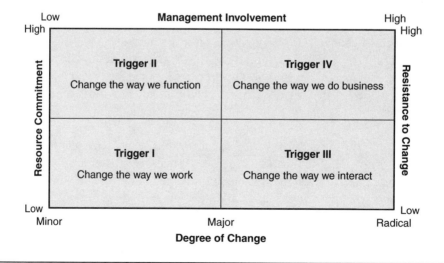

Figure 1.1 The triggers of change.

in change, one needs to be cautious and try to minimize the risk of failure. The best change is one that minimizes the intensity of the four variables of successful change, thus reducing the stress and strain on the organization undergoing change. This approach optimizes the possibility of successful change occurring.

Change has always been with us in one form or another. In the past we had the luxury of changing at a leisurely pace—our pace. Where it used to take 18 months to move from an idea to a marketplace product or service, it now takes five months or less, as shown later in this chapter. Change, like marketplace ideas, has also accelerated to this new pace. What would have been a long process of changing a culture now has to be a shortened process or the organization might be gone if it takes too long to change. In today's Internet pace of change, the rule is *"Change quickly, change often, or cease to exist."*

In the past, the rule used to be that the whole was greater than its parts—it was called synergy. Training and consulting firms used to tell us that the whole organization pulling together could accomplish more than any individual. That is not completely true in today's techno-world because the old paradigms do not apply in this new world of rapid-paced change. Employees are capable of more changes, more often because they have made an individual investment in techno-change over the past ten years. Employees in the workplace are working in ways that are very different from what we used to consider "traditional" employment. Their work week now goes beyond nine to five and Monday through Friday—they are approaching 24/7. They are wired, wireless, connected, and can contact anyone, anywhere in the world with a keystroke at any time of the day or night, and possibly get an immediate response. It is almost as if no one sleeps anymore and we are constantly at work.

WHY DID EMPLOYEES MAKE THIS INDIVIDUAL INVESTMENT IN CHANGE?

In today's business world, individual professional employees are capable of more change themselves than is the organization as a whole. This has come about for certain groups of employees who embraced each technological enhancement, gradually helping them work more efficiently and effectively. Not all the technology change of the past few years came at once. Individuals have changed in a constant and steady mode in response to technology, however. They tried the Internet, personal digital assistants (PDAs), cell phones, laptops, and so on and integrated them into their work life to make themselves more effective and efficient. They did this in a creeping reinvention, changing how they worked, when they worked, and where they worked. These "techno-individuals" were able to change and reinvent their work practices, work hours, work locations, and work interactions very easily by doing it gradually, consistently, and constantly. The more "techno" they became the more they changed and the more they could accomplish. Most of us, as we are reading this, are remembering people like that. They do not work for us anymore because we did not change fast enough or with them. They took their skills and ability to change to a new organization where they felt more comfortable.

People change when they see benefit to themselves for the near future. They are more willing to make gradual steady change rather than a massive upheaval. People resist a massive change because the variables of change are all at their maximum intensity level and require a great personal investment to make it happen. People have learned over the years that massive upheaval to make a change is seldom successful, and if it is partially successful the new situation is not the type of place in which a person wants to work.

WHY ARE THESE "CHANGE INDIVIDUALS" SO WILLING AND MOBILE?

Part of this recent "Internet-speed" change has been a change in the entire definition and concept of "job security" and "employee loyalty" for organizations. Security and loyalty in one's job used to mean that you worked for the largest employer on the block; that you did whatever your boss told you to do; that you kept your head down when things started flying; and that you were guaranteed a job if you did not make any mistakes and watched out for your bosses' best interests. How this has changed in the new "world of work and change" paradigm!

Techno-professional job security now means that you know how you contribute to the bottom line; your skills are sharp and up to date; and you can define and detail your role in making things faster, cheaper, bigger, better. Your sphere of knowledge and influence includes your boss, your largest customers, your major competitors, and your most significant vendors. You know who else would pay for your services and how much they would pay, both inside and outside your present company. Loyalty is now to oneself and not the organization. Finally, you know what your skills are and how they benefit your present employer. You know what the next level of skills are that will be required by the marketplace, and how and where to market them. If you keep these skills "fierce and flexible," you will still be changing while former employers are waning or have gone out of business.

WHY HAVE PAST CHANGE EFFORTS NOT BEEN SUCCESSFUL?

In the '90s, corporations started to lose their patience with "water and wait" change and Total Quality methodologies. The training and consulting companies would tell us that the process was important, and given enough time it would deliver the desired results. Very few organizations ever reaped the benefit of "water and wait." Today, organizations need to change quickly and constantly. There is no time to wait. It used to be that we had to sell people on change, but in today's fast-paced marketplace you either get with it or move on. Change is a core competency for even the most basic jobs. Now there is no time to coddle individuals.

If you are still purchasing "water and wait" change training and consulting that begins with large assessment processes of the current state, do not read any further. You may be beyond hope and would be better off using the time updating your resume. Giving people classes on how to change is a waste of time since the whole organization never reaches a point where everyone is trained to change, nor can you afford to stop work and train everyone. The best way to train people on how to change is on-the-job training. Teach them to change like the techno-professional; a little change all the time. Individuals become great change agents when they are actually practicing changing on a regular and consistent basis.

HOW DOES AN ORGANIZATION APPROACH CONSTANT CHANGE?

Organizations must approach change just as the most successful techno-individuals have, by constantly reinventing and making many minor changes so they are always positioned for the next wave of change in the marketplace. This way their workforce views change not as a strange phenomenon to resist but as one to embrace and not fear. It is normal to change if one is always doing it. Do not waste time developing facilitators or change agents to deploy into the organization, but rather make everyone an agent of change. Just developing change agents skilled only in the philosophy of change is a waste of resources since they have never actually done it but have only talked about it in the abstract. Putting employees through two to three days of mock exercises in change is another waste of organizational resources. In both cases there is no link to reality—nothing beats doing it for real. Save your "water and wait" training and consulting dollars and invest them in the first three triggers of change and not the fourth one. This approach has a higher potential return on your investment.

The New World of work is changing faster than the old one. There is little time to congratulate yourself on "getting it" because "it" will probably have changed again by the time you're done celebrating.

WHAT BEHAVIORS CAN LEADERS USE TO SUPPORT CHANGE ON AN INDIVIDUAL LEVEL?

At the end of each week, the leadership and employees of an organization should be asking themselves "How have we changed this week? How must we change next week?" Many successful employees are competent at dealing with change, yet do not know it or choose to deny it. Instead, they seize up when faced with an "official" change notice, acting out as victims or critics, more often than not in anticipation of their unrealistic negative perceptions becoming real. Conversely, when presented with the facts regarding their past history of successes with numerous individual and organizational changes, employees are given the opportunity to become empowered by recognizing their actual record of success and ability at coping with change.

Leaders can encourage potential innovators to emerge, and early adopters of change to continue by nurturing, facilitating, and protecting creative and worthwhile ideas in addition to appropriate responses to change. Leaders can provide this support by standing behind the creative employee's ideas, finding resources within the organization to put their subordinates' new ideas into action, and publicly recognizing individuals who exhibit the organization's preferred response-to-change behaviors. When leaders fail to support and find resources for new ways of doing business, these ideas and adaptive behaviors can wither and die before their potential benefits are ever considered, and before others can observe and emulate the early or successful adopters of new changes.

In addition, maintaining a high level of positive employee motivation is essential for effective leadership in response to change. Doing so effectively involves a number of leadership behaviors. Active listening validates employee involvement and can alert management to potential pitfalls. Maintenance and enhancement of employee self-esteem facilitates attempts of new behaviors, and overcomes mistakes and errors that might otherwise cause employee paralysis. The focus on specific behaviors and outcomes helps to avoid a bias toward status quo activity versus results. Influencing employees through recognition and reward reinforces the organization's preferred response-to-change behaviors by holding them in bas-relief, or highlighting them, in addition to supporting repetition and emulation. Communicating the benefits of certain employee behaviors by linking them to the big picture speaks to everyone's best self-interest. Setting specific goals and follow-up dates goes along with the proven concept of "that which gets measured gets done."

Helping innovators, early adopters, and successful adapters of change should be one of leadership's primary functions on a regular basis. Leaders often have the singular opportunity to cultivate change by helping individuals convert ideas into action, thus encouraging organizational growth and preparing the ground for large-scale change initiatives.

WHEN MUST YOU MOUNT A CONSISTENT AND SUSTAINABLE CHANGE EFFORT?

Do you wait for disaster? Or do you have foresight? The four triggers of change shown in Figure 1.1 are set up in four quadrants bounded by the four variables of successful change at different levels of intensity. The four variables of change—management involvement, degree of change, resource commitment, and resistance to change—are elements that need to be thought through in advance of starting any change effort, defining how much we can realistically accomplish and in what time frame.

The fourth trigger of change, "change the way we do business," is total cultural change and the most difficult to accomplish in a short time frame. In this approach you change the entire way you do business. This is the "desperate" trigger of change. In fact, when an organization pulls this trigger of change, it usually shoots itself in the foot. When an organization undertakes radical quick change it is usually as a knee-jerk reaction to being caught flat-footed in a changing marketplace or surprised by a competitor that is fierce and flexible. Massive upheaval usually results. The resistance to the change internally is high and sometimes rebellious. Management must heavily involve itself in making the change, patching up the mistakes caused by engaging in this massive change, and possibly defending itself against charges of incompetence. The philosophy that is espoused is to quickly link the organization to a new vision and possibly a new business model that may or may not be well thought-out. Thus the possibility of successful execution of a total cultural change is small and very few have ever done it.

The fourth trigger is the only level where all four variables of successful change must be at their maximum level of intensity. We all know from experience that running four things at their maximum level and expecting them to mesh and turn out the desired result is foolish. At least one or two of them will have a misstep and throw the rest out of synchronization. When this happens, we are never able to reach our desired goal, much less recoup our effort or loss.

Organizations have better success with change if they use the other three triggers of change since the four variables of change are at different levels of intensity—some low and some high. The odds of success are higher when you only have to deal with one or two variables at high intensity levels.

The first level of change focuses on the way the organization works gradually. This is a continuous improvement approach trigger of change. At this first level of change, all four variables of successful change function at their lowest level of intensity. In this approach, each part of the organization is making gradual and continuous improvement in the way it works. This is a great way to train individuals in how to change. This is on-the-job change training for employees at the most basic level.

The second level of change is a structural approach that changes the way the organization functions. This type of change has both management involvement and resistance to change at the highest levels of intensity. This change can be accomplished quickly since it usually is a reorganization that can be isolated to specific departments and business units. Usually the resistance is confined to a specific area in the organization and can be controlled and monitored. The resistance to change may be isolated to a few individuals that can be coached or consulted into joining the effort. This type of change should happen whenever certain functions are no longer needed, the organization needs to be flattened, a key manager or employee leaves, a business unit is sold, or a product or service line is discontinued. This type of change is healthy for an organization in the long run since it repositions the organization to focus its employees and resources on new tasks or new businesses for the future.

The third level of change is a behavioral modification approach that changes the way we interact with each other in the organization. This type of change has the degree of change and resource commitment at the highest levels of intensity. This type of change involves having a very clear philosophy statement of why we need to change the way we interact and support each other in the organization. This new philosophy of change could be a new mission, vision, values, or goals for the organization. The degree of change is high since people will be required to act and behave in totally different ways in order to meet the new goals.

If organizations are constantly working on the first trigger of change and are occasionally making trigger two and trigger three changes they will, in effect, over time accomplish a level four change in an organized manner while reducing the stress on the organization that a complete level four radical change entails.

HOW DO YOU ENGAGE AN ORGANIZATION AND ITS EMPLOYEES TO SUCCESSFULLY SUPPORT A CHANGE EFFORT?

Once you decide which trigger of change you must initiate in your organization, the next step is to engage everyone fully in the change effort. As shown in Figure 1.2, there are steps that the organization and the individual must accomplish to make for a successful change effort.

When a change effort begins, both the organization and the individual employees struggle with the "translation spectrum" shown in Figure 1.2. The translation spectrum introduces stress and anxiety into an organization. This stress and anxiety results from an organization not completely defining what they are trying to achieve with their change effort. If the concept of "what change will accomplish" is not clear and compelling, then the individuals in the organization cannot envision what the end state will be and how they fit into that picture. When individuals cannot picture a future reality that clearly includes them in the big picture, they begin to feel stressed and anxious. Successful change results when an organization helps its employees move seamlessly through the translation spectrum. Concept to reality is easier when the end state is clearly defined rather than one that each individual may interpret incorrectly.

Why don't people change? Much has been written about the human species' reluctance to change, even in the face of continued survival concerns. While there is no single, definitive reason, we consistently see several versions of the same few reasons played out in the workplace.

For example, leaders may encounter resistance to necessary and logical changes from their technical professionals, sometimes even from those employees most vocal about and invested in the changes. Contrary to many leaders' initial impression, this resistance is not necessarily caused by a dislike of the change or its perceived failure to succeed. On the contrary, many technical professionals are often favorably disposed to

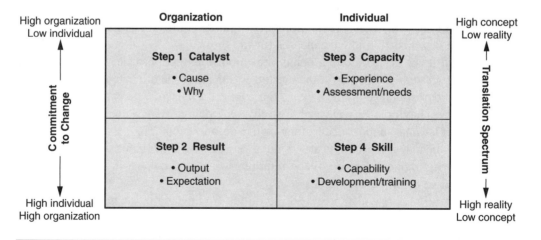

Figure 1.2   Change commitment continuum.

change, since they know it can lead to activities that they covet, such as challenge and variety. Often, resistance stems from our need for completion. For a number of professionals, once committed to a project or course of action, they want (or are driven) to finish it. They may perceive change as disrupting their ability to see projects through from beginning to end. Frustration and eventual job dissatisfaction can occur when a preponderance of projects or initiatives are either significantly modified midstream or terminated prior to conclusion.

Another reason is priority stress, a condition that results from the lack of clear focus on core priorities. Priority stress arises from role ambiguity ("I don't know what to do"), role conflict ("I have competing and conflicting things to do"), and role overload ("I have too much to do and not enough time to do it"). Some employees respond to competing priorities and resource limitations by reducing the areas in which they are willing to operate. Others slow up their activities and push decision making up to senior management, which often produces the type of decision making that blocks timely and effective resolution of problems and adoption of necessary changes.

A third example refers to the perceived powerlessness to act that employees feel when they believe that three factors exist in their organization: unclear accountabilities, overcontrol, and/or inadequate resources. Unclear accountabilities exist when people in an organization are not clear who has the responsibility for solving problems and implementing solutions, which leads to a chain of events that inevitably consumes leadership time and effort. Overcontrol is when employees believe that there are too many levels of authorization and overly tight controls that inhibit the capacity to act. This may be further compounded by the way in which some managers respond to performance pressures. Some managers feel pressured to show improved performance during times of stress and change, and do so by becoming more controlling, thereby reducing the autonomy and capacity to act of those reporting to them. The third component of powerlessness involves the absence of the resources needed to implement timely and effective solutions.

What are the triggers to decreasing stress, anxiety, and tension in individual employees? There are four primary questions that need to be answered to an individual's satisfaction before they can even attempt to "give it their all" when faced with change. Two are organization issues and two are individual issues.

All four of these areas need to be addressed to an individual's satisfaction to ensure that individual will wholeheartedly move with the change. If any one of the areas is perceived as unclear or threatening, as seen from the individual's perspective, then they will be less likely to move with the change and more likely to drag their feet, work at partial speed or energy, sabotage the change, or simply not participate in the change. The likelihood of successful change decreases further when more than one of the areas are seen as threatening, unclear, or negative.

Organizational imperatives explain the "what" and the "why" of change to an employee. While organizations are improving their ability and consistency in addressing these issues, the individual imperatives that speak to "how" the change will be made are often assumed or overlooked. One only need look to Maslow's Hierarchy of Needs to understand that the individual's issues are the root of greater anxiety and stress, hence, the more common and frequent reasons why change efforts are not successful in organizations.

Consequently, when addressing the capacity for change, we must look to the past experiences of the individuals and the organization. How much change have they experienced? What types of changes have occurred? How have individuals and groups reacted? As a first step toward a proactive stance, management needs to determine how small changes can be built into the daily, weekly, and quarterly regime of individuals and work groups. In many cases, these changes are occurring now, but the capability to handle them rapidly, with an economy of energy, and productively, requires a singular focus be put on what is happening, how people are reacting, and what the expectations are for output.

HOW DO YOU REALLY ACCELERATE CHANGE?

Individual behavior provides us with four signposts for rapid and successful change. Let us use the change from a written daily schedule book to a PDA device as an example.

Why would someone want to make a change from his or her traditional, comfortable scheduler to an electronic device? Usually, there is a catalytic event that provides the energy or impetus to change. Perhaps the individual lost their schedule book. Or their schedule book has become so bulky and filled with loose scraps of papers and notes that it is difficult to carry. Or they double-booked a time slot or misread a phone number due to their poor handwriting, thereby costing them time and money. Without the pain or anticipated pain of a catalyst, the necessary commitment energy will not be present to drive through the discomfort of change.

Next, the individual forms an image of a better, future state as an antidote, or alternative, to the flawed status quo condition. Their scheduler will weigh only a few ounces and fit into their pocket. They will clearly see when current appointments exist and when there are potential conflicts. All entries will be very legible and highly accessible. There will be a backup schedule available in case of disaster, with rapid and complete recovery of schedule and contact information. Again, without the promise of substantial improvement, the inertial energy required for successful change does not exist.

These first two steps are fairly conceptual in nature. They set the stage for the following two steps by building the urgency, energy, and commitment needed to take personal action and commit individual resources. Successful framing, within these first two steps, is not a guarantee that change will be implemented or successful, but the absence of one or both is a strong predictor of failure or flawed change.

Capacity consists of the individual taking stock of their current knowledge and resources and performing a gap analysis between present capacity and the future state. Also, deciding what information or skill or ability is needed to determine a new course of action and ensure that it will be successful. Are there alternatives to a written schedule book? What are they? How much do they cost? What are the start-up costs? What did I do before I used a schedule book? How did I move from the previous device to a schedule book? What do other people use? Comparing my present state to my ideal future state, what is needed to bridge the gap?

Finally, the individual fills the gaps between status quo and future ideal with skill development, knowledge, practice, training, and application. These are what facilitate the move from flawed status quo to making the future ideal state the new reality. Learning how to use PDA software. Practicing how to write with a stylus. Reading about and implementing a backup plan from their PDA to their personal computer. Using the schedule book and the PDA in tandem until the future state seems real.

The latter two steps are concrete, action oriented, and increasingly labor intensive. The chance for failure, errors, mishaps, recriminations, second guessing, and other various forms of personal pain and discomfort all exist here with higher possibility and probability. Consequently, this is where an individual requires the most support.

Building up a reserve of energy and commitment during the first two stages only carries one so far. These wells are depleted rapidly and can only be revisited sparingly with positive, recharging outcomes. The memory of the pain of the catalyst and the intangible promise of the future fade in light of present discomfort, awkwardness, pain, and energy requirements.

Invoking the catalyst and the future expectation can deliver renewed commitment for a short while. Eventually it is seen as a hollow gesture, which is ignored because it does not alleviate the pain and discomfort that goes hand in hand with learning, skill development, and making mistakes. Finally, it can controvert the change effort by standing as a reminder of the golden past, when expectations were known, results were easily within reach, and expertise was always present.

So, within each of the four triggers of change there is a four-step subset of the change commitment continuum, as shown in Figure 1.3.

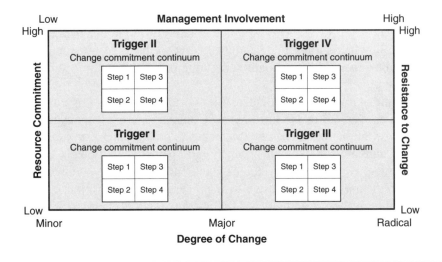

Figure 1.3   Four-step subset of the change commitment continuum.

The first two inquiries frame the change imperative by answering the questions "Why change?" and "Towards what result?" It is primarily the responsibility of the organization to set forth these answers in a clear and compelling manner so that the individuals making the changes have the necessary energy reserves and commitment to move forward with their work. The organization then needs to facilitate, resource, and reward the individuals for engaging in the subsequent two stages, "assessing needs" based on gap analysis of current capacity and future state, then "building capability" to meet that capacity through skill development.

HOW DO I BECOME A FIERCE AND FLEXIBLE COMPETITOR?

Building the capacity for successful change, as opposed to making changes in business and people, is a key differentiator and necessary competency of the fierce and flexible competitor. In the past, business leaders have been reluctant to change the way social and technical systems operate within their businesses. In fact, avoidance of change ("If it ain't broke, don't fix it!") is often a primary business mandate or value in some organizations.

Unfortunately, this approach has historically disabled people and businesses. In fact, it stands as a core differentiator between old line and new age business. Change for change's sake is exactly what is needed to survive and compete in today's world. In the September 2000 issue of *Fast Company* magazine, an article by George Anders entitled "Power Partners" discusses the challenges engendered when Wells Fargo, a company with a 100-year history, partnered with Internet start-ups and other new age companies with less than one year of existence. Included in the new rules for "partnerships that prosper" is "Take chances on almost everything."

In 1966, it took approximately six years to create a consumer product, from the concept in the mind of the inventor to the kitchen table in the house of the consumer. In 1996, the time line had shrunk to 18 months. Now we have seen many dot-com companies go from a concept to a company with three million customers to nothing in less than a few years.

One example of how to operationalize this shorter change and implementation cycle can be seen in an element of the Ford Motor Company's current management training program. By institutionalizing change it manages to create a separate capacity and ability for change unrelated to its results, which end up succeeding precisely for this reason. Each participant chosen for the management program is required to identify, project plan, and implement a change to a process so that the process is improved. During the tenure of their training class, participants begin the project and apply many of the lessons of the program to their process improvement project. This ingrains in each of them the mind-set, as well as skill set, necessary for seeking change, planning change, being comfortable and educated in the change master role, and ultimately results in the integration of change and change projects into quarterly goals.

SUMMARY

Building the capability and capacity to change needs to be unbundled from the results of change as well as the need to change. The tools, ability, and desire to change must be viewed as essential to individual success in the same way as is the ability to write, use a PC, or work on a team. Thomas J. Stanley, in his best-selling books, *The Millionaire Next Door,* co-authored with William D. Danko, and *The Millionaire Mind,* has shown an inverse correlation between conventional academic approaches to problems and entrepreneurial success. It turns out that the more risk-averse among us are less likely to become millionaires, and those of us most able to change have the best chance of fiscal success. Successful change follows a very similar pattern.

Organizations must approach change just as the most successful techno-individuals have by constantly reinventing and making many minor changes so they are always positioned for the next wave of change in the marketplace. This way their workforce views change not as a strange phenomenon to resist but as one to embrace and not fear. It is normal to change if one is always doing it. Organizations must constantly be asking themselves "What do we need to change to be a fierce and flexible force in our marketplace?" "How have we changed this week? How must we change next week?" Organizations have to build a workforce that is willing to take risks and try new ways. It is a never-ending cycle of change, change, and more change in today's techno-world.

SUGGESTED READING

Kotter, John P. *Leading Change.* Boston, MA: Harvard Business School Press, 1996.

Senge, Peter M. *The Fifth Discipline: The Art and Practice of the Learning Organization.* New York: Currency/Doubleday, 1990.

Tichy, Noel M. *Managing Strategic Change: Technical, Political, and Cultural Dynamics.* New York: Wiley-Interscience, 1983.

2

Problem Solving and Decision Making for Continuous Improvement

Grace L. Duffy

One of the first things we learn to do as leaders is to solve problems. We are encouraged to find solutions by doing things a new way. "If you always do what you have always done, you will always get what you always got." The business world is driven by the latest market trends and the belief that the latest initiatives are the best ones. We are often tempted to move to new options before focusing on finding efficiencies in our existing environment. Some of the greatest organizational improvements, however, have come as a result of addressing issues previously ignored. The subject of organizational problem solving may not seem a priority, but the overwhelming cost and performance implications associated with unsolved or chronic problems deserve a closer look.

Problem solving is a skill required in almost every aspect of life. Executives are constantly bombarded by requests from customers, stakeholders, and associates to solve problems inherent in the nature of market competition. At least some level of standard problem solving must be defined within the organization to allow the executive and senior leadership to direct others in the research and resolution of issues.

There are several problem-solving models useful to organizations. Figure 2.1 describes a generic model based on the work of Dr. Joseph Juran and Frank Gryna.[1]

The generic problem-solving model assumes a rational approach based on existing organizational assumptions, standards, and culture. Before a problem can be solved, it first must be defined. It is human nature to ignore a possible change until we become uncomfortable in our current state. Unless there is some difference between the status quo and the observed situation, there will be no discomfort in the organization to alert the leadership that a problem exists.

Step	Characteristics
1. Define the problem	• Differentiate fact from opinion • Specify underlying causes • Consult each function involved for information • State the problem specifically • Identify what standard or expectation is violated • Determine in which process the problem lies • Avoid trying to solve the problem without data
2. Generate alternative solutions	• Postpone evaluating alternatives initially • Include all involved individuals in alternative generation • Specify alternatives consistent with organizational goals • Specify short- and long-term alternatives • Brainstorm on others' ideas • Seek alternatives that may solve the problem
3. Evaluate and select an alternative	• Evaluate alternatives relative to a target standard • Evaluate all alternatives without bias • Evaluate alternatives relative to established goals • Evaluate both proven and possible outcomes • State the selected alternative explicitly
4. Implement and follow up on the solution	• Plan and implement a pilot test of the chosen alternative • Gather feedback from all affected parties • Seek acceptance or consensus by all those affected • Establish ongoing measures and monitoring • Evaluate long-term results based on final solution

Figure 2.1   Generic problem-solving model.

The model described in Figure 2.1 involves four basic steps. The first step is to define the problem. This involves diagnosing the situation so that the focus is on the real problem, not just on its symptoms. Flowcharts for identifying the expected steps of a process and cause-and-effect diagrams for defining and analyzing root causes are helpful at this stage. *The Quality Improvement Handbook* by Bauer, Duffy, and Westcott is a useful reference for detailed information on these and other problem-solving tools.[2]

The steps for defining problems are identified in Figure 2.1 under Characteristics. These steps support the involvement of interested parties, use of factual information, comparison of expectations to reality, and a focus on root causes of the problem. What is needed is to review and document how the processes currently work (who does what, with what information, using what tools, communicating with what organizations and individuals, in what time frame, using what format, and so on). Then, by considering problems, inefficiencies, redundancies, and bottlenecks, we can evaluate the possible impact of new tools and revised policies in the development of a model of "what should be."

The second step is to generate alternative solutions. This requires postponing the selection of one solution until several alternatives have been proposed. Starting with the "desired result" is very tricky. Having a standard with which to compare the characteristics of the final solution is not the same as defining the desired result. A standard allows us to evaluate the different intended results offered by alternatives. When one tries to build toward desired results it is very difficult to collect good information about the process. Working with desired results has another aspect to it that can be difficult. Well-defined desired results depend on a well-defined process and that usually does not exist. Generally defined, probably, but not well defined.

Considering multiple alternatives can significantly enhance the value of the final problem solution. Once the team or individual has decided the "what should be" model, this target standard becomes the basis for developing a road map for investigating alternatives. Brainstorming and team problem-solving techniques are both useful tools in this stage of problem solving. These new alternatives should reflect current and projected business rules. If the analysis is done at the level of the functional processes, it is very likely that there will be some significant opportunity to capture insights from other organizations.

Many alternative solutions should be generated before evaluating any of them. A common mistake in problem solving is that alternatives are evaluated as they are proposed, so the first acceptable, although frequently not optimal, solution is chosen. If we focus on trying to get the results we want, we miss the potential for learning something new that will allow for real improvement. See further in this chapter for related decision-making techniques.

The third problem-solving step involves careful weighing of the advantages and disadvantages of the proposed alternatives before making the final selection. Skilled problem-solvers use a series of considerations in selecting the best alternative. They consider the extent to which:

- They will solve the problem without causing other unanticipated problems.

- All the individuals involved will accept the alternative.

- Implementation of the alternative is likely.

- The alternative fits within the organizational constraints.

Given the natural tendency to select the first satisfactory solution proposed, this step deserves particular attention from problem-solvers.

The final step is to implement and follow up on the solution. Leaders may be called upon to order the solution to be implemented by others, "sell" the solution to others, or facilitate the implementation by involving the efforts of others. The most effective approach, by far, has been to involve others in the implementation as a way of minimizing resistance to subsequent changes. Chapter 7 discusses some useful techniques for team involvement in organizational improvement and change.

Feedback channels must be built into the solution implementation to produce continuous monitoring and testing of actual events against expectations. Problem solving is an effective activity in the organization only if the solution remains in place and is updated to respond to future changes. Juran and Gryna describe a basic feedback loop using several of the concepts already discussed in identifying and solving problems. See Figure 2.2 for an illustration of a feedback loop.

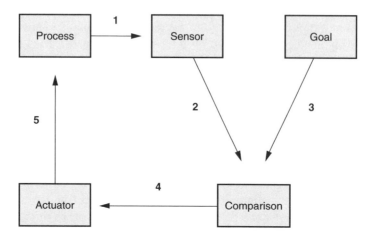

Figure 2.2 The basic feedback loop.

This general feedback process applies to all levels, from the chief executive to line workers. The sequence can be applied anywhere to understand and run everyday problem-solving and decision-making processes. First, the individual or team chooses the process to be studied or improved. A comparison is made at step (2) between an observation of selected characteristics of the process and a standard (3). As a result of the comparison action is taken (4) to change or improve the process to meet the stated standard or goal. Once the action has been tested and approved, the change is integrated into the formal structure of the process and maintained for future benefit of the organization. Finally, the feedback loop is completed when the approved changes are integrated into the process and become standard.

Reactive problem solving occurs when the gap between the status quo and current situation is large enough to cause noticeable discomfort to either internal or external customers of the organization. Chapter 12, Customer Satisfaction As a Driver for Improvement and Change, describes several approaches to identifying wants and needs of customers which, when left unmet, may cause such a level of damage.

Several barriers to effective problem solving often appear among organizational leadership teams. These barriers are:

- Inertia

- Loyalty

- Blinders

- Complacency

- Fear of the unknown

Many people are uncomfortable with change. Inertia in an organization encourages us to stay with what we already understand. Denial causes us to ignore the signs of discomfort and change until they are so glaring that we must respond from a position of weakness rather than strength. Proactive monitoring of our customer environment is essential to energize the organization toward continual improvement.

Misplaced loyalty to traditions and processes of the past may cause us to miss opportunities for improvement. This barrier also includes the "not invented here" phenomenon. If it isn't our idea, it isn't worth considering. Leaders must always encourage new thinking and reward those who are open to different alternatives.

All of us wear blinders from time to time. When situations become complex, it is natural to focus on only a few areas at a time. By involving multiple stakeholders in problem solving, we allow a broader perspective on many alternatives. The more we communicate between ourselves, the less we will close our personal views to new ideas.

Finally, complacency causes us to ignore that which does not generate immediate discomfort. Unless we are uncomfortable, we generally will not accept change. Fear, ignorance, insecurity, or just plain mental lethargy often get in the way of new solutions to existing situations. Executives should be key players in energizing the organization out of the doldrums of fear and indecision.

The best approach to problem solving is to use it as an advance indicator of opportunities for change and improvement within the organization. The model identified in Figure 2.1 can be used in conjunction with benchmarking, statistical process control, or general market research to identify influences affecting the organization. Proactive problem solving relates closely to the techniques described in chapter 3 on cost of quality by diverting resources usually expended on resolving failures to activities focused on failure prevention or creative improvement of the organization.

The models described in Figures 2.1 and 2.2 are based on the concept of problem solving. Often change and improvement can be most effective when initiated before problems arise. The discussion thus far has included decisions made regarding solutions to identified problems. What about a model that applies when there are alternatives, but not necessarily problems? How do we identify opportunities for improvement before discomfort begins?

INTRODUCTION TO DECISION MAKING

Decision making is one of the most exciting activities managers do amid the changes of business today. Much is written about continuous improvement and how to make it happen. Not all the literature addresses the decision-making process that goes along with that improvement. Some of those decisions are not easy. This chapter considers some of the ways that managers can maximize their skills in both strategic and operational decision making to better support the long-term success of their organization.

WHO MAKES DECISIONS?

Everyone makes decisions at some time in their career. Often we make decisions by choosing *not* to decide. This abdication of responsibility can be the most disastrous form of decision making for the organization. Unless we, as managers, take control of our environment, understand the current situation, and plan for required changes, we will not achieve the success that is imperative in the competitive world.

Fortunately, the trend toward employee involvement and cross-functional teams is spreading decision-making opportunities to more members of the organization. Tom Pyzdek[3] has described the transition of organizational structures from the traditional hierarchical to modern cross-functional forms. It is apparent in these structures that not only operational decisions, but also tactical and strategic decision-making is being moved farther down the framework of the company. As more and more employees are involved in the process, it is important that models for effective decision making be identified and taught throughout the organization.

Many managerial and team training modules have been developed that address the details of both individual and group decision making. Numerous publishers and third-party consultants have books describing all or part of the process necessary to effectively move the organization forward toward a more competitive position in the marketplace. One need only join the American Society for Quality to have the benefit of excellent mailings from a whole spectrum of publishers and private authors on the subject of decision making for organizational improvement. The challenge then becomes choosing from among the hordes of alternatives available.

Goetsch and Davis[4] provide one model for improvement in their discussion on cultural change in the organization. Figure 2.3 illustrates the simple four-step process.

Before any change is made in the organization, it is important to understand the history behind the current culture. Decision making causes change. Change causes resistance from some members of the organization. We need to know where we came from as a company before we can chart an effective path toward improvement. Often tying recommended changes to past trends lessens the resistance encountered when making decisions for the future.

When making decisions for improvement, it is also important to show actual improvement of systems, not just change for the sake of change. Often, in the heat of the moment, managers are tempted to make any decision that shows action. These activities may not benefit the long-term growth of the organization. Decisions for improvement must be based on legitimate adjustments to an identified system or a breakthrough that will allow realignment with long-term competitive advantage.

Any decision to change the current environment will create feedback opportunities. It is important that the manager be prepared to listen to those involved in the improvement

---

- Understand the history behind the current culture.
- Don't tamper with systems, improve them.
- Be prepared to listen and observe.
- Involve everyone affected by the change in making it.

Figure 2.3   Generic improvement or decision-making model.

and observe the impacts that occur as a result of that decision. Systems do not change by themselves. People create the change. It is the people involved in the improvement that have the ability to observe issues, barriers, and opportunities that can then be fed back into the original plans. By taking advantage of all these avenues of input, the manager can both validate the worth of their decision and modify their process for greater effectiveness. Also, most employees who are encouraged to provide feedback tend to feel more closely aligned with the process in question. Managers can gain critical allies through listening to and observing those who are part of the operational change at hand.

Finally, it is important to involve everyone affected by the change. Rarely can the manager anticipate every contingency of an improvement during the planning phase. Involving those most closely affected by an improvement will allow them the opportunity to recommend "in-flight" adjustments. Although the manager may feel the ultimate responsibility for the improvement results, it is the affected workers who will see the modifications to their daily activities. It is critical that the manager elicit the support and buy-in of those most closely involved in the modification to assure long-term commitment to the updated processes.

TYPES OF DECISIONS MANAGERS MAKE

Organizational planning and decision making is usually divided into three different time frames: strategic, tactical, and operational. Strategic planning generally is directed at goals that shape the organization's long-range future and competitive market environment. Tactical decisions are more functional in nature, like redesigning processes or expanding physical facilities. Operational issues are usually concerned with the current year's activities or more immediate issues.

Continuous improvement opportunities exist in each of these three time frames. When working at the strategic level, the organization needs to involve a variety of internal and external participants to ensure that accurate information is available upon which to make effective decisions. Corporate executives often create partnerships with key customers to better anticipate direction in the marketplace. By listening to customers, suppliers, shareholders, competitors, and employees, the executives can better understand the priorities and direction for continued success. See chapter 4 for more information on the value of supply chain management and the relationships between its different members.

At the tactical level, managers must take the decisions made at the strategic level and translate them into functional requirements for the firm. Here it is important to actively involve employees from many levels of the organization to better understand the impact of changes in processes and policies. The process for this translation of long-range customer requirements into internal functions is well explained in the quality function deployment approach to organizational planning.[5] This approach uses a sequenced model that breaks long-term opportunities into specific, internal operations that can be assigned to personnel and measured for effectiveness.

Operational decisions deal more with the day-to-day issues of running the business. Employee input is critical in making decisions at this level. Much has been written of the benefits of employee empowerment and involvement in operational decision making. Modern management training strongly supports the use of departmental or cross-functional teams to assess current situations and make recommendations for improvement. Management's role becomes more that of resource provider and expediter than initial decision-maker.

GROUP VERSUS INDIVIDUAL DECISIONS

Work groups and project teams are the predominant decision-making bodies within organizations. In these situations, their presumed motive is one of cooperation in facilitating the best possible outcome for the organization.[6] Certainly, those who have had a part in making a decision are generally more receptive to the ensuing changes. One of the recommended approaches to facilitating change is to involve all those who may be impacted by the effects of that change.

The traditional manager has often been reinforced in their idea that success is simply a function of working harder. With the increase in global competition and new technology, this is no longer enough. Creative thinking and initiative from as many employees as possible will increase the likelihood of better ideas, better decisions, and, therefore, better competitiveness.[7] As employees ask questions, they also generate ideas for solutions, particularly when given the opportunity to regularly discuss their ideas in a group setting that is positive, supportive, and mutually nurturing.

There are times, however, when decision making must be a lonely responsibility. Some decisions are such that the situation requires either a hero or a victim, depending upon the final outcome. Other decisions are simply direct enough that it is not effective to involve others within the time frame or scope of the current issue.

Because both group and individual decision making is a constant in the corporate world, it is important to have models that are effective in each situation. Individuals, whether in the role of manager or nonmanager, need to have some reliable approach to the decision-making process that will allow them to better support the long-term direction of the company or the stakeholders involved. These individuals need to have a tool that supports their efforts whether they are part of a group or making their decision in the isolation of their own judgment.

Lee Roy Beach introduced two excellent models in his book, *Making the Right Decision*.[8] This small but incredibly powerful offering is, unfortunately, out of print and no longer available. These models should not be lost to the new decision-makers who have inherited the rapidly changing and competitive environment of the 21st century.

This chapter reintroduces these models as simple, easy-to-remember tools for decision making in an environment of change. They are general enough to apply to multiple situations. They are useful for both group and individual decision making. Each model considers the current organizational environment before addressing opportunities for improvement. They have been successfully used by those new to the business world as well as those more seasoned in traditional corporate environments.

TWO DECISION-MAKING MODELS

Beach's text identified these two models as appropriate for "progress decisions" and "adoption decisions." The Progress Model was developed for decisions considered to be in line with current business trends. The Adoption Model was offered for situations when more radical change is anticipated.

My use of these two models with clients and students of decision making over the last several years suggests that they might more directly be named the Evolutionary and Revolutionary Models for decision making. The Evolutionary Model assists in the situations where Beach saw progress along existing cultural trends, where the Revolutionary Model better describes situations where the organization must adopt new or less comfortable approaches to improvement.

THE EVOLUTIONARY DECISION MAKING MODEL

As stated earlier, the evolutionary approach to decision making assumes that changes or improvements resulting from the decision will be generally supportive of the current goals and strategies of the organization. In these situations, the traditional strategic planning process can be used as a reference from which to analyze relevant data and to plan for improvement of existing processes, products, or services.

The first steps to the Evolutionary Model (Figure 2.4) refer to the culture, vision, and activities already established for the organization. Here, the underlying beliefs, goals, plans, and actions serve as a gyroscope, keeping the organization moving straight ahead, toward current strategic objectives.

Gryna[9] provides an excellent approach to identifying the current opinions, beliefs, traditions, and practices held by employees and management in an organization. He

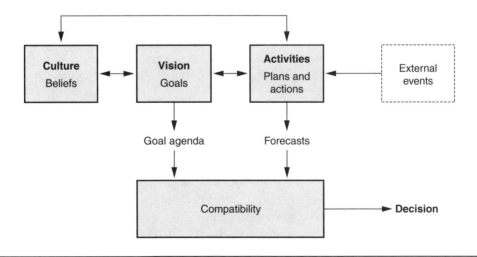

Figure 2.4   Progress (Evolutionary) Model for decision-making.

suggests a series of focused discussions with groups of employees and the use of written questionnaires to gather and maintain a much-needed base of assumptions from which to plan future change.

The author expands his discussion of culture and vision to include the broader organizational framework of customers, suppliers, and industry partners. Not only must the organization take the beliefs of their employees into consideration, but must also study the attitudes and perceptions of those outside the company who make up the total marketplace environment. As shown in Figure 2.4, it is often one or a series of events from outside the organization that provide the catalyst for improvement.

When external events begin to put pressure on the existing assumptions of the business, the organization can rally around their current culture to provide direction for improvement within proscribed parameters. These events may be new market opportunities, customer requirements, environmental regulations, or any number of other stimuli requiring decisions from the organization.

This application of current cultural parameters to external threats and opportunities is reflected in the model by the arrows tying the goal agenda and forecasts to a compatibility process. In an evolutionary decision-making process, it is usually possible to tie the new, external influences to already established expectations for long-term success of the organization. The individual or group need only select the one decision option that is most compatible with the current culture, vision, or activities. The model indicates this direct approach by the single arrow pointing to one best decision in response to the external stimulus.

The Evolutionary Model uses the same assumption as force-field analysis in supporting change as an extension of the existing direction of the organization. Where there are perceived barriers to change, discussion focuses on how modification of current activities can provide positive outcomes for those affected, thus reducing resistance. The closer an anticipated improvement can be tied to existing activity, the easier it is to elicit support from those who will be required to champion the change.

THE REVOLUTIONARY DECISION-MAKING MODEL

The Revolutionary Model (Figure 2.5) begins with the same relationship to the strategic planning activities of the organization as does the Evolutionary Model. Only through association of external pressures to the existing environment can the organization identify situations that go beyond the current trends, agendas, or forecasts.

When decision-makers discover that external events provide either an opportunity or threat that lies outside the current scope of their planning, the situation becomes more complex. Changes that radically differ from current assumptions often cause discomfort within the organization. Barriers to improvement are more likely to occur when decision-makers are faced with unknown input or outcomes.

Because of the potential for "unknowns," two decision-making opportunities exist with the Revolutionary Model. Like the Evolutionary Model, options can be considered in response to the external events which, although less comfortable to the organization,

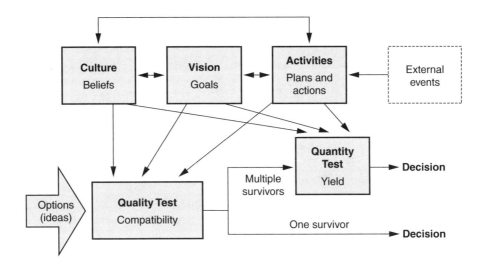

Figure 2.5 Adoption (Revolutionary) Model for decision-making.

still support the existing strategic direction. It is still quite possible, although more difficult, for management to tie the new opportunity or threat to the existing strategic direction of the organization.

Often group decision-making is most effective in this environment. Many of the existing quality management tools were developed specifically to support improvement decisions in the face of rapid change. Force-field analysis, nominal group technique, and cause-and-effect diagrams are all useful in helping groups of decision-makers to work through their initial emotions and see the relationship of new challenges to the existing plan. The simple process of thinking through these tools allows resistors to take a second, less emotional look at the opportunity for improvement.

For this reason, the Revolutionary Model shows compatibility as part of an initial quality test. If the decision-makers are able to work through their original reaction to the external events and tie those events to the current direction, then, again, one decision survives for implementation.

If, however, the situation diverges radically from existing assumptions, more deliberation is required. Here the Revolutionary Model refers to multiple survivors of the potential options in response to the external events. If more than one proposed option for improvement remains after the quality test, then the model suggests that a "best alternative" approach be taken. The quantity test looks at the surviving, possible options and quantifies the characteristics of each as having either the most positive or least negative impact to the long-term success of the organization.

As Beach recounts, "The problem lies in defining the point at which a candidate's violations are too important or too numerous; that is, in defining the rejection threshold."[10] Force-field analysis or matrix data analysis tools can be useful in either an individual or group decision-making process to help identify the relevant considerations for radical change.

Beach suggests a screening exercise to provide a quantitative threshold beyond which a remaining candidate option must be rejected from consideration. The rejection threshold tends to be rather unstable since the decision-makers' standards of acceptable change or impact may vary from day to day, but it provides some tangibility against which to proceed. Steps in the rejection threshold exercise are[11]:

- Only consider one candidate at a time.

- Do not make comparisons between candidates.

- Only take the candidate's violations into account.

- Do not attempt to balance nonviolations against violations; meeting some standards does not compensate for failing to meet other standards.

- Weigh the seriousness of each violation by the importance of the violated standard.

- Reject the candidate if its violations are too important or too many for you to feel comfortable with.

- Assign all survivors to a choice set.

- If, after all candidates have been screened, the choice set contains only one survivor, adopt it.

- If the choice set ends up containing two or more survivors, choose the best of them based upon relative quantities of potential outcomes.

It is helpful to involve as many affected stakeholders as possible when using the Revolutionary Model to support radical change in the organization. Since digression from current strategies is sure to create resistance, involving those who are most affected in the decision-making process establishes better support from them in the long run. The activities experienced in the quantity test are designed to involve stakeholders in the realities of the situation, so that they can each see the positive and negative effects of their own decisions.

It should be noted here that the best attitude to take while using the Revolutionary Model is that "criticism is a good thing." Be prepared to have decisions criticized.[12] In fact, encourage criticism as an effective tool for evaluation and feedback analysis. Group decision-making inherently contains this level of communication. Using the Revolutionary Model for individual decision-making may require an extra step of seeking out such review and criticism from others who will be impacted by the decision.

SUMMARY

Problem solving and decision making are two of the most important functions in business. Unless opportunities for improvement can be identified and acted upon, the organization has little chance of succeeding in the competitive environment of today.

Managers and nonmanagers alike have numerous opportunities for solving problems and making decisions. Recent downsizing and reorganizations have driven the decision-making responsibilities deeper down the organization chart. Employee involvement and empowerment programs have made it imperative that more training in problem solving and decision making be provided to all levels of the organization.

Cross-functional and departmental teams are now being given the responsibility for improving processes throughout the organization. Managers are required to be more involved at all levels in the strategic direction of the corporation. Data is more available through electronic data interchange and the Internet than ever before. The rate of change is such that problem solving and decision making can no longer be slow, deliberate activities. Each member of the organization must be more adept at gathering pertinent information, analyzing it in relation to strategic vision, and assessing requirements for relevant improvement and change.

This increased demand for improvement and change makes the availability of useful models all the more important. This chapter offered several models that were developed to provide broad approaches to both reactive and proactive improvements within the organization. These models have been tested in both individual and team situations. They are appropriate for both new leaders and the more seasoned corporate executive.

Problem solving and decision making are exciting parts of business. Only through involvement and accountability can each member truly be a significant player in the organization. It is through such involvement on a continuous basis that the organization can survive and grow in the competitive marketplace of today.

ENDNOTES

1. F. Gryna, *Quality Planning and Analysis* (New York: McGraw Hill, 2001).
2. J. E. Bauer, G. Duffy, and R. L. Westcott, *The Quality Improvement Handbook,* (Milwaukee: ASQ Quality Press, 2002).
3. T. Pyzdek, "Organizational Structures for Quality," in *The Essence of Quality Management*, no. 1 (Milwaukee: ASQ Quality Management Division, 1997).
4. D. L. Goetsch and S. B. Davis, *Introduction to Total Quality*, 2nd ed. (Englewood Cliffs, NJ: Prentice Hall, 1997).
5. J. Moran, J. ReVelle, C. Cox, *QFD Handbook* (New York: John Wiley & Sons, 1998).
6. M. H. Bazerman, *Judgment in Managerial Decision Making* (New York: John Wiley & Sons, 1994).
7. See note 4.
8. L. R. Beach, *Making the Right Decision* (New Jersey: Prentice Hall [out of print], 1993).
9. See note 1.
10. See note 8.
11. See note 8, p. 101–2.
12. See note 4, p. 258.

3

Quality Costs

G. Dennis Beecroft

Cost of quality (COQ) is not a new concept; it has been around for many years. Dr. Joseph M. Juran in 1951 in his Quality Control Handbook *included a section on COQ. The American Society for Quality (ASQ) established the Quality Cost Committee under the Quality Management Division in 1961 to promote quality cost techniques. However it was Philip B. Crosby who popularized the use of COQ because of his book,* Quality Is Free, *in 1979. Several current quality system standards, ISO 9000, ISO/TS 16949, QS-9000, and AS9000, reference the use of COQ for quality improvement.*

The term "cost of quality" may be confusing. What is being referenced are the costs due to the lack of quality or costs to ensure quality products are produced. Adding to this confusion is the fact that some authors refer to these costs as "cost of poor quality." Examples of these authors are; H. James Harrington's *Poor-Quality Costs* and Atkinson, Hawley et al.'s *Linking Quality to Profits: Quality Based Cost Management.* Other authors simply use the term "cost of quality," for example Jack Campanella (Ed.) in *Principles of Quality Costs,* Third Edition. Further complicating the situation, the automotive quality standard QS-9000, for example, uses poor-quality costs to refer only to the "failure" costs. Crosby has his own unique definitions and refers to the COQ costs as the "price of conformance"—the prevention and appraisal costs, and the "price of nonconformance"—the failure costs. Because of the varying terminology used, additional care must be taken when reading articles on quality costs to ensure understanding of the material being presented.

DEFINITION

Cost of quality (COQ) is the sum of the costs incurred by a company in preventing poor quality, the costs incurred to ensure and evaluate that the quality requirements are being met, and any other costs incurred as a result of poor quality being produced. Poor quality here is defined as waste, errors, or failure to meet customer needs and requirements.

It is also useful to think of quality costs in terms of the process approach that is being promoted today by many organizations. All work can be broken down into a process model. See Figure 3.1.

The process activities and resources can be separated into two groups. The first are those that are required to produce the output product to meet the needs of the customer. The second group is quality cost activities and resources (COQ costs) that have been put in place to ensure and verify that a quality product is produced.

These COQ costs can be broken down into the three categories of prevention, appraisal, and failure costs. The COQ Model is often referred to as the PAF Model after these three categories. See Figure 3.2.

• *Prevention costs.* The planned costs incurred by an organization to ensure that errors are not made at any of the various stages during the delivery process of a product or service to a customer. The delivery process may include design, development, production, and shipping. Examples of prevention costs include education and training, continuous improvement efforts, quality administration staff, process control, market research, field testing, and preventive maintenance.

• *Appraisal costs.* The costs of verifying, checking, or evaluating a product or service at the various stages during the delivery process of that product or service to the customer. Examples of appraisal costs include receiving or incoming inspection, internal product audit, inspection activities, inventory counts, quality administration salaries, and supplier evaluation and audit reports.

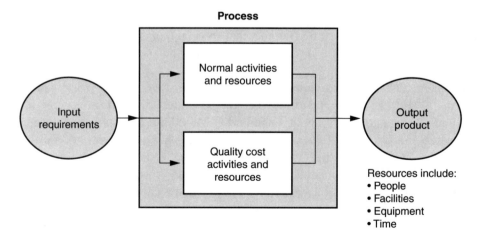

Figure 3.1 Process model.

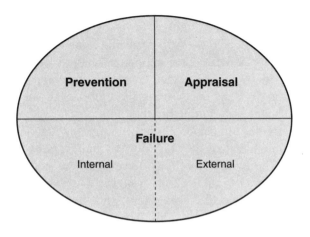

Figure 3.2 PAF Model.

• *Failure costs.* The costs incurred by a company because the product or service did not meet the requirements and the product had to be fixed or replaced, or the service had to be repeated. These failure costs can be further subdivided into two groups—costs due to internal or external failures.

Internal failures include all the costs resulting from the failures that are found before the product or service reaches the customer. Examples include scrap, rework, extra inventory, repair stations, redesign, salvage, corrective action reports, and over-time due to nonconforming product or service.

External failures are all the costs incurred by the company that result when the customer finds the failure. These external failure costs do not include any of the costs that the customer incurs. Examples of these costs include warranty fulfillment, customer complaint administration, replacement product, recalls, shipping costs, analysis of warranty data, customer follow-up and field service departments.

Many of the COQ costs are hidden and very difficult to identify by formal COQ measurement systems. Many of these costs, if identified, would be considered as the cost of doing business. Three major groups of hidden costs that are not considered in most COQ systems include customer-incurred costs, lost reputation costs, and customer dissatisfaction costs. While these costs are not captured by normal COQ systems, they are most important. Future purchasing decisions by both current and potential customers are very dependent on these costs. If external failures are eliminated, all of these costs are also eliminated. This puts a higher priority on elimination of the external failure costs.

IMPROVEMENT STRATEGY USING COQ DATA

COQ data is useful as a measurement tool. This data can be used very effectively to identify and prioritize improvement opportunities and then, once a change is made, track the impact of the change. The strategy for using COQ data for improvement is to attack the failure costs and drive them to zero. Implementing this strategy results in problem solving, and improving or changing the processes that produce the product or service. The money spent to investigate and correct the problems that result in the failure costs are prevention dollars. By capturing these dollars the organization can determine the bottom-line benefit of eliminating the failure cost.

Appraisal cost activities should be minimized, as they are non-value-added. They are defined as non-value-added, as they do not change the quality of the product or service being evaluated. The more inspections or verifications conducted, the less likely poor quality will be shipped to the customer; however these activities do not prevent poor quality from being produced. By spending more money on prevention activities, appraisal activities can be reduced, and this should also lead to lower failure costs. A Cost of Quality Model is shown in Figure 3.3.

The initial position is shown on the left and the ideal position is shown on the right. The initial COQ model consists of both *controllable* costs—prevention and appraisal costs, and *resultant* costs—internal and external failure, customer incurred, customer dissatisfaction, and lost reputation costs. An ideal model has zero failure costs. By eliminating the failure costs the customer incurred, customer dissatisfaction and lost reputation costs would also be zero. All the costs would now be controllable prevention and appraisal costs, with prevention being larger than appraisal. The ratio of prevention to appraisal would be very dependent on the type of business involved.

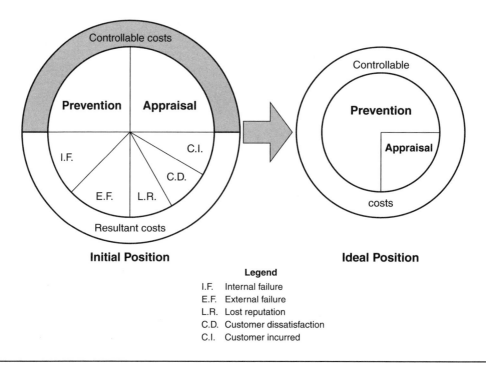

Figure 3.3 Cost of Quality Model.

BUSINESS STRATEGY/QUALITY IMPROVEMENT RELATIONSHIP

Quality improvement projects should be selected that link to the strategic business objectives and goals of the organization. For example, if the strategy is to increase market share, projects selected should focus on those areas that would have the greatest impact on future buying decisions of present customers and potential customers. However, if the business strategy is to increase profit in a particular product, the projects selected should focus on reducing quality costs by reducing errors, and eliminating non-value-added activities and waste. Another challenge for organizations to understanding this relationship is the definition of quality. Quality is meeting customer requirements, error-free, at the lowest possible cost. There is still a perception that quality can be too good. Upon investigation, this is usually a case of exceeding the requirements, therefore waste or "poor quality."

A byproduct of quality improvement is the improvement in productivity. By eliminating errors, non-value-added activities, and waste, resource capacity becomes available. However, this presents another management challenge. If these newly available resources are not deployed producing something else then there is no real impact to the bottom line. Management has learned through bitter experience that if these resources are laid off or let go then the improvement process is destroyed. Increased quality conformance reduces the production cycle time. It also decreases the use of machinery and equipment due to less rework. This results in a reduction in asset investment. Less materials are now required due to less scrap, rework, and waste.

Improving quality and productivity increases the profitability of the organization. Margins are increased due to these lower costs. Increased sales result due to higher conformance to quality, better on-time delivery, and the opportunity to reduce selling price. White-collar operating costs are also reduced due to elimination of poor quality, waste, and non-value-added activities.

Competitiveness of the organization is increased. Customer satisfaction increases due to improved conformance to requirements, better on-time delivery, and lower costs. Sales and market share will increase due to this improvement in customer satisfaction and increased perceived value. The organization will also be more competitive due to increased profitability.

COMMON APPROACH

Many organizations tend to treat strategic planning and quality improvement planning as two separate and isolated activities. Strategic planning is typically conducted on a regular basis, usually annually, using a formal structured approach. The output of this planning process is a formal document. Quality improvement planning, on the other hand, tends to be very ad hoc. Most organizations do not schedule quality improvement planning at regular intervals. In most cases, there is not any quality improvement planning documentation, if anything, only a list of improvement projects. When they finish their current improvement projects they then identify new ones. In most cases, improvement projects are added to the regular work of the individuals involved with the projects and therefore they tend to get worked on only when these individuals have time. This approach results in projects not being completed in a timely fashion, if they are in fact ever completed. Since projects do not get completed, there is no requirement for new quality plans.

Although strategic planning is conducted on a regular and formal basis, many organizations do not communicate these plans throughout due to their confidential nature. However, the organization is expected to achieve these plans even though they have not been communicated.

Improvement planning should be conducted as part of the strategic and business planning process. Improvement projects should focus on the needs of current and future customers and support the strategic and business goals of the organization. These improvement projects should be scheduled and resourced such that they can be completed before the next planning period. A common quality improvement problem is to identify too many projects then not being able to complete them.

DETERMINING STANDARD COST OF A FAILURE

As stated earlier, the strategy behind using COQ for improvement is to eliminate failures. This strategy is driven by the fact that all failures have root causes that can be eliminated. By eliminating the root cause of the failure, any future failures are prevented. The cost of preventing failures is many times less expensive than fixing a problem once it occurs.

The cost of failures is very different depending on where and what the failure is. Eliminating external failures is usually a higher priority than eliminating internal failures as the external failures impact the customer. Customer-incurred costs, customer dissatisfaction costs, and lost reputation costs also result from external failures. The customer's decision to buy future product is also impacted. When customers have problems with the products they purchase, they also tell other people, and some of these potential customers will not purchase based on the failures experienced by the existing customer.

When looking at the different types of failures that are occurring, it is important to be able to determine which has the highest cost and is therefore likely the highest priority for elimination. This can be done by determining a "standard cost" for the failure, then by multiplying this standard cost by the frequency that the failure occurs within, for example, a one year period. In this way a total annual cost of the failure can be determined.

To estimate a "standard cost" of a failure, first list all the activities and costs required to correct the problem for the customer. The next step is to determine the average costs associated with each activity. The time and cost likely vary somewhat with each individual incident, however, using the average cost allows sufficient differentiation between failures.

Let us consider the following example of shipping a defective part to a customer. The part costs $75 and sells for $150. First list all the activities required to correct the problem as in Table 3.1, column one. Any other costs associated with shipping the defective part are also listed in column one.

Table 3.1 Standard cost of failure.

Failure Shipping a defective part to customer	
Activity	**Cost**
1. Return of defective part	$ 50.00
2. Analysis of defect	$ 35.00
3. Disposition of defective part	$ 125.00
4. Take replacement part from next job	$ 75.00
5. Reschedule next job or work overtime	$ 50.00
6. Make new part	$ 75.00
7. Package replacement part	$ 25.00
8. Ship replacement part	$ 50.00
Other Costs	
1. Lost margin on replacement part	$ 75.00
2. Lost sales	Unknown
3. Customer "downtime" charges	$ 500.00
Standard Cost	$1060.00 plus lost sales

The next step is to estimate the average cost for each of the items in column one and record them in column two. The standard cost is the total of all the activity costs plus the other costs.

Now that a standard cost for shipping a defective part to a customer has been determined, it is necessary to estimate how often defective parts are shipped in a given year. It may be possible to determine the frequency of this type of failure by some other information that is currently being recorded. In our example, if it were required that for each returned part a report was completed on the analysis that had been made, it would only be necessary to count the reports to determine the frequency of shipping defective parts. Sometimes it is necessary to keep data for a period of time, usually a couple of months is sufficient, to determine the frequency. A simple checklist could be used to record each time a defective part was returned for analysis. Let us assume that the frequency is three times per month, or 36 times a year.

The total annual cost of shipping defective parts is calculated by multiplying the standard cost per failure by the frequency of the failures. In our example: $1,060 times 36 for a total annual cost of $38,160.

This same procedure would be used for each failure, and then the failure with the highest cost would be selected as the improvement project.

CONCLUSION

Not all failures have the same financial impact on an organization. As stated earlier, the external failures have a higher priority as they cause additional costs to your customers, which will impact their future buying decisions. Potential future customers will also be impacted because customers tell other companies about their problems, and some of the companies they tell will not buy as a result of those problems. By determining a standard or average cost for each type of failure, it is possible to select and prioritize failures to best support strategic business goals. The first step in establishing a standard cost is to list all the activities necessary as a result of the failure, such as getting the defective product back from the customer, producing a replacement product, and then getting it back to the customer. Once all activities have been identified, the cost of each activity is added and all the costs are then totaled. This cost multiplied by the frequency of the particular failure equals the total annual cost.

In conclusion, the projects selected for improvement should link to broader business goals. The business goals might be lower costs, improved profitability, or increased market share. The external failures that have the biggest impact on the business goals should be selected for improvement. Problem-solving activities must be completed to determine the root causes of failure. A solution must then be selected and implemented. Verification of the bottom-line impact can be determined by COQ data collection.

SUGGESTED READINGS

Atkinson, H., J. Hamburg, C. Ittner. *Linking Quality to Profits*. Milwaukee: ASQ Quality Press, 1994.

Beecroft, G. D. "What is Your Quality Costing You?" *IIQP Newsletter* (winter 2000).

———. "Cost of Quality and Quality Planning Affect the Bottom Line." *The Quality Management Forum* 27, no. 1 (winter 2000).

Crosby, P., *Quality Improvement through Defect Prevention*. Winter Park, FL: Philip Crosby Associates, 1985.

Campanella, J. (Ed.). *Principles of Quality Costs*, 3rd ed. Milwaukee: ASQ Quality Press, 1999.

Harrington, H. J. *Poor-Quality Costs*. New York: Marcel Dekker, 1987.

4

Supply Chain Management

Michael H. Ensby

Since the early 1980s and the "rediscovery" of Dr. W. Edwards Deming and the input of the other legendary "framers" of the modern quality movement, the search for a strategic, companywide philosophy of continuous improvement, constancy of purpose, and systems built on profound knowledge has intrigued many in leadership positions. The advent of newer approaches like Six Sigma and the Toyota Production System (TPS) have added to the body of knowledge regarding the original TQM methodologies. For the most part, companies have created, and even nurtured, pockets of persistence that can gather the apples from the ground and the other "low-hanging fruit" on the trees. Typically, these efforts focus on functionally specific processes, with more short-term benefit than long-term organizational change. The emergence of the supply chain management (SCM) focus across the globe has created new challenges, but even greater opportunities for the use of existing quality techniques and tools.

This particular chapter is written from the perspective that SCM is a strategic function in an organization. Regardless of whether the corporation is vertically integrated or merely virtual, establishing, monitoring, and modifying the various operations inherent in this new "chain of events" must be led from the very top of the "managerial mountain." The established pockets of persistence can make very little difference in mastering these increasingly complex systems. So the following sections will attempt to provide clarity in four areas:

- Viewing supply chains as multifunctional processes

- Aligning quality strategy within the framework of the SCM realities faced by every stakeholder in the chain

- Designing, implementing, and monitoring the environment for significant opportunities for change

- Measuring the "value add" aspects of the system to track true success

THE PROCESS OF SUPPLY CHAINS

This would be the best time to establish a couple of "operational definitions" lest the reading audience have one view of supply chain management and the author another (much like the flying public and airlines in terms of "on-time departure")! While many managers may view supply chain management and logistics as interchangeable, this is not the case. Below are the current definitions as stated by noted experts:

> *Logistics*—The process of planning, implementing, and controlling the efficient, cost-effective flow and storage of raw materials, in-process inventory, finished goods, and related information from point of origin to point of consumption for the purpose of conforming to customer requirements (Council of Logistics Management).

> *Supply chain management*— (SCM) is a set of approaches utilized to efficiently integrate suppliers, manufacturers, warehouses, and stores, so that merchandise is produced and distributed at the right quantities, to the right locations, and at the right time, in order to minimize system wide costs while satisfying service level requirements.[1]

A SHORT HISTORY OF SUPPLY CHAIN MANAGEMENT

While the concept of SCM can be traced back to the early 1960s, it wasn't until some 35 years later that it became a serious topic of study and discussion outside of academic and research circles. The initial supply chains, as they were identified back then by the National Council on Physical Distribution Management (NCPDM) were a two-factor endeavor: warehousing and transportation.[2] The meteoric rise of Wal-Mart as the dominant player in the consumer retail marketplace can be tied to a strategy built on superior logistics and an integrated network of information, some of it organic, but most of it shared by an increasingly broad collection of partners. The migration from stove-piped mainframe computers to networked desktops, riding a worldwide web of communications infrastructure (phone lines at first, and then the broader reach of the Internet) has resulted in a modern-day approach to SCM that leverages information technologies, operating on several levels. While this more robust approach is referred to as the "integrated SCM stage," others are advocating that the more optimal phrase should be "super–supply chain management."[3] What is occurring with more frequency is a series of processes, regardless of location or functional responsibility, operating in concert, driven by electronic rather than physical cues. As a result, organizations need to pay more attention to the efficiency and effectiveness of the process steps, and the intermediate and final outputs that do not necessarily have the "man-in-the-loop" oversight.

These newer and more complex "process webs" cut across functional areas, making accountability, responsibility, and authority much more difficult to assign, track, and evaluate. As seen in figure 4.1, there are many stakeholders (customers, suppliers, operators, strategic partners, and so on) in this "contact to cash" supply chain model. Referring back to the SCM definition presented earlier, this figure attempts to show the path to achieving a "perfect order."[4]

As demonstrated in Figure 4.1, what the customer expects from a supply chain and what businesses are attempting to achieve create a natural friction. These competing interests can become a positive or a negative, depending on how they are addressed. The last 20 years' efforts in continuous quality improvement have effectively run their course within traditional "stove-piped" functions. Most of their cycle times have been reduced within processes due to the application of qualitative and quantitative techniques, whatever you want to call them—"zero defects," TQM, or Six Sigma—so now it is imperative that companies find the next set of challenges to pursue, using quality-based applications. The complex nature of multilevel and multiple-player integrated supply chains is a prime target. The differences in sophistication between traditional quality systems and those in the SCM environment are presented in Figure 4.2.

Customer Focus: Quality, Cycle Time, Cost

Customer "need"	Manufacturing/ service system entry	Input supplies	Shipping/ delivery	Accounts receivable

Order receipt and entry	Credit approve	Manufacturing/ service complete	Customer receipt	Payment received

Business Function $ = Profit

Mktg, Eng, MIS, HRM, Ops, Procurement, Finance

Figure 4.1 Supply chain—contact to cash process management (PM) capable.

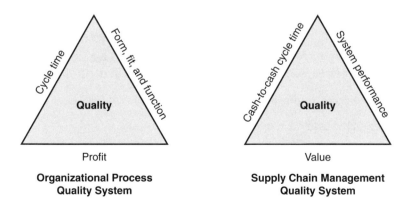

Figure 4.2 Traditional quality versus supply chain quality.

THE SUPPLY CHAIN BALANCING ACT

SCM-based processes have a series of inherent conflicts built-in. This is primarily due to the constant interaction of internal and external customers, many with competing interests and performance "success" measures. What follows is a representative sample of these conflicts, which can be referred to as supply chain tensions:

- Lot size versus inventory

- Inventory versus transportation

- Product lead time versus transportation

- Product variety versus inventory

- Cost versus service level

The balance between these interests can never be fully optimized, but the use of proven and systematic improvement techniques can reduce the amount of negative impact. A pragmatic executive will realize that the goal is not perfection, but reduction in suboptimization of the entire "contact-to-cash" supply chain (SC) system. Over the next few pages, we will take a look at indicators of "performance drift," how SC system leader–managers spend their time addressing these results, and how they can use the same amount of time to rein in variability through process management–based quality techniques.

INDICATORS OF SUPPLY CHAIN PERFORMANCE

First, we need to look at where people focus their efforts in relation to leading SCM activities. Figure 4.3 attempts to put this in perspective through the use of a modification of the more robust and complex "house of quality," the backbone of quality function deployment (QFD). While the quadrants are presented in a symmetric manner for purposes of discussion, this is rarely the case in evaluating supply chains in the real world.

When managers find the majority of their time, energy, and resources going to quadrants I and II, supply chain system performance suffers and incidences of suboptimization increase. Symptoms of this reality can be found in the following areas:

- Stock-outs and/or higher inventories

- Increases in cash-to-cash cycle times

- Higher return rates

- Unpredictable operating costs

- Poor service levels—Customer dissatisfaction

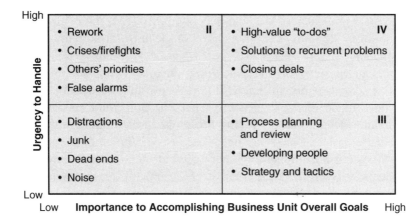

Figure 4.3 What people spend their time on in SC processes.

Adapted from: GE Capital Services, Center for Learning and Organizational Excellence, 1998. Used by permission.

While these same symptoms are evident in traditional "out of control" business processes, the impacts are even more glaring in integrated supply chains (refer to Figure 4.2.) The goal then, is for managers to focus on activities in quadrants III and IV. This will not be a revelation to anyone reading this, but the difficulty is also apparent. As leader–managers, we want to be proactive, designing, operating, and improving high-performing SC systems. However, day-to-day malfunctions sap us of the energy to work on the optimization issues presented in the model.

The one thing about presenting models like the one in Figure 4.3 is that it looks appealing, but the reality is that models don't magically appear in practical application. The first step in integrating the proactive supply chain is to identify the root causes of system nonperformance. The lack of a true process management approach can be categorized into three distinct areas: (1) information management; (2) design and strategy; and (3) operational control. Let's examine each one in more detail.

In evaluating information systems, not just computers, servers, and Internet connections, we see some very glaring weaknesses in dysfunctional SC processes. For example, the metrics may be scattered at best, or measure the wrong indicators at worst. Typically, cycle time is measured within subprocesses and managed at functional levels. However, the idle time between processes is rarely tracked. For example, it takes the average automobile 15 days to travel from the factory to the dealer, but the actual time-in-motion is only one-third of this elapsed duration.[5] Traditionally, managers in organizations are evaluated on the activities that occur within their functional sphere of control. But who is watching the handoffs? Another deficiency in evaluating performance metrics is found to be inadequate definitions of SC service level. Since the breadth of the typical chain is so extensive, what qualifies as the standard in one stage rarely "sticks" throughout. Again, this lack of standard operational definitions can be traced back to an overall lack of singular accountability from the beginning to the end of the process—from the initial communication of the need through the point where the cash changes hands.

As to design and strategy, the overwhelming weakness in any supply chain relates to inventories. The advent of just-in-time (JIT), kanbans, and the notion of the "ideal lot size of one" have made physical inventory "persona non grata" in many businesses. While there is little debate that increasing inventory turns ultimately reduces carrying costs, capturing true ordering costs has never been easy. While the advent of information technology is assisting development of more accurate SC cost structures, it remains a challenge, especially given the large number of variables from the raw materials stage through to final delivery. Idle time of work-in-process inventory is one example of the factors that make capturing total inventory costs so difficult. Another weakness results from a contention by many managers that supply chains are primarily outgrowths of logistics and distribution networks. While transportation, handling, and other movement-related costs are significant, the back end of the process is where the real focus should be. Cash collection to complete the process typically takes 30–45 days, down from nearly 90 days as recently as the early 1990s. Needless to say, there is ample room for reducing this cash-to-cash cycle even further.

Finally, we come to issues of operational control. The biggest hurdle is quantifying the impact of uncertainty and risk across the entire spectrum. Given the complexity and numerous variables in play, the ability to perform effective analysis is difficult at best. The many handoffs, numerous internal players, and physical and cultural distances at work make monitoring and controlling an inexact science. Poor coordination between functional areas further exacerbates the problem. The lack of effective control results in bigger gaps between the ideal state and the level of suboptimization in the system.

Difficult problems require strong structures. In order to properly address the three root cause areas presented above, the concept of process management (Figure 4.4) becomes a driving force.

As pointed out in the "macro" process management model in Figure 4.1, the ultimate goal of an effective supply chain is customer loyalty. The systematic nature of a process management system works well to address the potential weak links in the chain—strategy and design, information flow, and operational control. As we will see in the following section, there are tools that can assist senior leaders. These combine strategy and tactics, with a focus on organizing efforts around key operational objectives. At the decision-making level, the key to success lies in identifying important process variables and comparing them discretely in sets of two.

For example, Figure 4.5 presents a method for evaluating various potential distribution strategies against the factors that impact key SC performance criteria. For certain strategy–attribute combinations, there are potential benefits to be gained if included in the process design. Specifically, in the case of leveraging the distribution component of this particular chain, cross-docking (the movement of in-transit goods between containers at distribution points) can result in the elimination of holding costs. If the inventories in question come with significant holding costs (for example, cold

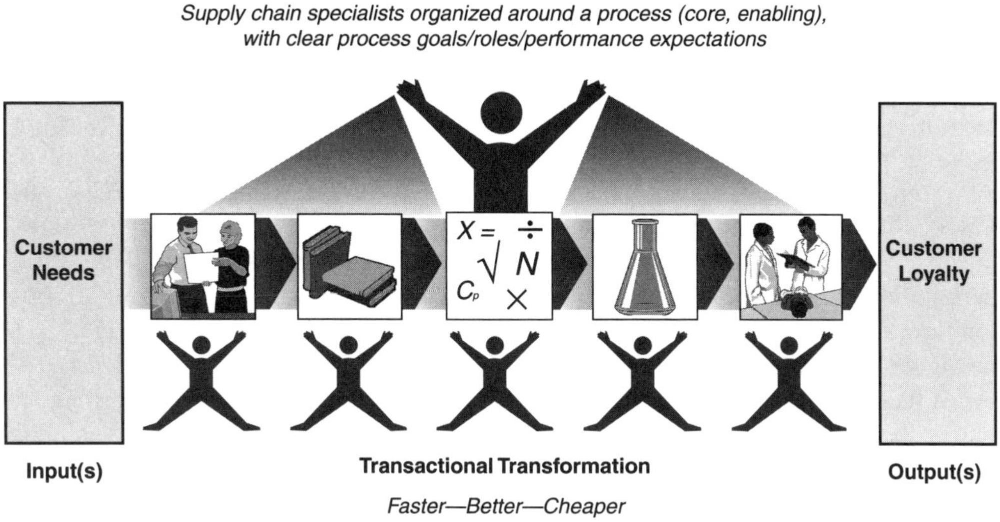

Supply chain specialists organized around a process (core, enabling), with clear process goals/roles/performance expectations

Figure 4.4 Components of a process management system.

Adapted from: GE Capital Services, Center for Learning and Organizational Excellence, 1999. Used by permission.

For Example: Distribution Processes

Strategy Attribute	Direct Shipment	Cross Docking	Inventory at Warehouses
Risk Pooling			Take advantage
Transportation Costs		Reduced inbound costs	Reduced inbound costs
Holding Costs	No warehouse costs	No holding costs	
Demand Variability		Delayed allocation	Delayed allocation

Note: a blank box denotes there is insufficient "value" to pursuing
a particular strategy–attribute combination.

Figure 4.5 Evaluating cross-functional SCM processes.

Adapted from: D. Simchi-Levi, P. Kaminsky, and E. Simchi-Levi, *Designing and Managing the Supply Chain: Concepts, Strategies, and Case Studies* (New York: Irwin McGraw-Hill, 2000). Used by permission.

storage), keeping them in motion through to the final point of delivery may realize considerable savings. This may be desirable in some, but not all applications. The results of evaluating process variables tied to performance outcomes better define the scope of the supply chain.

IMPLEMENTING SCM PROCESSES

Once performance variables are defined, evaluated, and selected at the macro process level, it becomes easier to carry the "message" down to the executable stages. In the examples presented in Figure 4.6, you can incorporate the process goal of "no holding costs" into the inventory management core process. When the manager in charge of supplier qualification develops the sequence of activities to achieve the particular process objectives, a critical criterion in evaluating potential suppliers will be to demonstrate their ability to cross-dock when it comes to cold storage items. The resulting information flow and control points (process metrics) will be easier to establish and stay tied to the higher-level core process.

At the micro process level, the technicians who carry out their duties and responsibilities should have no doubt as to the outcome if the system of processes is in alignment. Let's stay in the inventory management core process. When it comes time to execute a contract for a particular supplier who provides refrigerated goods, one of the key measures of performance becomes the use of cross-docking to ensure that no carrying costs are incurred during the lifecycle of those particular goods. The fulfillment of this metric, along with any other pertinent measures, is reported back up through the next higher-level processes. Taken in the aggregate, all microprocesses, if planned from the top down and executed from the bottom up, will ultimately perform with more consistency and be in alignment with the overarching goals and objectives of the systems, creating a "value chain." The reason is fairly simple. Design of processes is tied to strategy, and operational and tactical execution occurs as a natural outcome of planning. Feedback focuses on the key performance measures at each process level, with operational control in the hands of the appropriate experts. For those organizations that have undertaken process management approaches to SC design, measurement, and control, the gains are impressive and will be discussed at the end of this section.

In recent years, the number one reason for the increased focus on SCM as a strategic competitive advantage is the enhancement of information technologies (IT) as a core enabler. Simply stated, the ability to turn data into information and leverage it as knowledge in complex environments is the engine of the "new economy." If you accept the

Process Subdivision

(Level 1) Core	(Level 2) Subprocess	(Level 3) Subprocess	(Level 4) Microprocess
Transportation	Qualify carriers	Route scheduling	Product delivery management
Inventory management	Raw material supplier management	Supplier qualification	Supplier contracting
Billing and collections	Order input	New orders	Key in customer information

Figure 4.6   Hierarchy of supply chain process structure.

premise that SCM is a key to future business success, then it is important to understand how IT fits.

One of the biggest problems in the IT–SCM merger is misalignment. Enterprise resource planning (ERP) software is the standard by which SCM is measured these days. Business literature is overflowing with case studies of ERP implementations at companies big and small. Some tout the value of these centralized databases as the driver of success. On the other side there are an equal number of "horror stories," incidences where companies were virtually brought to their knees, ultimately scrapping IT investments running into the hundreds of millions of dollars. Why the disparity? How can one company achieve breakthrough success with their ERP systems, and yet others suffer devastating economic and market loss through implementation of the same software? The answer lies in preparation.

Before an organization begins the investment in ERP-driven IT, its senior leadership must understand the nature of its supply chain. All too often, organizations are guilty of "chasing" technology to achieve business success, only to be sorely disappointed after spending a significant portion of the capital budget and not yielding the expected return on the investment. Why is that? Is there anything that can be done to improve the "hit rate"? Figure 4.7 provides a way for executives to analyze their current supply chain complexity within the context of existing IT capability. For example, if a firm is currently operating in a "low tech" environment, both from supply chain and IT perspectives, there is no reason to invest heavily in information infrastructure. Consider this analogy, "why go squirrel hunting with an elephant gun!" In the low-complexity quadrant (I), the "KISS" principle works best. It is no sin to handle communications with paper, and physical handoffs do not appreciably diminish supply chain effectiveness. Many local and regionally-based companies can be extremely effective (and profitable!) without LANs, WANS, and extranets. This doesn't mean that an organization should stay in this quadrant forever, but in order to move elsewhere in the grid, it should do so with purpose, not for "flavor of the

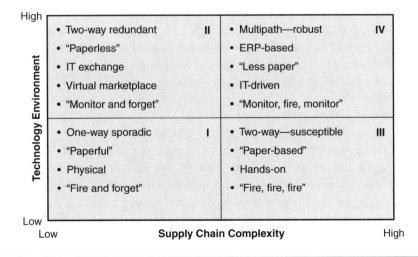

Figure 4.7   Supply chain communication management.

week." Conversely, a company that is in the middle of the global commerce war would be well-served to fully analyze its domain to ensure that the IT capability can meet the challenges of a complex supply chain environment. If that analysis determines that the firm is relying too much on paper for its communications, the chain sometimes experiences breakdowns due to lack of information, or worse, conflicting messages, and other indicators of quadrant III characteristics, then the senior leaders would be well-served to consider a comprehensive strategy for moving to quadrant IV. The bottom line is, most companies aren't hindered so much by a lack of communication, but rather, by a lack of *effective* communication. Going through an exercise similar to the one demonstrated in Figure 4.7 will assist an organization's leadership in better managing supply chain communications; it's better than the alternative of being managed by the missing information.

In his article "Demystifying Supply Chain Management," Peter Metz identifies five key success factors that enable continuing supply chain management accomplishments:

1. An overriding customer focus

2. Use of cross-functional teams

3. Attention to human factors and organizational dynamics

4. Quantitatively based performance management

5. Advanced use of IT[6]

When you look at the first four factors, the ability to master the fifth drives the others. Take for instance the cross-functional nature of SC operations, with both physical and virtual teams working together on the design, operation, and control of SC activities. From the 1960s well into the 1990s, individual members of these teams would be limited by the many legacy (multiple functional database) IT systems. In many cases, similar data would be in conflict or difficult to reconcile, making it useless to the team. With the advent of ERP and Internet technologies, team members can focus on using their functional expertise to evaluate common information from various perspectives. As a result, design, operation, and control activities become better defined and managed.

Similarly, customer relationship management (CRM) and organizational dynamics can gain by the use of IT systems. The parsing and cross-tabbing of data is invaluable in deriving root cause. Computer power allows marketing and HR analysts the freedom to create multiple "what if" scenarios, making assumptions, rearranging variables, comparing results, assigning risk, and, ultimately, customizing SC activities to better maximize returns to both internal and external customers.

Finally, IT can assist in the "management by fact" aspect of SCM. Previously, metrics were managed and reported at the functional level. Manufacturing, distribution, and transportation managers drove operational data, with a focus on evaluating the operations function. Likewise, marketing and sales leaders maintained their vigilance over market share and customer satisfaction indices. At the other end of the spectrum, accounting and finance professionals kept busy determining the flow of accounts receivable and payable. All of these are critical performance measures, but they are truly enhanced when the discrete measures are integrated into a systematic decision-making process.

Since the mid-1990s, IT has reached a level of sophistication that can move SCM forward to the point where integration becomes easier. The tools are relatively robust, user-friendly, and more importantly, "customizable." For example, until recently, ERP systems like SAP R/3 were relatively rigid. Organizations were required to adapt their processes to the rules of the data structures, sometimes with the effect of increasing suboptimization in specific functional areas, or even worse, across the chain. Now, with flexibility built into ERP, software like ASAP allows the information architecture to "fold around" the SC process architecture. The stage is set to get "management by fact" faster, better, cheaper.

KEY SCM METRICS

The next two sections set the stage for additional quality methodologies. Specifically, Figure 4.8 establishes the key metrics for integrated SCM. The supply chain operations reference (SCOR) model offers three key result areas, each with specific system metrics, and their corresponding units of measure. With a balance between efficiency and effectiveness, the SCOR model brings together two of Metz's five factors directly, with the other three receiving indirect benefits. Additionally, the SCM definition of "quality" becomes possible with this merger of measurement and technology. Going back to process management, upstream and downstream design, operation, and control are tied to one evaluation platform via centralized IT and integrated performance measures.

At this point we can revisit the two-by-two matrix, which is ideally suited to determine two aspects of SCM performance. First, senior leaders can evaluate current conditions and get a sense of whether the chain is properly aligned, that is, are the measures appropriate for the level of SC sophistication. The second and more important benefit

Key Result Areas	Metrics	Unit of Measure
Supply Chain Reliability	• On-time delivery • Order fulfillment lead time • Fill rate • Perfect order fulfillment	• Percentage • Days • Percentage • Percentage
Flexibility and Responsiveness	• SC response time • Production flexibility	• Days • Percentage
Assets/Utilization	• Total inventory days of supply • Cash-to-cash cycle time • Net asset turns	• Days • Days • Turns

Figure 4.8   Supply chain operations reference (SCOR) model.

Adapted from: P. J. Metz, "Demystifying Supply Chain Management," *Supply Chain Management Review* (winter 1998): 2. Used by permission.

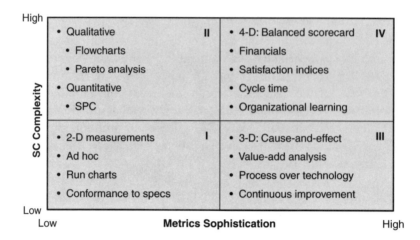

Figure 4.9   Supply chain performance management.

is knowing what attributes are best suited for SC performance management as the chain moves forward. Figure 4.9 provides general guidelines for these two evaluations.

For example, a firm that is low in its use of quality tools and techniques in its SCM but is fortunate to be in a low-complexity environment would be well served to focus on moving from quadrant I to quadrant II instead of trying to stretch into III or IV. Eventually, the chain may increase in breadth and depth, necessitating the addition of more robust quality methodologies. In contrast, those organizations with increasing SC complexity but a relatively unsophisticated ability to measure, control, and improve will face increasing risk of suboptimization and ultimately SC failure.

CONCLUSION

A properly aligned supply chain has incredible value to those firms engaged in its operation. The model presented in Figure 4.10 is the essence of Deming's exhortation to senior leaders back in 1986—constancy of purpose, profound knowledge, and continuous improvement. Metz admits that it's not a matter of "rocket science," but rather science and the art of due diligence.

Leaving this discussion, let's put a final perspective on the value of integrated SCM in terms of real gains[7]:

- Inventory reductions of up to 50 percent

- Total cost share of revenue reductions of 20 percent

- "Contact-to-cash" cycle time reductions of 27 percent

- Revenue enhancements of nearly 20 percent

- Inventory turns doubling, with stock-outs reduced by a factor of nine

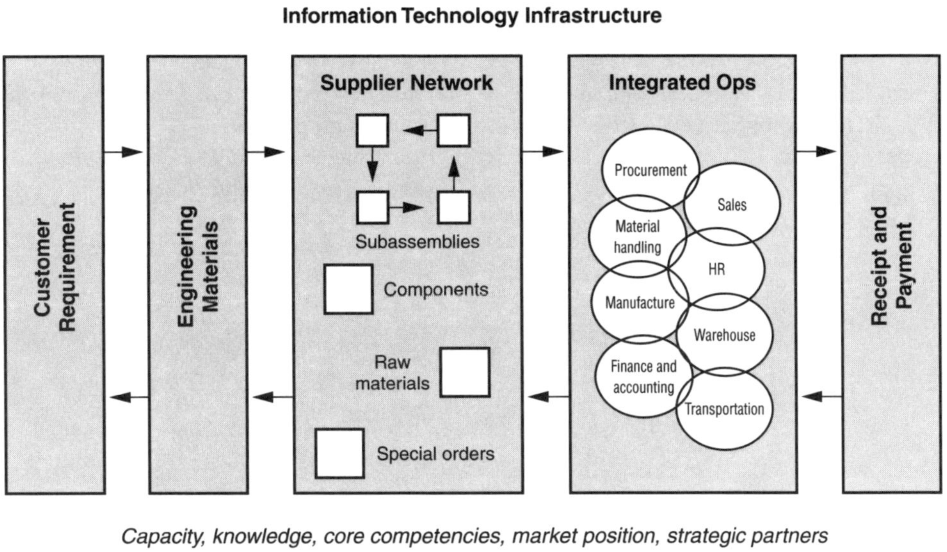

Information Technology Infrastructure

Capacity, knowledge, core competencies, market position, strategic partners

Figure 4.10 Integrated supply chain model.

SUMMARY

Whether an organization decides to implement TQM, Six Sigma, TPS, or any of the other variations on the quality systems management theme in its supply chains, the real key to success is to establish profound knowledge of its systems. The tools are only as useful as the understanding of the issues. A global supply chain in the automotive industry is no more valuable or better than a local chain that gets the wheat to the local grinding mill and the flour to the local bagelry and the piping hot bagels to the morning's customers. As long as the tools and rules fit the problem space, then the SCM is appropriate. In the final analysis, SCM rises or falls on three aspects—design, operations, and control—all ideally suited for the application of proven "soft" and "hard" quality tools.

ENDNOTES

1. D. Simchi-Levi, P. Kaminsky, and E. Simchi-Levi, *Designing and Managing the Supply Chain: Concepts, Strategies, and Case Studies* (New York: Irwin McGraw-Hill, 2000).
2. P. J. Metz, "Demystifying Supply Chain Management," *Supply Chain Management Review* (winter 1998): 2.
3. See note 2, p. 3.
4. D. J. Bowersox, D. J. Closs, and M. B. Cooper, *Supply Chain Logistics Management* (New York: Irwin McGraw-Hill, 2002).
5. See note 1, p. 5.
6. See note 2, p. 4.
7. Ibid.

REFERENCES

Brassard, M., and D. Ritter. *Sailing through Six Sigma: How the Power of People Can Perfect Processes and Drive Down Costs.* Concord, NH: Brassard & Ritter, 2001.

Lawrence, F. B., R. Krishnamurthi, and N. Clark. "Performance Metric for a Connected Supply Chain," *Review of the Electronic and Industrial Distribution Industries* 1, no. 1. The NEDA Education Foundation, 2002: 139–61.

Part II

Paths to Implementation

Chapter 5 Corporate Planning Models

Chapter 6 Core Process Redesign and Management

Chapter 7 Using Teams to Achieve Organizational Improvement

Chapter 8 The Management and Utilization of External Resources in the Workplace

Chapter 9 Quality Management Systems

Chapter 10 Environmental Management Systems

Chapter 11 Lean Enterprise

5

Corporate Planning Models

G. Dennis Beecroft

National Quality Award criteria are being used by thousands of organizations to improve their quality and business performance. The criteria are used as corporate business planning models. Annual assessments using these models are being conducted as part of the organization's business planning process. These assessments track their current performance and identify opportunities for improvement. These opportunities are then incorporated into action plans.

BACKGROUND

The Union of Japanese Scientists and Engineers (JUSE) introduced the Deming Prize in 1951 to honor W. Edwards Deming, who had been invited to Japan to present one- and eight-day courses on quality control. They hoped that recognition of Japanese companies who had successfully implemented quality control in their own organizations would assist and encourage others in their implementation efforts. In 1984 the regulations for the Deming Prize were changed, allowing overseas companies to apply for this award. Florida Power and Light became the first non-Japanese company to win this award. Additional information on the Deming Prize can be obtained from the Union of Japanese Scientists and Engineers in Ichiro Kotsuka, Japan.

The Japanese national quality award, the Deming Prize, led to the development of national quality awards by the United States (1988), Canada (1989), and Europe (1992). Other countries, states, provinces and cities soon copied these national awards with their own local prizes and awards. An "Annual Quality Awards Listing" of current quality awards was published in the American Society for Quality's August 2002 issue of *Quality Progress* magazine by Corinne N. Johnson, editorial assistant, and is listed in appendix B.

These national quality awards have in fact become corporate planning models used by many organizations on an annual basis. Three of these national quality award models, the Malcolm Baldrige National Quality Award, Canada Awards for Excellence—Quality and the EFQM (European Foundation for Quality Management) Excellence Award, will be presented here in some detail.

MALCOLM BALDRIGE NATIONAL QUALITY AWARD

The Malcolm Baldrige National Quality Award was established in 1988. The award was created under the Malcolm Baldrige National Quality Improvement Act of 1987—Public Law 100–107. The Baldrige Award was named after Malcolm Baldrige, who was the U.S. secretary of commerce from 1981 until his tragic death in a rodeo accident in 1987. The naming of the award in his honor was recognition of his significant contribution to long-term improvement in efficiency and effectiveness of the government. The purpose of the award is the recognition and promotion of quality improvement, and is contained under the "Findings and Purposes Section" of Public Law 100-107 and stated as:

1. The leadership of the United States in product and process quality has been challenged strongly (and sometimes successfully) by foreign competition, and our Nation's productivity growth has improved less than our competitors' over the last two decades.

2. American business and industry are beginning to understand that poor quality costs companies as much as 20 percent of sales revenues nationally and that improved quality of goods and services goes hand in hand with improved productivity, lower costs, and increased profitability.

3. Strategic planning for quality and quality improvement programs, through a commitment to excellence in manufacturing and services, is becoming more and more essential to the well-being of our Nation's economy and our ability to compete effectively in the global marketplace.

4. Improved management understanding of the factory floor, worker involvement in quality, and greater emphasis on statistical process control can lead to dramatic improvements in the cost and quality of manufactured products.

5. The concept of quality improvement is directly applicable to small companies as well as large, to service industries as well as manufacturing, and to the public sector as well as private enterprise.

6. In order to be successful, quality improvement programs must be management-led and customer-oriented, and this may require fundamental changes in the way companies and agencies do business.

7. Several major industrial nations have successfully coupled rigorous private-sector quality audits with national awards, giving special recognition to those enterprises the audits identify as the very best.

8. A national quality award program of this kind in the United States would help improve quality and productivity by:

   a. Helping to stimulate American companies to improve quality and productivity for the pride of recognition while obtaining a competitive edge through increased profits

   b. Recognizing the achievements of those companies that improve the quality of their goods and services and providing an example to others

   c. Establishing guidelines and criteria that can be used by business, industrial, governmental, and other organizations in evaluating their own quality improvement efforts

   d. Providing specific guidance for other American organizations that wish to learn how to manage for high quality by making available detailed information on how winning organizations were able to change their cultures and achieve eminence

The foundation for the Malcolm Baldrige National Quality Award was established, with prominent leaders from U.S. organizations serving as foundation trustees. The primary purpose of the foundation is to raise funds to permanently endow the award program.

The U.S. Department of Commerce is responsible for the Baldrige National Quality Program and the award, and the National Institute of Standards and Technology (NIST) administers them. The American Society for Quality (ASQ) assists in administering the award program under contract to NIST.

A board of examiners, who completes feedback reports to submit to a panel of judges, evaluates award applicants. The judges who are part of the board of examiners make award recommendations to the director of NIST. In 2002, there were approximately 400 board members consisting of nine judges appointed by the secretary of commerce, and approximately 60 senior examiners. The board membership consists of leading U.S. business, education, and healthcare experts.

The Baldrige National Quality Program now includes the three categories of:

• Business

• Education

• Healthcare

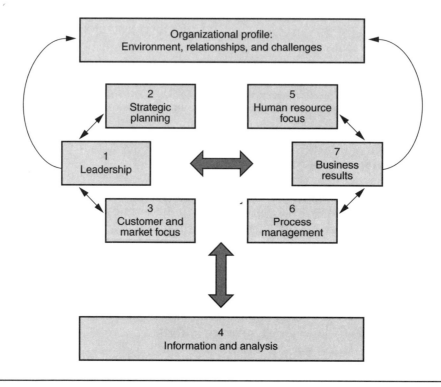

Figure 5.1   2002 Baldrige Award Model.

The 2002 Baldrige Award Model is shown in Figure 5.1. Detailed review of the criteria is not presented, as it is readily available from the NIST Web site, which I have listed below. Included later in this chapter is a comparison of Baldrige, Canada Awards for Excellence—Quality, and the EFQM Excellence Models.

Additional information and materials on the Baldrige Award and criteria are available on the NIST Web site: www.quality.nist.gov .

CANADA AWARDS FOR EXCELLENCE—QUALITY

The Canada Awards for Excellence (CAE) were established by Industry Canada, a department of the federal government, in 1983. The program was originally called Canada Awards for Business Excellence (CABE). The initial awards program recognized the following areas, however did not include a quality category:

- Entrepreneurship

- Environment

- Industrial design

- Innovation
- Invention
- Marketing
- Small business

With the introduction of the Malcolm Baldrige National Quality Award in the United States in 1988, Canada decided it was necessary to also create a national quality award. The quality category was first offered as an award in 1989. Until 1992 the Canada Awards for Excellence were funded and administered by Industry Canada; since then it has been the responsibility of the National Quality Institute.

In 1992 the National Quality Institute (NQI) was created as a not-for-profit organization "to provide strategic focus and direction for Canadian organizations to achieve excellence, enabling Canada to set the standard for quality and healthy workplace practices throughout the world." The NQI is funded through corporate sponsorship and fees for service activities.

Currently the Canada Awards for Excellence has two awards:

1. Quality
   a. Public sector
   b. Private sector
2. Healthy workplace

The CAE quality model called "Canadian Framework for Business Excellence" is shown in Figure 5.2. Further explanation and details on awards are available from the National Quality Institute.

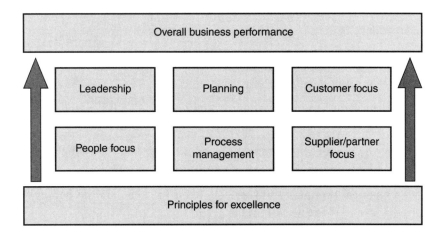

Figure 5.2 Canadian Framework for Business Excellence.

The CAE awards selection process is conducted in three steps. A pre-selection committee reviews all applications and determines if a site visit is warranted to further assess the organization. If so, a verification team meets on-site with employees from various levels throughout the organization. The initial application is reviewed and updated based on the findings of the visit. The pre-selection committee again reviews all the site visit evaluations. A report with award recommendations is prepared and submitted to a selection jury panel. The selection jury panel makes the final determination for trophies and certificates of merit winners. All applicants receive detailed feedback on their submission and may also meet with a member of the pre-selection committee to discuss their results.

Additional information and materials are available on the National Quality Institute Web site: www.nqi.ca .

THE EUROPEAN QUALITY AWARD

The European Quality Award was first awarded in 1992. It was established by the EFQM (European Foundation for Quality Management), founded in 1988, as a not-for-profit membership foundation of some 14 major European companies with the endorsement of the European Commission. Today EFQM has more than 800 organization members in 38 countries of Europe.

The EFQM and the European Organization for Quality (EOQ) administer the award. There are currently four categories for the award:

- Large businesses and business units

- Operational units of companies

- Public sector organizations

- Small- and medium-sized enterprises

  - Independent

  - Subsidiaries

The award was established to:

- Provide consistent European-wide recognition that can be extended to organizations beyond those currently recognized as top achievers

- Maximize the number of organizations who are able to apply the principles of the EFQM Excellence Model for organizational improvement

- Provide practical products and services that help organizations achieve improved levels of excellence

The EFQM Excellence Model is shown in Figure 5.3. Again, this chapter will not discuss the model in detail, as information is readily available from the EFQM Web site at: www.efqm.org .

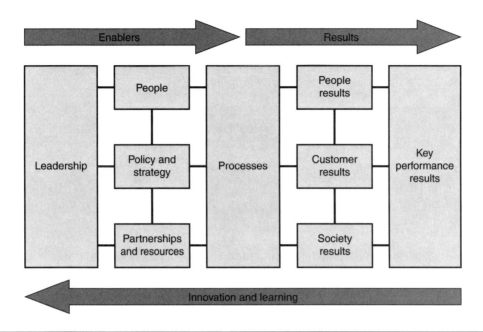

Figure 5.3　The EFQM Excellence Model.

A team of approximately six independent award assessors evaluates all award submissions. Assessors are usually selected from experienced practicing managers in European countries but may also include some academics and quality professionals. The submissions are evaluated and scored to determine if sufficient points have been awarded for a site visit. If a site visit is made, the evaluation is refined as necessary and a report is prepared for the award jurors, where the final decision is made on the winners.

All applicants receive a feedback report at the end of the assessment process. Part of the process will include a meeting with one or more of the assessors to discuss the feedback report.

A unique aspect of the award process is that each applicant is required to submit the names of four assessors that are added to a pool. This has several advantages: it spreads expertise across Europe, assessors can be provided at a minimal cost Europe-wide and the training associated with the assessors will result in a greater understanding of the award model within the organizations that apply for the award.

PRINCIPLES, VALUES, AND CONCEPTS

Each of the national award models is driven by a set of principles, values, or concepts. It is interesting to compare them. There is very much in common; little is unique. The main criteria titles may be somewhat different; however, when the details are analyzed, the criteria include the same things. Common values and principles include: involvement of leadership team, customer focus, results orientation, valuing of employees, management by fact, employee involvement, and innovation and improvement. Table 5.1 shows the comparison of the three award models.

AWARD CRITERIA

The award criteria for each of the national models evolved over time, some much more than others. However, as with the principles, concepts and values, the criteria are very similar. Common to all three award models are leadership, planning, results, customer focus, people focus, and process focus. When the criteria details are further studied, the overlap of the criteria becomes even more obvious. Table 5.2 shows the criteria comparison for the three award models. The criteria numbering and ordering that is used in the table are the same as that used in the award model.

Table 5.1 Values, principles, and concepts of the three major quality award models compared.

Baldrige Award	CAE—Quality	European Quality Award
Values and Concepts	**Principles**	**Concepts**
• Visionary leadership	• Leadership through involvement	• Results-oriented
• Customer-driven excellence	• Primary focus on stakeholders/customers and the marketplace	• Customer focus
• Organizational and personal learning	• Cooperation and teamwork	• Leadership and constancy of purpose
• Valuing employees and partners	• Prevention-based process management	• Management by process and facts
• Agility	• Factual approach to decision making	• People development and involvement
• Focus on the future	• Continuous learning and people involvement	• Continuous learning, innovation, and improvement
• Managing for innovation	• Focus on continuous improvement and breakthrough thinking	• Partnership development
• Management by fact	• Fulfill obligations to all stakeholders and society	• Public responsibility
• Public responsibility and citizenship		
• Focus on results and creating value		
• Systems perspective		

Table 5.2 Award model criteria comparison.

Baldrige Award	CAE—Quality	European Quality Award
1. Leadership • Organizational leadership • Public responsibility and citizenship	1. Leadership • Strategic direction • Leadership involvement • Continuous improvement	1. Leadership
2. Strategic Planning • Strategy development • Strategy deployment	2. Planning • Plan development • Plan implementation and review • Continuous improvement	2. Policy and Strategy
3. Customer and Market Focus • Customer and market knowledge • Customer relationship and satisfaction	3. Customer Focus • Customer, market, and product knowledge • Management of customer relationships • Continuous improvement	3. People
4. Information and Analysis • Measurement and analysis of organizational performance • Information management	4. People Focus • Human resource planning • Participatory environment • Continuous learning • Employee satisfaction and well-being • Continuous improvement	4. Partnership and Resources
5. Human Resource Focus • Work systems • Employee education, training, and development • Employee well-being and satisfaction	5. Process Management • Process development • Process control • Process improvement • Continuous improvement	5. Processes
6. Process Management • Product and service processes • Business processes • Support processes	6. Supplier/Partner Focus • Partnering • Supplier/partner management • Continuous improvement	6. Customer Results
7. Business Results • Customer-focused results • Financial and market results • Human resource results • Organizational effectiveness results	7. Overall Business Performance • Customer focus • People focus • Process management • Partnerships • Responsibility to society • Owner/shareholder focus	7. People Results
		8. Society Results
		9. Key Performance Results

SCORING FOR MODELS

The award models each use a different scoring system to reflect the importance of the individual element criteria.

The Baldrige assessment process is based on a total score of 1000 points. The 2002 Baldrige Award is shown in Table 5.3. There is a very dominant results focus (almost 50 percent of the total score) in the current scoring of the model.

Scoring for the CAE—Quality model is very similar to the Baldrige model. However the point distribution is different for the public and private sectors. Table 5.4 shows this comparison. The private sector scoring is very results-dominated while the public sector is more "process" focused.

Scoring for the EFQM Excellence Model uses a tool that is referred to as RADAR logic. This same RADAR logic is the heart of the EFQM Excellence Model. RADAR logic consists of four elements:

1. Results

2. Approach

3. Deployment

4. Assessment and Review

Table 5.3 Baldrige Award scoring.

Category	Point Value	Percentage
1. Leadership	120	12.0%
2. Strategic Planning	85	8.5%
3. Customer and Market Focus	85	8.5%
4. Information and Analysis	90	9.0%
5. Human Resource Focus	85	8.5%
6. Process Management	85	8.5%
7. Business Results	450	45.0%
Total Points	**1000**	**100.0%**

Table 5.4 CAE—Quality scoring.

	Public Sector	Private Sector
Category	Percentage	Percentage
1. Leadership	10	10
2. Planning	10	8
3. Customer Focus	17	9
4. People Focus	17	14
5. Process Management	17	11
6. Supplier Focus	5	6
7. Organizational Performance	24	42
Total Points	**100**	**100**

To apply this logic, an organization must follow the following four steps:

1. Determine the *results* that are planned as part of its policy and strategic process. The results should include the performance of the organization, both financially and operationally, and the perceptions of their stakeholders.

2. A set of integrated *approaches* are then developed and planned to achieve the results that were determined in step 1.

3. The approaches are then *deployed* systematically to ensure complete implementation.

4. The organization then *assesses* and *reviews* the approaches by monitoring and analyzing the results achieved. Based on the results, the organization then identifies, prioritizes, plans, and implements improvements as required.

CORPORATE QUALITY IMPROVEMENT PLANNING

The largest impact of these national quality awards is derived by the award winners being required to share information on their performance and quality strategies with other organizations. For example, since the Malcolm Baldrige award was established 14 years ago, hundreds of thousands of companies, educational institutions, healthcare organizations, and government agencies have taken advantage of this requirement and learned from the winners.

The national award criteria have been used by thousands of organizations to improve their quality and business performance. Many organizations conduct annual assessments against the criteria as part of their business planning process. To assist organizations in this assessment process, the Baldrige National Quality Program has a free booklet available, Getting Started with the Baldrige National Quality Program Criteria for Performance Excellence: A Guide to Self-Assessment and Action. The National Quality Institute provides training and assistance on its use for self-assessment on the CAE—Quality award. The EFQM has also produced materials to assist with the implementation and evaluation of the EFQM Excellence Model. Books on the EFQM model have also been published.

Several organizations and consultants are also available to provide training on the criteria and assistance in conducting assessments. An excellent book is available through ASQ—*From Baldrige to the Bottom Line* by David Hutton—for additional detailed information on the assessment process when using the Baldrige model.

CONCLUSION

The natural question to ask might be "which is the best quality model?" In fact, there have been various articles written to determine this. However, the correct answer is likely "all of them." Each has its own unique differences. The similarities of these models far outweigh their differences. The best model for your organization is the one that you can implement successfully and sustain over the long term. Sustainability, or, to use one of Deming's 14 points, "constancy of purpose" is one of the most difficult challenges for any organization. Short-term focus and demand for immediate results interfere with efforts to promote these planning models over the long term.

REFERENCES

Beecroft, G. D. "Deming? Malcolm Baldrige? or CABE—Quality?" *IIQP Newsletter* (winter 1992).

The Canada Awards for Excellence—Quality, National Quality Institute, www.nqi.ca .

The Deming Prize. www.deming.org/demingprize/ . Union of Japanese Scientists and Engineers (JUSE), access English language references through The Deming Prize page of The W. Edwards Deming Institute: www.deming.org .

The EFQM Excellence Model. The European Foundation for Quality Management, www.efqm.org .

Hutton, D., *From Baldrige to the Bottom Line.* Milwaukee: ASQ Quality Press, 2000.

The Malcolm Baldrige National Quality Award. The National Institute of Standards and Technology (NIST), www.quality.nist.gov .

6

Core Process Redesign and Management

Richard A. Waks and John W. Moran

The purpose of this chapter is to give an overview of the fundamentals of successful process redesign. Core process redesign[1] is a five-phase team-based methodology that helps institute a systematic process of improving how work is done in organizations. This methodology asks two key questions at every phase:

1. *Does the process under study support the organization's strategic mission?*

2. *Is the process under study necessary to meet the demands of our customers?*

We have found from our experience with redesign that these questions are seldom asked or answered. Often processes not necessary to attaining the strategic mission or to meeting customer demands are redesigned and improved when they should be eliminated.

Other chapters in this book (chapter 14, Measurement—The Balanced Scorecard, chapter 2, Problem Solving and Decision Making for Continuous Improvement, chapter 1, The Challenge of Successful and Sustainable Organizational Change, chapter 7, Using Teams to Achieve Organizational Improvement, chapter 12, Customer Satisfaction As a Driver for Improvement and Change, and chapter 16, How to Get Results: Setting Goals and Hitting Targets) all provide in-depth discussions of topics mentioned in this chapter.

WHAT IS PROCESS REDESIGN?

"The fundamental rethinking and radical redesign of the entire business system to achieve dramatic improvements in critical measures of performance."

—Michael Hammer, *Reengineering: The Implementation Perspective Workbook*, 1994

Core process redesign (CPR) is a team-based action learning methodology for improving what and how work is done in your organization to enhance customer satisfaction, business performance, and the competencies of those who do the work. Whether it is called process reengineering, process redesign, or simply process improvement matters less than applying a systematic team-based approach to exploring, and hopefully refining, the systems people engage in to deliver on customer needs. It is a structured process for self-developed, large-scale change. It is *not:*

- A quick-fix approach
- An "outside expert" approach
- A passing fad or program
- Downsizing or "rightsizing"
- Inflexible to changing needs
- Very fast or easy

WHEN AND WHY REDESIGN?

Every organization struggles with the decisions of when to launch a major process redesign initiative, how to focus it, and who to involve. The identification of redesign opportunities is the purview of senior management. To decide on which areas to focus the effort requires that a thorough analysis, both quantitative and qualitative, be completed. Once this analysis is completed, the data must be utilized to prioritize the areas that have the critical processes most in need of a redesign to align them to the organization's and customer's needs. From our experience it is necessary to redesign when:

- It becomes clear that incremental change will not get the organization to its goals.
- Improvement of functions and departments alone will not achieve the results desired by the organization or its customers.
- The reengineering of just one organizational system will not achieve the results desired by the organization or its customers.

Whichever processes an organization chooses to work on, redesign teams must keep in mind the strategic intent or *focus* of the organization (its values, strategy, and goals) and the other components of the organization it may choose to redesign. When teams make a design choice about changing a work process, it must be in concert or *aligned* with these other organizational characteristics.

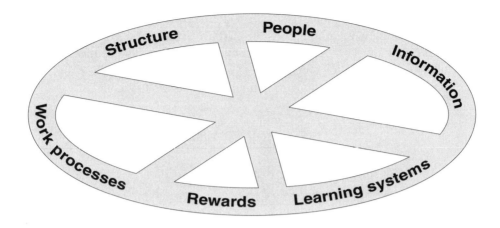

Figure 6.1   Six areas critical to successful business outcomes.

ORGANIZATIONAL REDESIGN CHOICES

When a redesign team begins the CPR process they need to keep in mind the six redesign areas shown in Figure 6.1. These six areas are critical to successful business outcomes, since improving these in the redesign ensures that the changes being made really take hold in the organization. The six areas are as follows:

1. *Information* deals with the types of information provided by the organization to its personnel, its accessibility, and timeliness in making decisions. Information also encompasses the critical measures the organization uses to assess its performance to determine if it is successfully meeting the needs of its customers and employees.

2. *Structure* looks at how the organization is organized and what are the roles, responsibilities, and accountability of each area of the organization.

3. *People* is the total human potential of the organization. This is the process of how the organization acquires, develops, and retains its personnel.

4. *Rewards* focuses on how the organization formally and informally compensates its personnel for their time and effort. The reward structure must align the process with the organization's goals. There is an old saying, "that which gets rewarded gets done." Organizations need to ensure that the compensation and reward systems drive the behaviors they desire.

5. *Learning systems* help improve processes since they help improve the organization's people's capabilities. These are the processes that help people acquire, transfer, and improve their knowledge base.

6. *Work processes* helps the organization and its personnel focus on the concept of a process view of what it does to satisfy internal and external customers. A process view does not replace a functional view of work. The process view shows how the functional components are linked together or flow together to transform a series of inputs into value-added outputs to customers.

THE CPR PATHWAY

The systematic CPR methodology for exploring and refining central work processes involves five phases, as shown in Figure 6.2.

Phase 1—Focus

The first real step in an organizational redesign effort is to select those processes that have the highest potential payoff if redesigned. These are the processes with the largest gaps between performance and customer requirements or those processes most centrally linked to the success of organizational strategy. Senior management usually undertakes this focus step as the result of an organizational assessment and thorough data analysis. Here they wrestle with existing strategy and goals, cost data, customer data, and staff input.

Once these high-priority processes have been chosen, the senior managers of an organization sponsor teams of employees to tackle the work of redesign. They *focus*

Phase 1: Focus	Phase 2: Assessment	Phase 3: Negotiation	Phase 4: Redesign	Phase 5: Implementation
Form team	Map process	Identify unmet customer needs	ACT • Analyze • Conclude • Test	Analyze implications Seek approval
Focus team • Mission • Scope • Objectives • Strategic ties • Measures	Assess and validate customer needs	Negotiate valid requirements Set improvement targets and success measures		Refine Monitor and measure
Outcome: Establish the change imperative and guiding principles	*Outcome:* Understand the current business situation	*Outcome:* Define real requirements and gaps in performance	*Outcomes:* Develop the change plan Pilot testing Refinements	*Outcome:* Dramatically improved performance

Figure 6.2   A core process redesign pathway.

organizational resources on improving the processes they have selected. In addition, as teams meet for the first time, they must *focus* on management's requirements of their work together. Hence, phase one is called *Focus*. There are two key activities in this first phase.

During the first phase of CPR, each team formed by management must (1) identify the scope of its proposed work and (2) document its agreements with its sponsor (in management). This means drafting a team charter and reviewing it with the team's sponsor before any further work, thus ensuring alignment of mission, scope, objectives, ties with strategy, and measures of progress and success. Figure 6.3 shows an example of a CPR team charter the authors have used successfully in many organizations.

The team charter is a dynamic document. It is updated as necessary so that as the team moves through the CPR process it actually reflects what is being focused on, the

1. Team Charter		
❏ Project		
❏ Task Force			

2. Team Name: Safety Process Team	3. Version: 01	4. Subject: Improved process dynamics

5. Problem/Opportunity Statement: Review and revise the "as is" safety processes to bring into compliance with current regulatory requirements.		

6. Strategic Alignment: To create a safe work environment for all employees at XYZ. "To always work safely and encourage each other to do so" in everything we do.		7. Team Leader: R. Waks

8. Team Sponsor: J. Moran, H.R. Manager	9. Team Facilitator: G. Duffy

10. Team Members:	Area of Expertise:
1. Hal R.—Construction Supervisor	Construction
2. Mary M.—Network Manager	Network
3. Tom S.—Maintenance Supervisor	Maintenance
4. Herb M.—Installation/Repair Manager	Installation/repair
5. Donna T.—Safety Secretary	Safety office
6. Others as required	

11. Performance Improvement AIM (Mission):   Initiate an aggressive safety plan at XYZ, raise employee awareness, and create an accident-free workplace.

12. Scope (Boundaries):   To have all internal and external work performed for XYZ be accident-free.

Figure 6.3 Example of CPR team charter.   *continued*

continued

13. Customers (primary and other):	Customer Needs Addressed:
• Employees	Update and train employees on safety practices.
• External customers	Job site safety: equipment use and work processes
• Insurance carrier, OSHA officials, and other agencies	Record keeping, filings, responds to changes.
• Contractors	Identify Gulf safety practices.

14. Objectives:

- Provide proper training in all areas of safety.
- Develop a smooth handoff procedure to process owners for safety policy, practices, and procedures.
- Follow up with documentation and auditing.
- Create safe work environment. Develop new employee or transfer orientation.
- Comply with all OSHA, DOT, State, and local requirements.

15. Success Metrics (Measures):

- Reduce lost-time accidents from 1–2 per month to an accident-free workplace.
- Compliant facility audit and compliant job site audit.

16. Considerations (Assumptions/Constraints/Obstacles/Risks):

- XYZ will be a safe place to work.
- Employees are complacent.
- Process owners will fail to communicate safety process.
- Risks are accidents, severe injuries, and loss of extremity or life.

17. Team Member Time Commitments: 2 hours/week	18. Available Resources: Process owners and/or designated employees

19. Key Milestones:		Date:
• Completing team charter		3 weeks
• Flowchart safety process "as is " state.		4 weeks

20. Communication Plan (Who, How, and When):
Weekly meeting minutes to H.R. manager, team, president, process owners.

21. Key Stakeholders:	Area of Concern (as it relates to the charter):
• VP of HR	Safety
• Process owners	Each business process
• Employees	Employee injuries

Figure 6.3 Example of CPR team charter.

goals to be achieved, and the time frame for implementation. This is an excellent review document for senior management since it concisely states the team's mission to be accomplished.

Phase 2—Assessment

This is where the real work begins! Phase two of CPR starts by gathering baseline data along two dimensions:

1. Process capabilities

2. Customer needs

Determining *process capabilities* (what it can do or deliver) involves mapping the flow of activities as they *currently* occur and measuring the input, output, and value added of these activities, separately and in total. This gives the team an important baseline against which it can later evaluate redesign options. As the team develops its flowchart of the current state, many times they find unnecessary work being performed or reports developed, and eliminate them during this step. This process is a dynamic one, and improvement opportunities do not have to wait until the end of the process to be made. If it is not useful, eliminate it.

Assessing *customer needs* (what they believe they want or require) is, of course, critical to measuring the success of a process. Customers are the *raison d'être* of a work process. They are for whom the team does what it does. This component of assessment involves identifying the internal and external customers of the process, documenting what the team knows these customers currently need and might expect in the future, and planning how they will close any gaps in their knowledge and understanding.

These two key dimensions of assessment are best done simultaneously because *organizational success* (for example, goals such as good product innovation/quality, customer satisfaction, and financial performance) is a function of aligning process capabilities with customer needs. There are two paths to organizational success: closing performance gaps and/or taking risks to leverage growth opportunities.

There are two types of misalignment to consider as teams move on to phase 3—negotiation:

1. *Performance gaps.* These occur when a process is not delivering on customer needs. Teams must work to close these gaps by improving the capabilities of the process or renegotiating the validity of customers' needs. (Needs are not valid requirements unless you are willing and able to commit to fulfilling them.)

2. *Growth opportunities/risks.* These present themselves when a process is delivering above and beyond what customers need. Teams may or may not want to leverage these opportunities; doing so is a risk. If the process is functioning in anticipation of true, future customer expectations, this performance can be a company's competitive advantage. If the team is wrong about the future, customers may see the process as "goldplating," adding value that is not and will not be appreciated nor requested.

Analyzing Process Performance

Once the team has described the process in phase 2, it can use the description as a framework for understanding how well each component is working when it analyzes the root causes/drivers of performance gaps in phase 4. Three aspects of performance are important in this context:

1. Process time (cycle or throughput)

2. Costs (fixed and variable)

3. Rework and/or defects (product or service quality)

The team may want to study all three dimensions of performance in relation to its particular process, or it may for the moment be interested in only one or two of them—it depends on the mission of the team.

If the process performs well on all three of these dimensions and has been built to meet the appropriate customer requirements, then customer satisfaction should follow.

It is important to note that these three aspects of performance are internal or "self" measures—ones that the team and the company care about improving. On the other hand, customers use a completely different set of measures. Their *perception* of an organization's speed, integrity, competence, flexibility, and so on, determines their level of satisfaction. They could care less about what it costs the company to get the job done or how much rework was involved. Customers care about product or service outputs and their interface with the people who deliver them.

Phase 3—Negotiation

Unlike most process improvement methodologies, in which a team draws maps of the "current process," goes out and asks customers what they want, and then dives into analysis of how to make it happen, CPR spends a whole phase in the middle on "negotiation." By negotiation, we do not simply mean "haggling" with customers, but drawing them in as process *partners*.

Critical to an understanding of process partnership is the idea of negotiating the *validity* of customers' needs. As noted in phase 2, needs are not valid requirements unless you are willing to commit to fulfilling them. Getting to a point where both operators (suppliers) and customers of the process both feel as though their concerns are being addressed involves discussion, joint ownership, and collaborative problem solving. The actual redesign of the work process begins during these discussions, not in a back room crammed with flipcharts and Post-it notes.

Since redesign may involve great changes in who does the work and how it is done, this phase concludes with a reconsideration of targets. With growing pressure to reduce resources and increase productivity—doing more with less—it is essential that the team is very clear during Phase 4 about what it is going after. As we all know, the days of unending TQM teams spinning their wheels or missing the mark are surely an endangered species in today's rapidly changing business environment.

Validating Customer Needs

In the previous phase, the team made some assessments based on its collective assumptions about customer needs and process capabilities. Before it can use these decisions to focus its redesign efforts, the team must *validate* (confirm) these assumptions by talking to its customers again.

The team must remember that *organizational success* (which includes goals such as product/service quality, customer satisfaction, and financial performance) is a function of aligning process capabilities with customer needs.

For a work process to function effectively, both customers (internal and external) and suppliers (those who operate the process) must have their needs and interests met. If customers feel that the value of an output or service is not worth the price, they will not buy it (or they'll get it outside the organization). On the other hand, if suppliers feel that they are not receiving a fair price, or the process is incapable, they will not sell it or deliver it.

Traditionally, suppliers within an organization have had a captive market in their internal customers, so they have not had to take their customers' needs completely seriously. However, other business units, departments, and even internal process partners are increasingly free to decide whether to procure their services within the company or purchase them outside from another vendor.

As customer needs increase and vital organizational resources diminish, it becomes ever more critical to redesign processes in ways that ensure alignment. From the perspective of the designer, this means soliciting, validating, and prioritizing customer needs through *negotiation*—a series of questions that build partnerships with customers:

- What are your basic, root needs?

- Which are more important than others? What can you live without?

- What would you consider ideal performance?

- How satisfied are you with current performance?

- Where do you feel there are gaps in performance?

- What do your customers need?

- Where do you see poor quality, wasted time, or unnecessary costs?

And a series of questions to ask the team:

- What is the process *really* capable of delivering?

- Where are the gaps?

- What's most important to fix?

- Which needs cannot be addressed?

Implied in these questions, on the low end, is the usual give and take of traditional negotiation. On the high end, it means forming new, less adversarial relationships with customers by building relationships based on collaboration, trust, and mutual problem solving.

Phase 4—Redesign

O! when degree is shaked,
Which is the ladder to all high designs,
The enterprise is sick.

—William Shakespeare, *Troilus and Cressida,* 1602

The idea of restructuring . . . combines continuity and innovation . . .

—Mikhail S. Gorbachev, 1987

This is it. This is the phase where the team must make decisions about redesign; how the process *might* work better. Decisions about what to keep, what to eliminate, and what to fix are really just a series of *educated guesses*. They are educated because they are based on the team's careful analyses of valid data; they are guesses because they are based on each member's experience, instincts, and intuition.

Many improvement methodologies (and their purveyors) promise that they can provide magic at a certain point during redesign efforts, as though there were some sort of trick built into step X of the work. CPR offers no magic except for the natural synergy of getting the right people in the room—those who know the most about a particular work process—and providing platforms, tools, and activities that can help a team tap into its members' creative and analytical capabilities.

In this phase of CPR, teams continue their analysis of the current work process by looking more closely at the root causes or *drivers* of key performance gaps and they start to explore options for closing them. This exploration entails asking a series of questions that will help the team focus on which options will give it the best improvements—lowered costs, reduced process time, and improved output/service quality.

The team already has many of the answers to these questions. By describing the current process, measuring its capabilities, and comparing this data with negotiated (valid) customer needs, it has already identified some of the shortcomings of the process. Undoubtedly, they have also started to draw conclusions about where they can change things to meet stated customer needs.

However, they need to be careful about their initial conclusions. This phase involves a very basic principle, a form of scientific method: make a hypothesis and run a scenario analysis. For every change the team proposes making in how the process operates, it will need to look carefully at the potential *consequences* of the change. For example,

- If the team takes out one step (activity, task, approval, handoff, and so on) to lower costs, what might happen to output/service quality? How might it impact other processes it supports?

- If they reroute the process around other steps to improve cycle time, what might happen to coordination?

- If they add steps somewhere else to increase output/service quality, what might happen to the overall costs?

Every change imaginable has consequences, intended and unintended. The goal as a redesign team is to find optimal solutions by identifying consequences and making careful choices through "laboratory" scenario testing. The questions are endless, but the variables are not. If team members keep their collective eyes on costs, time, and quality, they can better manage the unintended consequences of change that will invariably pop up during implementation.

One tool we have found useful for CPR teams to use in this phase is "ACT" (Analyze—Conclude—Test).

The main activities of new design can be broken down to three basic steps:

1. *Analyze* the work process to look for the root causes or drivers of performance gaps.

2. Draw *conclusions* about what changes will close these gaps.

3. *Test* your conclusions about whether you have the right improvements and whether you have gone far enough.

As noted when the team was describing the current process, analyzing processes begins the moment you get a group of people together. Even drawing a basic flowchart will reveal quick fixes and immediate improvement opportunities. Maps drawn for basic descriptive purposes are analytical in nature. Beyond basic descriptive maps, teams can use:

- *Cross-functional flowcharts.* These are flowcharts arranged into columns (or rows) that show the departments or functions that do each of the sequenced activities/tasks.

- *Handoff diagrams.* These cross-functional flowcharts focus on the "white space"—the arrows between activities or functions. They can help spot inefficient, unnecessary, or problematic exchanges of materials or information.

- *Activity analysis grids.* These charts help look at the gaps in the performance of individual activities in a work process along three key dimensions—time, cost, and quality.

- *Consequence analysis.* This simple analysis chart allows you to test the potential impact of eliminating or resequencing steps and activities in a work process. It is usually used toward the end of an analysis phase to help check the viability of different scenarios.

Remember, it is important to analyze three aspects of performance:

1. Process time (cycle or throughput)

2. Costs (fixed and variable)

3. Rework and/or defects (product or service quality)

Teams may want to study all three dimensions of performance in relation to their particular process, or they may, for the moment, be interested in only one or two of these variables—it depends on the mission/aim of the team.

There are tools that can help the team analyze one or two of the variables in isolation. Using them can be particularly helpful in measuring potential trade-offs. A few of these are:

• *Activity-based costing (ABC)*. This form of accounting analysis can be used to assess total and hidden costs of a work process. It involves looking at the fixed and variable costs of each step in the process; adding in the costs of personnel operating the process (for example, their salaries and benefits), the costs of the space used by the process, and out-of-pocket expenses; and thereby assessing the value of each activity relative to the time it takes to complete.

• *"Stat" analysis*. This tool allows a team to spot wasted time in a work process by comparing the actual time used in each of the steps when it is done "stat" with the total elapsed time it usually takes for each step in a process to cycle an initial (or "triggering") input into a final (or "terminating") output. The amount of time where information, a customer, or any other product/service is not being worked on (being "touched") is potentially wasted time. A simple form of this tool is to "staple yourself to a customer," where you literally walk with a customer through their contact with a work process. Here you can observe and measure the process as a real experience.

• *Control charts*. These traditional TQM charts are a measurement tool that can help teams spot patterns of variation in output quality. They involve setting control limits of normal/acceptable performance based on past performance, monitoring output over time, and looking for variations beyond the control limits.

Phase 5—Implementation

> *There is nothing more difficult to take in hand, more perilous to conduct, or more uncertain in its success, than to take the lead in the introduction of a new order of things.*
>
> —Niccolo Machiavelli, *The Prince*, 1532

Once the team has a proposed new work process, it is probably eager to see it in action—to test and finalize new structures and standards for how work flows through the process. This is natural, but premature.

Successful implementation of CPR is a carefully analyzed and orchestrated process that takes into account the anticipated effects of proposed changes on the people and systems of the organization. If the team can anticipate the implications of changing the work process on such things as the competencies of the people who do the work, the information needed to get the work done, and the types of reward mechanisms needed to drive appropriate behavior, it can minimize potential failure down the road. All too often, changes that seem appropriate at one level or place in the company wreak havoc somewhere else. To avoid fixes akin to "sticking your finger in the dike," while other leaks sprout, the team must step back and take a strategic view of the "whole dam."

Successful implementation of CPR is also an *iterative process.* After each step in implementation, the team must consider what modifications are needed to improve its design. Following are the steps and points of modification a team should go through before it can finalize its redesigned work process.

Redesign teams must think of themselves as expert consultants hired by their company. As such, they would go through a very similar contracting process (the focus phase of CPR):

- Conduct a capabilities and customer assessment (the assessment and negotiation phases)

- Develop initial recommendations (the redesign phase)

- Work with the client (the team's sponsor and senior management group) to finalize and implement its recommendations (this phase).

Just like outside consultants, the team must give senior management the most cogent information and its most well thought out recommendations, and be willing to modify its proposal to suit their needs. It is the senior management group's responsibility to consider the recommendations of multiple teams in the context of each other. Invariably, there will be conflicts that must be negotiated and modifications that must be made. Remember, changes to one process cannot be made in a vacuum; all processes must be coordinated and aligned so the entire system functions at an optimal level.

TRANSITION AND IMPLEMENTATION TO THE NEW PROCESS "RED ZONE"

Change does not occur all at once. Redesign will not simply be implemented one Monday morning. During implementation, those involved will go through a "red zone," where they are doing things partly the old way and partly the new way. This is a critical period where operations themselves are going through a transition, not just people's emotions. In a service organization, this period can have disastrous consequences. But careful monitoring, problem solving, and communication can minimize the risks involved.

Another potential problem midway through the changeover is the tendency to mix what is left of the old with the new, and produce a hybrid that will not achieve a company's objectives and may turn out to be worse than the old process the team is trying to improve. Staying attentive to the transition will ensure that everyone is kept informed, and as resources are freed-up from the old system, they can be redeployed to the new process in a planned, orderly manner.

CONCLUSION

The process described in this chapter for doing successful process redesign has a systematic team-based methodology as its core component for improving how work is accomplished effectively and efficiently in an organization. CPR is a structured process to deliver not only a redesign process but organizational change as well. We have used this CPR methodology successfully in manufacturing, financial services, healthcare, information technology, telecommunications, and service industries. This process adapts to the industry since it is focused on improving processes, which every industry has as its core for delivering its products or services to its customers.

Stated below are the "laws" we have learned from our involvement with CPR teams. We share them with you so that your redesign efforts will be successful.

The Laws of Process Redesign

1. All decisions must be driven by data; confirm all assumptions.

2. Stay focused on meeting (or exceeding) customer requirements and fulfilling organizational strategy.

3. Fix whatever you can immediately.

4. Use ongoing measurement (both process and results) to keep you informed and on target.

5. The phases of redesign are not completely linear—learn, recalibrate, and refocus as necessary.

6. Wallow in constructive conflict; arbitrate with data.

7. Avoid "analysis paralysis" by testing best guesses.

8. Keep people who are not on the team informed.

9. Improvement work is continuous—you are never completely done—but don't forget to celebrate your successes!

ENDNOTE

1. Core Process Redesign is a consulting and training product of RAW Consulting and is being used with permission as the basis of this chapter.

7

Using Teams to Achieve Organizational Improvement

Grace L. Duffy

Building teams has never been optional. The great heroes, no matter how self-sufficient, have a core of trusted associates around them when times get tough. Red Adair, the famous Texas Oil field engineer of the late 1900s, didn't shut down oil rig fires by himself, New York City police and fire workers all pulled together after 9/11, and Warren Buffet, the hero of Wall Street, checks his sources before buying and selling companies.

Executives become executives because we know how to work with others. Teams come in many different flavors; forever changing based on the goal of the situation. Every day situations happen that draw us together to use our common knowledge and skills for improvement and change. These situations become unifiers of people, uniting us in unique ways. People working together to make improvement within an organization is a concept that has been around for as long as organizations have existed.

Good teams require good leaders who value their employees' opinions, are not threatened by them, and reward workers when appropriate. Good leaders serve as coaches, not commanders. We realize, too, that we all benefit when teams for which we are ultimately responsible accomplish good work. We value our employees' opinions and facilitate rather than control problem solving and decision making.

Over the last two decades, team members have been given more autonomy within the team as companies struggle to become more competitive. The concept of teams has adapted to the requirements of business. Formal teams came into existence in the 1960s with the influence of global work methods. The Japanese concept of quality circles, individuals from the same work unit working together to improve their products and output, was very popular in the 1970s. Since then, the idea of groups of employees meeting together to solve problems affecting their work area has become increasingly common. Teams have been told that their opinions count and that they will be recognized for their good work individually and as part of a team. Successful teams today are effective because individual expectations are met and not at the expense of the organization.

The company's expectations are met, too, when a team is successful. Companies formulate teams for a variety of reasons. Mostly teams are asked to solve problems so an organization can become more competitive. More recently, with the pressure to reduce levels of management, teams have been given further authority and accountability for critical processes within the organization. Several other chapters in this Guide reference the benefit of team involvement in problem solving, decision making, Six Sigma projects, supply chain management, and other areas critical to business results.

Some of the most dramatic examples of teams effecting change involve simple problems. These are problems that are well understood by the average employee; the employee closest to the problem—perhaps better understood than by management. As an example, the faculty and staff of a South Carolina technical college banded together to answer telephones during open registration. This initiative began after Trident Technical College, which serves over 10,000 curriculum students, documented some 3,000 calls for which students or potential students received an "all lines busy, please call again" message. Through changes resulting from the efforts of one process improvement team, these 3,000 calls were reduced to 5 during a recent registration period.

This example shows the impact of employees and other team members banding together with a common goal. The situation, whether a crisis or just a good idea, provides an environment for growth. When teams are successful, they improve employee morale and ultimately contribute to a culture that helps keep employees satisfied with their work environment. This positive attitude helps maintain a low turnover rate within the organization, because individuals feel they have contributed, added value, and made a difference.

Individually, when people change their attitude at work, their personal lives are affected. Personal relationships developed at Trident Technical College have remained strong among the original team members nine years after the project was finalized and process changes integrated into the daily operations of the college. See chapter 16, How to Get Results: Setting Goals and Hitting Targets, for a complete description of the improvement culture developed by Dr. Thornley and her associates, using teams and leadership excellence, at Trident Technical College.

Building teams means creating the opportunity for people to come together to share concerns, ideas, and experiences, and to begin working together to solve problems and achieve common goals. There are some significant risks we take as executives when we encourage teams in our business. Involving others in decision making takes time. It is easier in the short-term to make choices on our own. Many of us fear the overwhelming wave of opinion and input that comes with supporting a team environment. Some of us are concerned about being confronted with evidence of our own fallibility or we just don't see teams as worth the time. Many of us have heard stories of instituting teams into the organization causing severe disruption. How do we circumvent these potential pitfalls and support the positive outcomes teams can offer?

The Stuck Organization	The Moving Organization
Internally-driven	Customer-driven
Functionally-focused	Process-focused
Management-centered	Employee-involved

Figure 7.1   Contrasting the stuck and the moving organization.

From J. H. Zenger, E. Musselwhite, K. Hurson, and C. Perrin. *Leading Teams, Mastering the New Role.* Burr Ridge, IL: Irwin Professional Publishing, 1994. Used by permission.

THE EXECUTIVE'S ROLE IN SUSTAINING TEAMS

Teams are essential to the customer-driven and process-focused organization. Other chapters in this Guide address the ongoing need to involve suppliers and customers in our efforts for continual improvement. Figure 7.1 contrasts the characteristics of the traditional organization with the organization now required for competitive success. Zenger et al., in their work of the mid 1990s, *Leading Teams,* talks about the 180-degree change that has occurred in the organization.[1] Organizations have radically altered direction in several ways to address heightened competition and economic pressures.

The stuck organization in Figure 7.1 represents the traditional top-down silo approach to management. When the rate of change was slower, we were able to look inside the organization for stable processes, long-term successful trends, and consistent management practices. Now that the rate of change has escalated, the organization must be constantly "moving" toward bigger, better, and faster ways of meeting customer expectations. The organization has moved from internally-driven to customer-driven, from functionally-focused to process-focused, from management-centered to employee-involved.

Why is this the case? Because the global economy has become totally interdependent. One organization can no longer live in its own world without considering the impact of what is going on around it. We are forced to anticipate customer needs, forced to consider the impact of processes that overlap all areas of the supply chain, forced to consider the valuable input to be gained from employees and partners.

If teams are essential to the new organization, skilled leaders are essential for effective teams. The executive in such an organization has a role that, like a fulcrum, must balance the load and support its weight. Leadership of the team environment is the very core of success. The executive and senior management team can be the life or death of teams in the organization. Critical elements of executive leadership are:

- Special training and skills in team leadership and support to reduce the risk of failure in the eyes of the individual teams and the organization as a whole

- Senior management support, attention, and training for the first-line team leaders

- Increased visibility of executive management in team activities and review meetings

- Clear charters from senior management for the roles, responsibilities, and authority of teams, especially where teams overlap established reporting structures

- Explicit assurance to first-line team leaders that their assignments are more than just an additional duty in their daily assignment

Without skilled leadership at all levels, teams can easily flounder, go too far or not far enough, lose confidence, or simply lose sight of the assigned goal. People who contribute to the direction and focus of the business with their ideas and suggestions feel a greater sense of ownership and involvement. Not only is the quality of work better, but also, as workers are more committed and involved, employees stay longer and commit at greater levels.

Many line and mid-level managers have been eliminated from organizations as an expense reduction, and yet this segment is an essential link in any improvement process. It is the middle manager that encourages the first line to share the things they learn about the business, customers, products, pricing, economy, trends, and anything else that allows them to contribute ideas for improvement. Make it easy for senior and middle managers to contribute and acknowledge the contributions of teams in your organization.

H. James Harrington writes in *Quality Digest,* (August 2002), "top management is essential to getting any improvement process started, but middle management keeps it going. If top managers truly accept their roles as planners and direction-setters, they distance themselves from day-to-day problems facing their businesses, which means it's middle managers who actually run their organizations and ensure that they continue to improve."[2]

Executives must not ignore the valuable common ground middle managers inhabit in the team environment. Top leadership must focus on the outside customer and stakeholders and yet remain supportive of the internal employees who keep the business going. Executives set the direction; middle managers take that direction and make it happen with the first line.

The executive's role in a team environment is complex. Using the senior and middle management structure to cascade team behaviors from the executive office to the first line supervisor and line worker enhances this role. Figure 7.2 lists some behaviors suggested by Harrington to maximize the effectiveness of the senior management team.

A key part of any change process is cascading sponsorship. Without a concentrated effort directed at transforming the senior management team, creating the team environment throughout the organization will fail. Employees at all levels of the organization must feel motivated to participate in the team environment.

A basic principle in relationships is that one person cannot "motivate" another. Motivation comes from within and is a consequence of one's environment. This environment may consist of past experiences, the present situation, competency to do the job, working conditions, degree to which one feels empowered to act on behalf of

- Developing close working relationships with and understanding of their customers
- Focusing on the big picture and managing it
- Focusing on process rather than the actions
- Recognizing continuous improvement as well as meeting targets
- Rejecting requests to make decisions that should be made at lower levels
- Providing role models for first-level managers and employees
- Maintaining honesty
- Sacrificing departmental performance when necessary to improve total organizational performance
- Proactively stimulating upward communication
- Sharing data openly at all levels
- Practicing consensus decision making whenever possible
- Communicating priorities and holding to them
- Establishing networks that identify potential negative trends
- Placing a high priority on problem prevention
- Treating everyone as equally important
- Demonstrating the importance of meeting schedules and getting the job done without compromising quality
- Handling negative situations with a smile more often than with a frown
- Being a good listener

Figure 7.2 Executive behaviors for encouraging middle management team support.

the business, and so on. Each person has a unique set of needs that, if fulfilled, helps them feel motivated. An effective leader provides an environment in which teams may feel motivated.

To do this, Russell Westcott, co-author of *The Quality Improvement Handbook,* suggests using the "six Rs":

1. *Reinforce.* Identify and positively reinforce work done well.

2. *Request* information. Discuss team members' views. Is anything preventing expected performance?

3. *Resources.* Identify needed resources, the lack of which could impede effective performance.

4. *Responsibility.* Customers make paydays possible, all employees have a responsibility to the customers, internal and external.

5. *Role.* Be a role model. Don't just tell; demonstrate how to do it. Observe the team's performance. Together, critique the approach and work out an improved method.

6. *Repeat.* Apply the above principles regularly and repetitively.[3]

The executive sets the stage for a motivating environment. The development of a team culture creates the climate in which motivation can grow. Since those within the organization always notice the senior management team, our behaviors are critical to the establishment of effective team behaviors throughout the company. Figure 7.3 identifies a number of techniques that have proven to be effective team motivators.

TEAMS COME IN DIFFERENT FORMS

A team is a group of individuals organized to work together to accomplish a specific objective. An organizational work group may not necessarily function as a team. However, a team may be comprised of members of a work group. When a group comes together in a synergistic whole to accomplish a common goal, those individuals become a team.

A team cares about achieving common goals. Teams are formed with the understanding that improvement can be achieved using the skills, talents, and knowledge of appropriate individuals. Several different types of teams are described following.

- Catch team members doing something right and positively reinforce the good behavior in that specific situation.

- Use mistakes as learning opportunities.

- Reward team leaders and members who take risks in changing, even if they sometimes fail.

- When discussing situations, listen closely to the team leader or member. Respect their opinion, even if it must be modified.

- Acknowledge the team's reason for action, but don't agree to it if it's inappropriate.

- When giving performance feedback, reveal reactions *after* describing the behavior needing change, not before it.

- Encourage members to make suggestions for improving. Always give credit to the team or member making the suggestion.

- Treat teams with even more care than other business assets.

Figure 7.3 Leadership techniques for effective team motivation.

Departmental or Work Team

A departmental team is comprised of persons having responsibility for a specific process or function and who work together in a participative environment. The departmental team is a permanent group generally reporting to a single, common management. Employees, as a group, assume added responsibility for solving problems and making improvements within their own department or function. The team leader is generally the one responsible for the function or process performed within the work area.

Improvement Team

Process improvement teams (PITs) focus on creating or improving a specific business process. A PIT may attempt to completely reengineer a process or work on incremental improvements. If addressing a major improvement, the team is usually cross-functional, with representatives from a number of different functions. Managers often assign a problem to a temporary group of employees selected for specific skills or characteristics related to the issue or improvement.

Cross-Functional Team

People from different functions or departments meet regularly to address mutual problems or issues; hence the term "cross-functional." Process improvement teams will often become cross-functional if the objective of the PIT is to effect a major improvement or change.

In some organizations, cross-functional teams carry out all or nearly all of the functions of the organization. In such cases, the organization resembles a matrix- or project-type organization. Organizations, in attempting to eliminate internal competition among functional groups, have adopted cross-functional teams for many areas, including administrative support, information systems, facilities management, and so on.

The smaller the organization, the more employees are required to work together, often backing each other up as needs arise. Each employee develops a set of overlapping skills in several technical areas. In recent times, larger organizations have come to recognize the value of smaller, cross-functional teams. These flexible teams can move more quickly than larger competitors by reconfiguring themselves to meet changing needs.

Project Team

A project team is formed to achieve a specific mission. The project team's objective may be to create something new, for example, a new product or service, or to accomplish a complex task, for example, upgrade the human resources database.

Typically, a project team employs full-time members on temporary assignment for the duration of the project. The project team operates in parallel with the primary organizational functions. The project team may or may not be cross-functional in member composition, depending upon its objectives and competency needs. Often the project leader may be the person to whom the ultimate responsibility for managing the resulting project outcome is assigned.

Self-Managed Team

Self-managed teams are intact work groups that handle most daily operational issues with minimal supervision. Often called high-performance work teams, these teams offer employees a broader accountability and process ownership. The members often select their own team leaders.

Because of the level of empowerment afforded, careful planning and training is key to a successful self-managed team. Self-managed teams must be enabled first or they are simply leaderless groups of individuals. Establishing self-managed teams is easiest in a new function with little established history. Transforming a traditional work culture to self-management is a difficult process and may be quite disruptive to the organization.

Virtual Team

Virtual teams are groups of two or more persons, usually affiliated with a common purpose. Team members often are not from the same company or organization. The virtual team either partly or entirely conducts their work via electronic communication. Virtual teams may or may not be cross-functional in skills or reporting structure. These teams may or may not be self-managed. Typically the virtual team is geographically dispersed.

ESSENTIAL CHARACTERISTICS OF ALL TEAMS

No matter what form teams take, there are common characteristics of all successful teams. The organization must focus on integrating these characteristics into the work environment *before* implementing the team concept. Much has been written about these components of effective team building, so only the basics will be identified here.

John Zenger[4] includes the following as some crucial characteristics for members when first initiating a team environment:

Common goals

Leadership

Involvement

Self-esteem

Open communication

Power to make decisions

Planning

Trust

Respect for others

Conflict resolution

These characteristics are major contributors to high employee morale. They also positively influence customer satisfaction, whether internal or external. The same skills we executives are required to use work well at all levels of the organization. Figure 7.4 summarizes many of the characteristics and elements of dynamic and successful teams.

LEADING TO GET THE WORK DONE

A team cannot function effectively unless the members individually function well. The performance of each person acts as a catalyst to the others. It goes back to the cliché about the whole being more than the sum of the parts. Synergy is critical in realizing the benefits of a team environment.

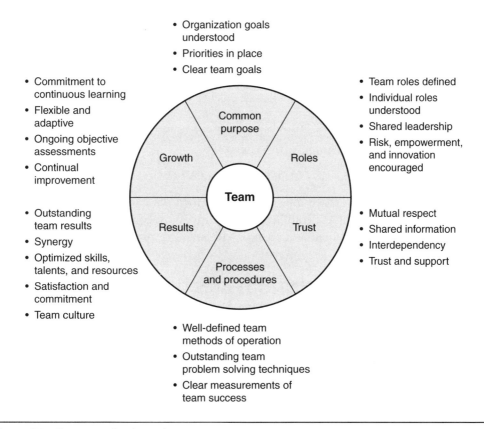

Figure 7.4   Elements of a dynamic team.

Effective teamwork supports three of the most important motivating factors in the workplace. For most people to feel involved in their jobs they must be:

- Excited about the work

- Fully committed to the work outcomes

- Qualified to do their work

Good leadership generates happy and productive people. Executives are the lifeblood of the attitude within an organization. How the workforce sees the executive behaving sets the stage for what happens throughout the organization.

As leaders, we focus on two main areas: tasks and people. The more we provide an environment in which our people can excel, the less effort we, as executives, need to personally put into the tasks. Create good people, get them working together with the right direction, resources, and authority, and the tasks will get done in a way that delights the customer and other important stakeholders.

The best approach executives can take is to:

1. Reassure

2. Challenge

3. Empathize

4. Inform

5. Explain

6. Direct

7. Guide

8. Delegate

Supporting an effective team environment requires all of the above approaches. For people to work comfortably in teams we must answer yes to each of these three questions:

1. Do the employees really want to be here?

2. Is the objective something worth doing?

3. Does the employee really want to do this task?

If the answer to these three questions is yes, then we can safely start expending resources to provide resources, training, leadership, and recognition to the teams, and feel confident that improvement and change will be the result of their efforts.

MAXIMIZING TEAMS DURING IMPROVEMENT AND CHANGE

Maintaining a strong team environment is difficult in quiet times. It becomes a full-time job during times of revolutionary improvement and change. The executive becomes the ultimate coach. Change reduces productivity, which affects profitability. Teams become distracted by surrounding pressures and lose focus. Some get angry, some try to grab power, some simply retreat into their own shells. Everyone looks to the top to "fix" the discomfort. Even the people who are excited about change and are willing to help don't always agree on the next plan of action.

Trust becomes critical when change escalates. Just when the industry wants innovation, the human response is to entrench into what we already know. Many of us fear the unknown. Trust is best built by letting individuals know "what is ahead" whenever possible.

Conventional team-building techniques may not even be enough. Powerful, energizing leadership is required to help handle the increased pressure of change. The best time for growing trust is when people are being tested or challenged. Only then do we get a chance to really prove anything. Will we keep our word? Are we consistent in our behavior? Are we fair in implementing policies and recognition? Are we visible and involved when the teams need us? Will we put ourselves at risk for the sake of the teams and the company?

Teamwork always carries an element of risk, even in the best of circumstances. If teams do not trust their executive leadership, the risk factor climbs so high that it becomes a barrier to cooperative effort. Individuals start looking out for themselves, at the team's expense, doubting that the group will adequately protect them.

The actions of senior leadership can either encourage or destroy the trust required for an effective team environment. We must not become careless with small actions. Take every chance to create a climate of trust. Actions such as sharing information, following through on commitments, keeping people informed, and helping teams see how their actions directly support bottom-line results, will encourage a climate of trust.

Some major "trust busters" have been identified by Jeff Dorman & Associates, Inc.[5] See table 7.1 for a summary of their suggested indicators of potential team destroyers and corrective approaches.

USING CONFLICT TO STRENGTHEN TEAMS

Conflict is a recognized stage in the team development process. Scholtes, Joiner, and Streibel describe the four phases of team development (forming, storming, norming, and performing) in "The Team Handbook."[6] Since conflict will happen during most change processes, we might as well benefit from it.

Conflict between team members can occur at any of the stages, but is more likely to surface during the *forming* and *storming* stages. Conflict is common and useful. It is a sign of change and movement. Conflict is neither good nor bad. The effort should not be to eliminate conflict but to refocus it as a productive rather than destructive force. Conflict can be a vital, energizing force at work in any team. When conflict occurs within teams, do not ignore it. Address the conflict, use it to find the friction that change has created within the team, and use problem-solving techniques to resolve and improve the situation. See chapter 3 for more on problem solving and team decision-making tools.

Table 7.1   Trust busters and team destroyers.

Indicator	Symptom	Corrective Approach
Purpose of the team is no longer linked to strategic goals of the organization.	The team is excluded from corporate planning. It may not understand its role within the greater organization.	Keep team informed of changes in strategic goals. Involve teams in deploying organizational changes and improvements.
Management commitment and personal involvement has slipped.	Team leadership is unable or unwilling to use a team approach and does not encourage the use of team-building activities. He or she often uses a "command" decision style rather than a "consensus" decision style. The leader does not share his or her power or leadership responsibilities.	Leadership training for all team leaders and supporting managers. Provide strong executive support to those leaders who exhibit team behaviors and reward the same in their employees.
The team is facing a hostile or indifferent environment.	The team's climate discourages members from feeling comfortable, from being direct and open, and from taking risks.	Establish and maintain a strong climate of trust in the company. Reward trusting behavior at all levels of leadership.
Assigned members lack needed knowledge, skills, experience, or attitude.	Team members are not qualified, pro-fessionally or socially, to contribute to the team and thus do not help it to achieve its goals. Team members do not have the specific skills sufficient to meet their assigned task responsibilities.	Initiate or expand a systematic process of skills analysis, training, and development in technical and communication skills for teams and their leaders.
Team coaching is not available or is inadequate for the new tasks.	In order not to upset team members, neither group nor individual errors or weaknesses are addressed directly enough so they are eliminated.	Train team leaders and managers in addressing and correcting issues on a timely basis. Support their efforts.
Team leadership is inadequate to help the team meet objectives.	The team may not understand its objectives; and if it does, it may not believe they are worthwhile. It may set targets that are either uninspiring or unreachable. Team member's performance may be reviewed only infrequently.	Work with senior leadership to establish clear charters for team objectives. Establish review processes to keep targets and progress in view of all involved parties.
Team building is nonexistent or inadequate.	Teams that are required to work together compete rather than collaborate. Because teams do not meet to compare agendas, their priorities may conflict.	Establish and maintain a cycle of communication and team reviews. Train all teams and leaders on meeting skills.
The team process is ignored or improperly managed.	Problems that are faced by the team are not solved effectively and efficiently.	Hold team leaders and facilitators accountable for addressing team problems.
Members are not behaving as a team.	Team members are not committed to the aims and purposes of the team and are reluctant to expend personal energy on meeting the team's goals.	Look for barriers to team commitment. Use senior management to reinforce and recognize good team behavior.
Team members are unsure of what's expected of them.	Team member's roles are not clearly defined, efficient communication procedures have not been developed, and administrative procedures are not supportive of the team's efforts.	Train and implement team facilitators to help teams define roles and responsibilities. Take personal interest in the roles of individual team members.
Recognition and reward for work done well is nonexistent or inappropriate.	Team members do not generate new ideas, perhaps because risk-taking is not encouraged and rewarded by the organizational climate.	Restructure the organization's reward and recognition system to support the new, more effective team environment.

Leaders, with guidance from a facilitator if needed, can help transform a conflict into a problem-solving event by:

- Welcoming differences between teams and team members

- Listening attentively, with understanding rather than judgment

- Helping to clarify common goals among the conflicting parties

- Acknowledging and accepting the feelings of the individuals involved

- Offering support to the parties in resolving the differences

- Reinforcing the value of each of the parties to the organization as a whole

- Creating appropriate means for communication between those involved in the conflict

SUMMARY

Nurturing a team environment is one of the major success factors of any growing business. Just as the entrepreneur must reach out to partners as his or her business expands, so executives in larger organizations must develop a climate of trust in the whole team to maintain competitive results.

The benefit of teamwork is available at any level within the organization. The executive team is one of the most visible, while teams at the line-worker level may provide the best return on investment. The techniques for initiating, maintaining, and rewarding teams are pretty much the same at all levels. Choose the right people, train and mission them appropriately, support and recognize them. Certainly this is easier said than done. The value of the effort is well worth it, however. No one can lead a large and complex organization alone. We need each other to succeed in this environment of rapid change and improvement.

ENDNOTES

1. J. H. Zenger, E. Musselwhite, K. Hurson, and C. Perrin, *Leading Teams, Mastering the New Role* (Burr Ridge, IL: Irwin Professional Publishing, 1994).
2. J. H. Harrington, "Creating New Middle Managers," *Quality Digest* (August 2002): 14.
3. J. Bauer, G. Duffy, R. T. Westcott, *The Quality Improvement Handbook* (Milwaukee: ASQ Quality Press, 2002): 53.
4. See note 1.
5. J. Dorman, *Creating and Leading Effective Team Building Sessions,* Student Guide from Seminar (Charleston, SC: JD&A, 1994).
6. P. Scholtes, B. L. Joiner, B. Streibel, *The Team Handbook,* 2nd ed. (Madison, WI: Oriel, 2000): 6-4 to 6-7.

SUGGESTED READING

Scholtes, P., B. L. Joiner, and B. Streibel. *The Team Handbook,* 2nd edition. Madison, WI: Oriel, 2000.

Zenger, J. H., E. Musselwhite, K. Hurson, and C. Perrin. *Leading Teams, Mastering the New Role.* Burr Ridge, IL: Irwin Professional Publishing, 1994.

8

The Management and Utilization of External Resources In the Workplace

Jeffry Mead, John W. Moran, and John W. Moran III

This chapter is focused on helping managers to successfully engage external resource services, measure benefits received, evaluate the success of the engagement, manage the external resources, and audit performance.

———————————————

Once the decision has been made to bring in resources external to an organization, every manager needs a tutorial on how to manage those external resources so that their organization actually receives what it contracted for in the first place. Too often, organizations engage external resources to help them in a problem situation and then at the end feel they never really received the benefit they expected from the engagement. Many reasons exist as to why external consulting engagements fail or come up short of the client's expectation. Some of those reasons are:

- Initial RFP (request for proposal) was vague in its description of needs.

- Scope of the project changed often, and little documentation was kept on the scope change.

- No benefits were clearly defined.

- Resources, both internal and external, kept changing—lack of continuity on the project.

- Conflict between the engagement manager and client manager.

- No measurement of benefits being received was in place.

- Weekly progress meetings were not held.

- Client did not understand how to manage the external resources.

- The external resources managed the client.

- Conflicts arose between the internal and external resources.

- Client did not provide timely or accurate data.

The list of why projects involving external resources fail is endless. It is our intention in this chapter to provide some techniques that will ensure successful projects when external resources are being utilized.

Every consulting firm has a handbook and course entitled "How to Manage the Client Relationship." Every consultant in the firm takes this course before they go on their first engagement—client management is the lifeblood of a consulting firm. If you can manage the client's behavior and expectations, a successful project will be the result.

The following list of topics are the normal list of what is covered in the "How to Manage the Client Relationship" course:

- Developing, presenting, and winning the contract from the proposal

- Delivering quality client service

- Building client relationships

- Evaluating the client's strengths and weaknesses

- Developing and staffing the work plan

- Presenting progress—verbal and written

- Maintaining worth

- Facilitating client change

- Work papers

- Billing and collecting fees

- Closing out the engagement

- Extending the contract (add-on work)

Guess who they are managing?—*You.* Guess what they are managing?—Your expectation of their work. Guess why they do this?—To maximize the engagement's return to their firm.

The authors do not pretend that there is anything wrong with this approach. It is sound business management on the consulting firm's part. What the authors will do in this chapter is give you, the manager of the external resources, some tips on leveling the playing field so that you, the client, are in charge.

The remainder of this chapter will cover:

- The danger signs when using external resources

- Consulting management versus client management

- The primary aspects of an RFP (request for proposal)

- The types of external resources

- What to look for in the consulting firm and its employees

- What to use external resources for

- What not to use external resources for

- How to track progress and benefits

- How to compensate external resources

- Work papers

DANGER SIGNS WHEN USING EXTERNAL RESOURCES

Bait and Switch

The team that shows up the first day of the project is not composed of the same people who made the assessment and presentation. Those people were knowledgeable and impressed us with their level of actual senior experience in our industry. Instead we got a group of freshly minted and overly aggressive, irritating, and experienceless MBAs.

You met the "rainmakers." Those who hunt and get the work. They do the first part of the job—secure the engagement so others in the firm can work. You will hear that this new team is just preparing the data for the rainmakers, who will analyze it and help develop the recommendations. Do not allow bait and switch; before the contract is signed in writing demand to know the following:

- Who is going to be on the project.

- Their relevant qualifications.

- The duration of their assignment—whole project or certain phases.

- What they will be doing—responsibilities and deliverables.

- What other engagements they are on at the same time as yours—it's not unusual to assign resources to multiple engagements.

- Potential conflicts that may result from the other engagement.

- Which engagement has priority when push comes to shove.

- Make sure you review each potential team member's experience and background. Interview each proposed team member and if you do not like any particular one, have them get another that is more suitable to your needs and organization.

The Trainee

Every firm needs to develop new talent but not at your expense. Before any engagement starts, be sure to know what relevant worth each member of the consulting team brings to the project. Allow them to bring on all the new hires they want to train, but do not pay for them. The old story is that they are developing the databases. Database developers cost a lot less than $1500 per day plus expenses.

Boilerplate

They make a presentation to you on the first-pass results and two slides have your major competitor's name on them. It really is boilerplate consulting and they have had the first draft presentation prepared from the start. This has happened many times. If it happens to you, fire them and do not pay them for any work to that point. This is fill-in-the-blanks consulting. The boilerplate exists so that they can present a first draft of their findings quickly. They just fill in the new client's numbers and have an instant first draft analysis.

Data Explosion

They build databases faster than our IT department can add servers to keep up with the demand for storage space. You receive 300 pages of 10-point Excel spreadsheets per day. They slice and dice your internal data every which way—top to bottom, sideways, diagonally, bottom to top, inside and out, and you do not have a clue what it means. Then they apply benchmarks, overlay goals, and compare best practice data to these spreadsheets—more columns and more confusion. The more times you ask "What does this all mean?" the more spreadsheets you get.

You should ask for a one-page executive summary of the data that clearly draws the top five conclusions contained in the data. If benchmarks are being displayed, asked what is the appropriate level of performance for your organization against the top 10 benchmarks. If it is best-practice data, ask in which best practices you are behind and what it will take to close the gap.

Do not let the data explosion scare you off from asking questions. There is nothing wrong with asking dumb questions or requesting simple summary reports.

Part of the Family

Did we hire him/her? He/she has been here so long they seem like a regular employee. They attend our meetings, give out assignments, demand results, comanage some departments, have the best offices, have access to the top corporate officers, and the latest equipment, bought by our company, which we are told is on hold until this mess is straightened out. They even attended our annual employee picnic and won all the prizes in the raffle.

What has happened is they have created a niche with a top executive or manager. They have convinced someone that they are invaluable to the organization and this person or persons have come to depend heavily on them to keep their job. You need to begin asking yourself, how much are we paying for this help versus hiring them full-time?

Work Assignments

They are assigning your people work, setting goals for them to achieve, monitoring their progress, and presenting their results. This is a sign of a consultant in charge. This person is a forceful manager who knows how to get things done. The only problem with this is that *you* should be in charge giving them assignments and holding *them* accountable. If you sense this problem, reverse the situation immediately and start giving them assignments, set reporting goals, and monitor their progress.

Travel

They all leave on Friday afternoon to travel home. Do you pay your regular employees to travel home? Then, do not pay them either. Set the expectation up front that we work a full 40 hours per week—travel on your own time. Stop the clock when they leave or are not on the site. One other approach is to look for firms that have local offices so the resources are local and may only need to be augmented by some out-of-state workers occasionally. If the entire team is from outside the local area, travel will be an issue every Friday and the day before any holiday. Request in the contract that the majority of the resources are local and that paying for travel expenses is something you do not wish to do, or that you are only willing to spend a certain amount on them.

Meeting Schedules

You have to rearrange your schedule to meet with them since they have to manage their travel schedule. Guess who is managing whom at this point.

The Intern Is in Charge

"We will be back on Wednesday after we clean up a little problem with our last client. But our intern will be here if you have any questions." In other words, we are lining up the next client and we are making the presentation. This is a popular danger signal, especially toward the end of the contract. You should demand that the resources contracted for are on site and not at another potential client site. If all the major players can leave and let the intern run the job, there probably is not too much left to be accomplished. Consider ending the contract sooner rather than letting it expire with the contract end date.

Draft for Discussion Purposes Only

Every document that they present to you has this on it. Why do they do this? Organized crime had its motto—"Never write when you can speak, never speak when you can wink, and never wink when you can nod." "For discussion purposes only" is their method of making sure that if there is a mistake, or you object, the document was only a draft and for discussion only. It is their safety valve in case you question or find a flaw in their analysis. "We were just sharing our preliminary thinking with you and will make all corrections as we review the data with the team." In other words, we thought we would see how you react to our proposals and then we can keep fine-tuning them until you agree with them. Then, the final report will be completed.

The Surprise Visit

"You are in luck! Our most respected national partners are able to be on-site today. They are in such demand. We are indeed fortunate they can join us." In other words, they were not billable anyplace else so we will slide them both in here for a day at $3000 each to help them meet their billability targets. Be generous and let the partners visit the engagement anytime for free. Do not fall for this one. As with the trainees, tell them to feel free to visit the engagement anytime, offer their expertise, and review your team's progress, but do not expect you to pay anything for it. Pay for value-added services only.

Blame Shift

"The project deadline is slipping and it's your fault—your people are not providing the data on a timely basis." In other words, we underestimated the job and this is a way to get more billable hours. At the outset of the project, have a clear delineation of what your responsibilities are to the external resources. Review these responsibilities weekly and make sure they are being met. Do not wait until the first major deliverable is due to find out that the blame shift game is being played. This is a key parameter you need to be monitoring at all review meetings, and stay on the alert throughout the length of the engagement.

Gifts

All of a sudden, you are invited to their corporate box at some sporting event, a dozen golf balls are delivered, an invitation to a golf tournament, tickets to a dinner show, or maybe a concert are offered. What should you do? Refuse? Accept and go out with them to get to know them better in a nonwork environment? The bigger question is why gifts now?—What is wrong? Is this part of some type of early damage control? Look into why the beneficence at this point in the contract. It is a danger sign worthy of concern on your part.

Planting Seeds

Every consultant is trained to find areas of opportunity within your company to win add-on work. They are excellent at finding weaknesses in the company and offering services to solve these problems (remember, this is their livelihood). However, the real trick to this is that they plant seeds in your head and start growing them so it seems like your idea to hire them and solve this problem. This could be a sign that they are nearing the end of their contracted work and want to find more to do to increase their sales numbers. Their suggestions might be good and improvement might be needed, but be sure to weigh the cost benefit of the work to be done, because every company has its weaknesses.

THE REQUEST FOR PROPOSAL PROCESS

This is an important process that many organizations do not spend enough time on before they start to engage external resources. The request for proposal (RFP) process can be broken down into the following (not inclusive) general topics.

Overview

Includes the name of the project and a description of the problem to be addressed.

Objectives of the Proposal

In this section the organization needs to be as specific as possible as to what it wants to achieve with the requested assistance from an outside consulting firm. Spend the time to think out in detail what you really want. The more detailed you are, the better the chance you will get what you want.

Each objective should be quantifiable and measurable. This requires specificity. Take the time to make sure each objective stated is measurable so it can be used in auditing the vendor's performance once the project has begun. Furthermore, it can also be used to determine if they actually completed their work and if payment should be made.

Estimate of Proposal Cost

In this section, estimate what you think the cost of the proposed scope of requested work should be. It is reasonable to let those bidding on the work know that you will not pay more than $100,000.

Period of Performance

In this section, give those bidding on the work an idea of how soon you expect the work to be completed from the date of the signed contract.

Schedule of Deliverables

This section should tie back to the objectives of the proposed work and should detail expected milestones and completion dates. Once an external consultant has been selected, this section should be detailed out, with measures, to both parties' satisfaction. This is the measurement vehicle used to determine if the requested work is being completed as agreed upon. This is the weekly review list and project-tracking tool.

Instructions for Responding to RFP

In this section, detail what you want from each vendor responding to the RFP. Make the sections straightforward so you can make vendor-to-vendor comparisons easier. Usually the following are the general categories requested:

• *General statement of the vendor's capabilities.* A general statement of the proposed vendor's knowledge, capabilities, work history, and other qualifications in the relevant practice areas in which you are requesting assistance. Place a two-page limitation on this section. You want a concise overview.

• *List of proposed project personnel.* Request a list of each individual proposed to be on the project team or who will have substantial part-time involvement in the performance of the project. Put their names on the contract and at this time state that no substitutions of personnel may be made during performance of the contract without the express written advance approval of the hiring organization. No bait and switch.

• *Relevant projects.* Do they have any experience in the area in which you are requesting assistance? Ask for a brief description of up to five relevant projects in which one or more of the personnel to be on the project team has had significant, substantive participation. In the descriptions, request the name and a description of the project, a brief description of the nature of the tasks performed on that project by the proposed personnel, the dates of the project, other relevant project data, and the name and telephone number of a reference for that project. Again, place a two- to three-page limitation on each write-up.

• *Resumes.* Request a detailed resume on each proposed team member, indicating work experience and education. Review each one thoroughly and before the contract is signed, ask to interview each of them. You need to make sure that they will fit with your organization's culture.

• *Billing rates.* For each individual identified in the core project team, request that the vendor indicate the fixed billing rate to be charged during the project.

• *Other charges.* Just like credit card companies, check for any hidden charges that may surprise you later during the contract stage. Ask for a schedule of any and all other charges that the vendor normally invoices during an engagement. These could be for office support, travel, entertainment, and so on.

• *How to respond.* Detail how a vendor is to respond to the RFP. Make it a standard response so it will facilitate comparison of the different vendors. Detail the format, font size, and type that should be used in the response. Indicate the maximum size allowable of the response—35 pages. Also indicate if brochures or addendums are allowed. Indicate the number of copies required and the latest date for submission after which no proposals will be considered.

EVALUATION FACTORS FOR COMPARING THE PROPOSAL

Let the responding vendors know how you are going to compare and contrast the proposals to make an informed decision. Listed below are the most common evaluation tools for your consideration:

- *Conforms to the RFP proposal guidelines for submission.* Meets the format requested.

- *Technical evaluation criteria.* Itemize any technical criteria to be used.

- *Relevant experience criteria.* Past performance of the firm or proposed key personnel in relevant areas, and other technical merit/professional qualifications.

- *Price evaluation criteria.* Is price the most important?

- *Other internal organization specific criteria.* Describe.

The RFP process, when done correctly, forces the organization into an introspective look as to why external resources are needed, the scope of these resources, the specific areas or problems to be addressed, how success will be defined, time lines, and the internal involvement necessary. Consider the RFP as a first step in fully understanding your needs before you present them to external firms to analyze. As firms respond to your RFP and make proposals, continue to update and modify the document as you gain new insights into your internal needs. This document can be an important basis for setting up the benefits to be delivered.

TYPES OF EXTERNAL RESOURCES

The Big Five

In the past they were tied to a "big five" audit firm but in the recent past have been spun off as an independent unit. Normally they have in-depth expertise in selected industries and usually do not do contracts under a million dollars. Excellent at large project management, they usually have large databases to pull from, have local offices, and well-experienced and educated talent to draw upon.

The Training Consultant

This is a spin-off from a training firm that tries to sell consulting services based on their training experience. Trainers and external resources are very different individuals. A good trainer does not necessarily make a good consultant. A good consultant is usually not a good trainer. The best use for this service is if the trainer fits in with the organization and the consulting needs are general rather than specific in nature. Sometimes this resource is utilized to operationalize a training program. The trainer helps move it from the classroom into the culture of the workplace. Be careful if the consultant recommends more training since this may not necessarily be what you need but rather what they can deliver.

Independent Specialist

Usually former executives with specific industry experience who may have retired. This type of resource can be helpful by bringing another set of expert eyes to a situation needing remediation or change. Usually this is a local resource that may know your industry or market. They might be from a former competitor. This type of resource is excellent for a very specific knowledge-type problem.

Independent Generalist

Similar to the independent specialist but may have their experience in marketing, sales, strategic planning, HR, or the softer sides of the business world.

Interim Executive

A former executive who is available for short period fill-in assignments. These fill-ins can be for senior management or supervisory levels. Usually used when a vacancy needs to be filled quickly, giving the organization time to do an adequate search for the right person to fill the role on a permanent basis. These assignments are usually contractual for a period of three months to a year. This lets the organization have a seasoned person in place while a search is conducted for a permanent replacement.

Coaches

Coaches are used by organizations to help individuals having difficulty in a new assignment, trying to make a career change, trying to change their behavior or management style, or to get them through a substance abuse problem. Coaches are used when an organization has a person they feel needs help in changing and is worth the effort and cost to make the change.

Silver Bullet External Resources

These are the types that pick up on every new fad and tell you that it's the "silver bullet" that will solve all your problems. Six Sigma versus TQM is a popular theme today.

"Everything we taught you last year that did not work is out of style but this new one is the answer." The first thing to look at with fad consulting is what was offered last time. Is this the same book with a new cover? Do the tools look familiar but have new names? Fad consulting is a money-loser for an organization since it is usually being invented as it is being implemented and the benefits are often nebulous. All fad consulting requires enormous organizational resource commitment for training, oversight, auditing, steering committees, and so on. Organizations that use fad consulting usually have a senior-level executive as the internal champion that drives the fad. Once the executive either moves to a new position, tires of the fad, or gets promoted because he drove a major corporate initiative, the movement starts to die.

Academic Consultant

"But it works in the classroom." They just change uniforms. This is the new 21st century way to do it successfully. Local colleges, especially community colleges, have a wealth of training resources and programs that are usually very reasonably priced. The downside is that they are usually very generic but in some cases customizable to your specific needs. Make certain that the person(s) employed from a college have some relevant business experience to back up the academic experience. It helps establish credibility with your people.

The "Way" Consultant

A former executive of a Xerox, HP, Digital, Wang, Polaroid, Eastman Kodak, and so on, that will implement the "way it was done at XYZ." Take a look at XYZ today; where is it? Every well-known executive gets a book written on how they did it at XYZ. Just remember, your company is not XYZ. Your organization has a different culture, the time was at a different point in the economy, and your business may not be in the same business as XYZ. "Way" consulting is usually nothing more than a few pep rally speeches that are informative and entertaining. We recommend not investing much money or resources in "way" consulting.

WHAT TO LOOK FOR IN A CONSULTANT AND THE FIRM

You should look for the best in each of the following categories. Settle for nothing less since you are paying for it:

- *People.* Qualified personnel.

- *Experience.* Background of the people—you want specialists not generalists.

- *Results.* Proven and documented. Verify that they have done this type of work a number of times in similar industries.

- *References.* Obtain references in similar industries with successful and unsuccessful engagements.

- *Fee schedule.* Do not pay for mega overhead. Pay a reasonable rate for the resources provided. Realize that they have to maintain an infrastructure to support their personnel. Be careful of "The Phantom Partner" being billed to the engagement. Only pay for those providing direct service to the engagement. Review each bill carefully to ensure that the on-site resources are what you are paying for.

- *Measurement system.* Ask how they measure success on a project. Most firms will have a system to do this and will want you to use it. Make sure they are willing to modify it to fit your specific needs and add anything you feel is appropriate.

HOW TO MONITOR PROGRESS

When monitoring progress of an engagement of outside resources you need to watch the "burn rate" and the "return rate." The *burn rate* is how quickly the fees are being incurred by the resources—billing speed. The *return rate* is how quickly the organization starts to see a return on its investment in the resources. At the start of any engagement the burn rate will exceed the return rate since the engagement resources are working to uncover the opportunities that will give the organization a real return. At some point the return rate should begin to catch up with the burn rate and then exceed it. The return rate needs to be one that can be quantified. This quantification of return should be part of the contract. Have the return rate defined, a metric agreed to, and the timing required specified. If you are ever going to get the six-to-one return you need to monitor it.

Figure 8.1 is a tracking tool that can be used to monitor the burn and return rate weekly. You need to have a formalized process to monitor the burn and return rates, which benefits the external resources and the organization by allowing a weekly tracking (the billing cycle may also be used as the timing) to show what benefits are being returned.

Figure 8.1 presents a simple approach to monitoring the projects being undertaken by the external resources. The review items are as follows:

1. *Project summary.* A simple statement of what the project is supposed to accomplish. This summary should be part of the contract or referenced in the RFP.

2. *Start date.* When the project began.

3. *Project duration.* How long the project is going to take.

4. *Staff on project.* How many external resources we are paying for on the project. It's good to know how many people are on a project and their billing rates. You may also want to add a row to track internal resources from your organization dedicated to the project to track the full cost of all resources.

Review Item	Project 1	Project 2	Project 3
1. Project summary			
2. Start date			
3. Project duration			
4. Staff on project			
5. Total estimated benefits			
6. Benefits identified			
7. Benefits realized			
8. Percent of total benefits received			
9. Fees incurred to date			
10. Fee run rate per week			
11. Contracted fees for the project			
12. Percent contracted fees spent			
13. Net return			

Figure 8.1 Client project review matrix.

5. *Total estimated benefits.* Before the project begins, there should be an estimate of the total benefits expected from the project.

6. *Benefits identified.* Benefits that have been uncovered that may lead to realized gains at a later date. It is a good idea to compare the size of benefits identified versus what is actually realized. If $1,000,000 worth of benefits are identified at the project level but only $10,000 are actually realized, it is an indication of the quality of the analysis the external resources are conducting.

7. *Benefits realized.* Benefits that you have already put in the bank: costs that have been reduced, revenue that has been accelerated, or reductions in staff. These are real savings not potential ones.

8. *Percent of total benefits received.* Benefits received divided by total estimated benefits.

9. *Fees incurred to date.* How much the external resources have cost the organization to date.

10. *Fee run rate per week.* This is the burn rate. It is a measure of how fast the contracted dollars are being consumed by the external resources billing.

11. *Contracted fees for the project.* How much was allocated to this project from the total contract. It is a good idea when possible to break the billing down into specific projects so you can monitor progress at a subproject level and not an overall contract level.

12. *Percent contracted fees spent.* Fees incurred to date divided by contracted fees for the project.

13. *Net return.* Compare the percent of total benefits received against the percent contracted fees spent and see which one is moving faster. At the estimated midpoint of the project, the percent of total benefits received should be getting very close to the percent contracted fees spent. As you reach the halfway point of the project and notice a gap between the burn and the return rates, it is time for a major review to see if you will ever make the return projected.

HOW TO COMPENSATE EXTERNAL RESOURCES

There are many ways to set up the compensation schedule for external resources but the best one is to make them have a stake in the outcome. Summarized below are the primary ways most external resources are compensated:

- *Compensation by the hour.* Contract for so many hours of training at a set fee. Training is the easiest one to compensate since it is based on preparation hours, delivery hours, materials per student, and any related travel expenses.

- *Compensation by a contract.* You agree to a set fee that will provide you with a specified amount of resources to accomplish an agreed-upon objective.

- *Compensation by a contract plus a percentage of the savings.* Some firms will agree to a set fee, reduced by some percentage, plus a percentage of the savings they deliver. The difficulty with this arrangement is the calculation of the savings at the end of the project. Many disagreements will result on what the final savings actually are. This type of percentage contract needs to have the way savings are calculated clearly defined up front before the contract commences.

- *Fixed fee.* When hiring an interim executive you can set a fixed fee for a specified period of time.

- *Percentage of the savings.* This is common when firms are hired to go after aged accounts receivable. They collect a percentage of what they actually return to the organization. This is a performance-based approach, which is fairly easy to set up.

Note: If the vendor does not deliver what was stated in the contract, then you might want to think about holding payment until they fix their work. Furthermore, it would be wise not to pay for the extra work they do to fix their original mistakes. This can quickly become an ugly situation, which makes the earlier stated point about the type of objectives to put into the contract all the more important. The more quantifiable and measurable the objectives of the engagement are stated, the better. Furthermore, keeping work papers for just such a situation is discussed on page 110. Work papers are documentation that you keep on the engagement. Clearly defined goals and work papers will make it easier to defend your reasoning for withholding payment as well as measuring the performance of the contractors.

WORK FOR WHICH NOT TO USE EXTERNAL RESOURCES

- *Change management.* Only you can change yourself.

- *Fad consulting.* SPC, TQM, Six Sigma—it's being invented while you watch. Read a book on the subject and you will find only the cover is different and the topics are about the same.

- *Emerging concept consulting.* Knowledge management or customer relationship management—these are the bottomless pit projects. They sound good but no one knows what they mean. They hold conferences on the topic but the speakers all seem to contradict one another.

- *Assessments.* They tell you where you are. If you do not know where you are, it is time to resign.

- *Customized off-the-shelf training programs.* We will put your name on our generic product.

WORK FOR WHICH TO USE EXTERNAL RESOURCES

- *Short-term assignments* that are very definable in scope and outcome.

- *Specific technical problem* needing specialized skills.

- *Expert witness* for a court case.

- *Large-scale project management.* You need experience and a skillful person to run the project.

- *Coaching.* Saving good people.

- *Specific training projects.* Scope is controllable.

- *Off-the-shelf generic training programs.* One size does fit all—you customize it if need be.

- *Train-the-trainer programs.* Knowledge transfer to you on a specific set of skills your organization does not have.

- *Specific transitions and restructuring* of your organization where you may need experienced executives or managers to fill in slots that were vacated or are not yet filled.

- *Peak period fill-ins.* Staff for a baseline not a peak—using external resources to fill 15–20 percent of required project positions to add short-term flexibility. Example: in the Information Technology department to complete a software upgrade.

WORK PAPERS

Work papers are documentation that external resources keep on the engagement in case of a lawsuit or dispute of any kind. The sorts of documentation that are kept are important correspondences with the client (such as any directions or scope changes), deliverables, memos, and any other documentation that shows why the external resources did what they did. Most external resources have a good (and time tested) system of keeping documentation and you should do the same.

It is imperative to collect and keep documentation on the activities of the external resources. You should keep any important correspondence and meeting notes where direction or feedback is given to the external resources, as well as any important information the external resources send to you. Use this information to compare the direction they took as well as the deliverables they created from these meetings to ensure they are on track. Furthermore, do not let them take back the hard copies of any presentation, deliverable, or discussion document that you have notes on. You do not want to lose these notes.

Work papers are necessary, and if done properly you will be able to defend your position and more effectively manage the external resources. The work papers hopefully will not be needed, but they will be important if there is any dispute because the external resources will have their documentation. They are keeping track of you, so you should be keeping track of them.

SUMMARY

Every firm at some point needs to engage external resources to help them solve a problem, provide interim staffing, or to provide specific expertise. We hope this chapter has given you some tips and warning signs to help you engage those external resources in the most cost-efficient manner to ensure a successful outcome. The purpose of the chapter was to help you understand how to manage and monitor the external resources you might engage. Choose wisely, after all it is your money and your organization, and you are the one accountable in the end after they have gone.

We hope you liked this chapter and if you think something is missing, remember: this is a "draft for discussion purposes only."

9

Quality Management Systems

G. Dennis Beecroft

Many managers today are faced with two management systems in their organizations: quality management systems (QMSs) to address the quality of their products or services, and environment management systems (EMSs) to address control, usage, and disposal of all the gases and liquids, including water and air, that are present in their organizations.

The International Organization for Standardization (ISO) has developed two series of standards for these management systems. The ISO 9000 series addresses quality management systems and ISO 14000 series addresses environment management systems.

The ISO 9000 Quality Management Standards were the first to be developed in 1984. The ISO 14000 environment was described later in 1996. Both standards have undergone changes and continue to be revised.

In this chapter G. Dennis Beecroft will address the ISO 9000 Quality Management Standards. Randy Garrison will present information on the ISO 14000 Environmental Standard in chapter 10.

QUALITY MANAGEMENT SYSTEMS: ISO 9000

Background

ISO 9000 quality management standards have their roots in the procurement of military products. Military standards, such as MIL-Q9858A or U.S. Air Force—AF5923, were initially developed to define specific contracted quality requirements that suppliers were required to meet. The philosophy of the time was that the quality of the products being purchased would be better as a result of these requirements being imposed on the suppliers.

ISO 9000 was introduced in 1984 based on this original philosophy. Since its introduction it has gone through two significant revisions, the first in 1994 and the second in 2000. To better understand this early philosophy, current philosophy, and where it is likely going to be in the future from a quality improvement strategy viewpoint it is useful to refer to David Garvin's "four major quality eras"[1] which have been adapted in Figure 9.1. In era 1—"inspection," quality was seen as a problem that could be best solved through detection. The quality role in this initial era fell solely on the inspection department where the product was gauged, measured, graded, and sorted into good and bad categories. Problems generated at any point in the process were not detected until the very end of the process. This method was not only very costly but also ineffective in detecting unacceptable product, which then led to the "statistical quality control" era.

Unfortunately during this second era, quality was still viewed as a problem to be solved. The method used was to control the product and to prevent it from being shipped to customers. Inspections were added at the various steps of the process—incoming, in-process, and final inspection. The emphasis was on product uniformity and the reduction of inspections by the introduction of statistical techniques. Quality professionals were involved in problem solving and the application of the statistical methods for inspection. The quality responsibility was also transferred to the manufacturing and engineering departments, however the focus and approach was to "control-in" quality. The approach was reactive and considered "non-value-added" as it focused on the product after it was produced and did not impact the product's quality. If poor quality was produced, the best this approach could offer was to detect it and prevent it from being shipped to the customer. Increased inspection resulted in increased nonconformances being detected, however it did not address preventing the defect in the first place. This unsatisfactory situation led to the third era—"quality assurance."

The quality assurance era was revolutionary in that the emphasis shifted from trying to *detect* poor quality to an emphasis of *not producing* poor quality. This shifted the

Era 1	Era 2	Era 3	Era 4
Inspection	Stastical quality control	Quality assurance • Process focus • Prevention	Strategic quality management
Inspect-in quality	Control-in quality	Build-in quality	Manage-in quality
ISO 9000		ISO 9004	TQM
QS-9000			

Figure 9.1 Four major quality eras.

Adapted from David A. Garvin. *Managing Quality, the Strategic and Competitive Edge.* New York: The Free Press, 1988. Used by permission.

focus from the *product* being produced onto the *processes* that were used to produce the products, as it was determined that the only way to prevent poor quality was to control the processes used. This phase emphasized the coordination of all functions throughout the complete supply chain from design to ultimate customer and the contribution of all areas, particularly design, through the use of sophisticated tools, such as design of experiments and failure mode and effects analysis, to prevent quality failures. Quality improvement programs were used to address quality. The role of the quality professional changed to one of consultant in quality planning, quality measurement, and program design. The quality responsibility was now shared by all functions—engineering, manufacturing, materials, and quality, with the focus to "build-in" quality.

In era 4—"strategic quality management" the primary focus was the strategic impact on the organization with emphasis on the market and customer needs. The methods employed were strategic planning, goal setting, and the mobilization of the complete organization. The quality professional's role was goal-setting, education and training, and quality improvement consulting. In this era, top management were now included in the quality process and expected to provide strong leadership. Until now, management had been able to delegate the quality responsibility. The orientation of this era was to "manage-in" quality.

ISO 9000 and Total Quality Management (TQM)

ISO 9000 was issued as an international standard in 1987. The bulk of the initial registrations were in the UK because of the active role of BSI (British Standards Institute) in the development of this standard. ISO 9000's adoption in North America was very much slower.

Japan's Deming Prize led to the development of the Malcolm Baldrige National Quality Award (MBNQA) in the United States in 1987. Canada followed the United States by developing its own award, the Canada Awards for Excellence—Quality (CAE—Quality) in 1988. These national quality awards became in fact total quality management models. Please see chapter 5, Corporate Planning Models, for more information on these awards.

Many organizations saw ISO 9000 and TQM as competing programs. However, they were very different in their strategy and approaches. ISO 9000 focused on 20 very specific requirements emphasizing documented procedures to demonstrate compliance to the standard. While the standard has been used for both service and manufacturing organizations, the twenty elements were very "manufacturing" focused. TQM was very much broader in its focus and was really based on a set of quality management principles. While the Deming Prize, the Baldrige Award and Canada's quality award were slightly different, the principles were mainly the same.

The ISO task committee TC 176 addressed the philosophy and strategy behind the development of the ISO series of standards in their document ISO/TC 176/SC2/N336. Unfortunately this document has not been communicated very effectively. Figure 9.2 has been adapted from this document. The committee developed a three-level customer needs hierarchy of quality assurance, quality management, and TQM. Level 1 is the ISO

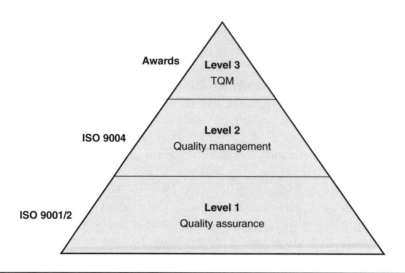

Figure 9.2 Customer quality needs hierarchy.

9001/2 quality management requirements, level 2 uses the ISO 9004 quality management guidelines, and level 3 implements the TQM principles using either Malcolm Baldrige or another national quality model.

The goal of level 1, quality assurance was to put in place an effective system to produce products conforming to customer requirements. Controlling product quality and eliminating customer failures and recalls prevents customer dissatisfaction. This is very much era 1 and 2 in Garvin's evolution of quality.

Level 2, quality management, addresses cost, efficiency, and effectiveness in meeting customer needs. Here the focus is on customer satisfaction by improving the complaint process, reducing cycle time, and waste reduction. The process and prevention focus of the quality management guidelines is equivalent to Garvin's era 3, quality assurance.

Level 3, TQM equates to era 4 in Garvin's model. Strategic quality management and TQM both focus on total customer satisfaction. This is achieved through employee involvement, long-range and strategic focus, and customer-driven designs. Please refer to chapter 6 for more information on customer satisfaction.

Strategy Unsuccessful

The implementation strategy has not been successful for a number of significant reasons:

Communication. The ISO task committees did not communicate the implementation strategy to a very wide audience. Most organizations are completely unaware of the "customer needs hierarchy" that the committee proposed. Even the guideline standard, ISO 9004, received very little attention. Registration is based on the implementation of ISO 9001 or 9002 requirements; therefore it was "not needed." Consultants and trainers, in most cases, did not promote the use of the guideline standard. In some cases, some registrars even discouraged the implementation of some of the ideas promoted in the guideline standards as "they might jeopardize" the quality system's registration. As stated earlier, TQM was seen as a competing strategy and not as a necessary step in meeting customer needs.

Compatibility. ISO 9001 and ISO 9004 were not compatible. The language in the requirements standard was totally different from the guideline standard. It was very difficult to incorporate the ISO 9004 guidelines into the organization's quality system.

Registration versus Improvement Focus. Likely the most significant barrier has been the focus of quality systems on *registration* rather than using the quality system to drive *improvement* in organizations. This registration focus has driven senior management in some organizations to minimize cost, minimize effort, and delegate their quality responsibility. By focusing on registration, the ISO 9004 guidelines and TQM principles are completely ignored or seen as additional burden. This has also resulted in the external auditor obsession. Organizations using their quality system with an *improvement* focus maximize value, reduce waste, and improve product/service quality through the senior management team's involvement.

Quality Improvement: Linking Principles, Strategy, and Tools

Most quality improvement efforts, including TQM, have been unsuccessful. One has to ask the question—why? Total quality management, for the most part, is really a set of principles. Successful quality improvement efforts require having a set of principles that drive a strategy and then using the appropriate tools for implementation. See Figure 9.3.

For example, a current successful quality improvement program is Six Sigma. The *strategy* is reducing variation, using a disciplined approach and a good measurement system. This is not a new concept or strategy, however, what makes Six Sigma successful is also the *principles* that drive the strategy. Six Sigma principles include: senior management–driven, major projects, weeks of training, and dedicated resources. Six Sigma is covered in detail in chapter 15.

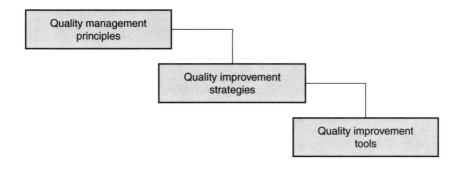

Figure 9.3 Linking principles, strategy, and tools.

The new ISO 9001:2000 standard includes eight quality management *principles:*

1. Customer focused organization

2. Leadership

3. Involvement of people

4. Process approach

5. Systems approach to management

6. Continual improvement

7. Factual approach to decision making

8. Mutually beneficial supplier relationships

The *strategy* of the revised standard includes:

- Increased base requirements

- Alignment of 9001 and 9004 documents

- Internal audit training includes TQM principles

- Required awareness of 9004

2000 Edition of ISO 9001

Likely one of the most significant changes is the move from a 20-element structure to a structure consisting of four parts based on a process model (see Figure 9.4). The four

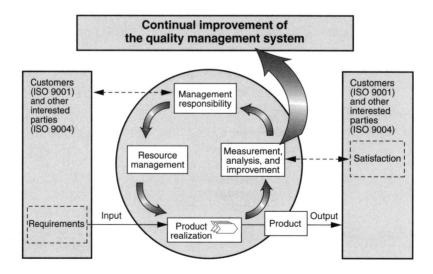

Figure 9.4   Model of the process approach.

Source: ANSI/ISO/ASQ Q9001-2000. Used by permission.

sections are: Management responsibility, Resource management, Product realization, and Measurement, analysis and improvement.

Management responsibility includes: policy, objectives, planning, quality management system, and management review. The Resource management section includes: human resources, information, and facilities. Product realization includes: customer satisfaction, design, purchasing, and production. The final section Measuring, analysis and improvement includes: audit, process control, and continual improvement. The 20 elements from the second edition have not been eliminated but rather incorporated into this new process structure.

The Revised Standards. The current second edition of the ISO 9000 standard series includes some 20 standards and documents. With this revision the number will be reduced to four:

1. ISO 9000 Quality management systems—Concepts and vocabulary

2. ISO 9001 Quality management system—Requirements

3. ISO 9004 Quality management systems—Guidelines

4. ISO 10011 Guidelines for auditing quality systems

All organizations will register to ISO 9001 because the current ISO 9002 and ISO 9003 will be eliminated. However, ISO 9001 has been restructured to allow for exclusions if the requirements do not apply (for example, the design requirements).

ISO 9001 and ISO 9004 have been designed as a "consistent pair." The sections of both are identical. While meeting ISO 9001 is all that is required for registration, it is hoped that the two standards will both be used as part of the QMS. While ISO 9001 focuses on effectiveness, ISO 9004 focuses on both effectiveness and efficiency. ISO 9004 includes the eight quality management principles that are part of the national quality awards such as Malcolm Baldrige, the European Quality Award, and Canada's quality award.

The language of the revised standards has been simplified for better understanding and use. The manufacturing bias of the second edition has been removed, making standards application simpler for all sizes of organizations in any sector.

Another major change is the significant reduction in the required documentation. Currently, organizations must have a procedure for each of the 20 elements. Many have also elected to include work instructions to support each of their procedures. The third edition requires only six documented procedures: control of documents, control of quality records, internal audit, control of nonconformity, corrective action, and preventive action.

Several new requirements have been added with this edition. Continual improvement has now been added. While many felt that the second edition already included this requirement, it is clarified in this revision. The role of top management has been significantly expanded. Meeting legal and regulatory requirements is now included. Quality planning now includes the requirement for having quality objectives. Organizations will have to collect and use customer satisfaction and /or dissatisfaction data. The training requirements now include the evaluation of the effectiveness of the training. There are increased requirements for measurement data at all levels—system, process, and product. Organizations will also be required to collect and use performance data on the QMS.

Conclusion. Compared to previous editions, the 2000 edition of ISO 9000 has simplified its language, reduced the required documentation, and made several changes based on customers' and users' feedback. This new edition is a standard that will be easier to implement, use, and upgrade from previous editions.

Internal Audits—Obstacles or Opportunities?

Internal auditing is a requirement of both ISO 9000 and ISO 14000. The audit process used for both is audit standard ISO 10011, which is currently under review. The internal audit process has the potential of either ensuring a very successful QMS or EMS or destroying the system. This section has been added to help explain the history behind audits and their negative effects. It also, hopefully, challenges your thinking to help create a more positive process, thereby achieving maximum benefit from your QMS and EMS systems. See chapter 13 for a full treatment of the audit function.

Introduction. Auditing is an old idea that has been used throughout history to examine finances, taxes, quality systems, and other complex entities. An *internal* audit, such as required by ISO 9000 quality system standard, is conducted by a company on itself to determine if its quality system is being followed and is effective. While the internal quality audit process has the potential to be highly destructive, it can also stimulate tremendous improvement within an organization and help create a "proactive" environment.

"Reactive" or Proactive" State? In contrast with the current state of many organizations, the *ISO 9004 Quality management system guidelines* focus on prevention, continuous improvement, and customer satisfaction (Figure 9.5). Despite our expending considerable effort to adopt these principles and achieve the "proactive" condition, we

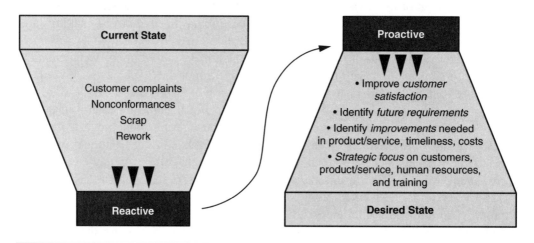

Figure 9.5 Comparing two states of organizations.

remain locked into our reactive, negative oriented ways of thinking—eliminating defects and fixing problems. A significant cultural shift such as this is difficult and will require many years of gradual progress. Why is this change in approach so demanding? We readily accept the proactive position as more positive, yet most of us continue to function in a "reactive" state. A key to adopting this "proactive" culture is our acceptance of the fact that there is likely a better way of doing everything. Since it is not feasible to be addressing everything we do, it is easier to remain in our reactive, negative thinking mode. Organizations concentrate on resolving customer complaints rather than freeing up the resources for identifying what is required to improve current customer satisfaction as well as determine their future needs and expectations. Likewise, vast amounts of company time and resources are spent trying to reduce scrap and fix nonconformances. Most would agree that it is far better to prevent the scrap and nonconformances in the first place, reducing waste while improving customer satisfaction. However, this again requires considerable additional resources, which are just not available in our "lean" organizations.

It is imperative that organizations concentrate on continual improvement—in fact, it has become a survival issue. Continual improvement is required in product or service quality, in timeliness, and in costs. Organizations that strategically focus on their customers, on the quality of products or services, and on the human development and training of their own workforces become the survivors. Internal audits can play a major role in shifting organizations to this more positive proactive state if done correctly and with a positive approach.

Changing the Negative into Positive. The negative view of the typical audit process is illustrated in Figure 9.6. This viewpoint is the result of how the audit was conducted, who conducted it, and how the audit findings were implemented.

For the internal audit to be constructive and viewed positively it is necessary to change not only the auditing process so that it is different from an external audit but also to name it differently, such as a "review." Today's perception of the internal audit is that it is (1) required by the quality system standard and that (2) its purpose is to discover and correct any problems before an "external" auditor finds them and sees reason to delay or deny the company its "registration." Understandably, this worry tends to drive a lot of "fear of failure" throughout the organization before and during any audit. Many organizations instruct and train their employees how to answer auditors' questions—answer only what is asked and don't volunteer anything. Auditors are usually escorted during their visit to ensure they talk only to the "right" employee and that they not find hidden things that will delay or prevent registration. While this approach may help guarantee registration, it does little to encourage genuine improvement in the quality system!

Management could instead promote the internal review as an opportunity to identify strengths and seek improvements, not just fix problems. The review is then turned into a positive experience that is anticipated with optimism rather than fear. Negative nonconformances identified during the usual external audit process often make people feel they have somehow failed. In contrast, by identifying strengths during the internal review, the workforce receives positive feedback and a valuable boost to morale. The strengths, once recognized, can stimulate similar improvements in other areas.

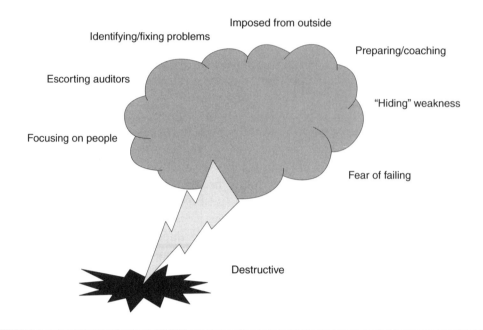

Figure 9.6   The typical audit process.

Many organizations have permanent auditors. In these cases the "owner" of the quality system becomes the audit department and its members are the "bad guys." Rather than "belonging" to a certain department, the quality system should be under the eye of the entire organization. Each function or department should determine the most appropriate procedures to put in place, as well as share responsibility for system maintenance and improvement. By sharing the review between the different departments each time, perhaps even with different individuals, ownership of the quality system is transferred back to the various departments. The downside of this role-sharing is that training is required prior to each review. However, such training would help create an involved workforce more knowledgeable about requirements and thus more likely to consistently meet them.

Process Improvement. Auditing is often practiced as a punitive process. Instead, the internal audit or review should examine the process rather than the people. The identification of nonconformances normally results in dwelling on why someone did not follow a particular process. While employees do occasionally neglect to follow a required process, all too frequently there is insufficient effort taken to learn the root cause of such a mistake.

When deficiencies are discovered or opportunities for improvement recommended, the review team should be involved in identifying solutions and their implementation. Their participation will increase the positive value of the internal review process by solving real problems or finding better ways of doing things for the workforce. An internal review is successful when the people performing the functions being reviewed feel the review team has made their jobs easier or eliminated some of their concerns.

1. Change process, change name.	5. Make recommendations.
2. Identify strengths.	6. Solve "real" problems.
3. Share responsibility.	7. Prioritize findings.
4. Focus on process.	8. Drive improvement.

Figure 9.7 Converting the audit into a positive process.

One of the biggest challenges of the internal review process is to prioritize the findings of the review team. It is easy to overload an organization with the work required in addressing the review findings. As the number of deficiencies or opportunities for improvement increase, the probability of implementing effective solutions decreases. It is far better to focus on a vital few areas than to take on too many changes and implement none. Therefore, a key role of the review team is to prioritize their findings and select for management's consideration those that have the biggest impact on driving improvement.

By addressing the key factors summarized in Figure 9.7, an internal review can be made more constructive.

Conclusion. Given our current reactive and negative oriented culture and the history of auditing with its many years of negative experiences to overcome, creating a positive internal review process presents a tremendous challenge. Transforming the audit process into a positive internal review is not a simple task and much has yet to be learned.

The internal review process is key to an effective quality system implementation. Successful organizations transform their internal reviews into positive experiences. The process is essential in moving their organizations from their current reactive state into the more preventive proactive state to assure their future position among business leaders.

ENDNOTE

1. D. A. Garvin, *Managing Quality, the Strategic and Competitive Edge* (New York: The Free Press, 1988).

REFERENCES

Beecroft, G. D. "2000 Edition of ISO 9001." *IIQP Newsletter* (winter 2000).
———. "Internal Quality Audits—Obstacles or Opportunities." *IIQP Technical Research Report RR-97-06 (NT)*.
———. "Implementation Philosophy—ISO 9000 vs. QS-9000." *IIQP Technical Research Report RR-97-04 (NT)*.
ISO Task Committee TC176, "ISO/TC 176/SC 2/N336."

10

Environmental Management Systems

R. J. Garrison, Jr.

THE ORIGIN OF ISO 14000

In August 1991 the International Organization for Standardization (ISO) established the Strategic Advisory Group on the Environment (SAGE). Its charge was to determine if a need existed for international environmental standards and to present a recommendation for such standards if a need existed. SAGE determined that there was a need, however, it reported that there could be possible barriers to international trade and commerce from such standards. As a result, SAGE concluded in its study that ISO establish a technical committee to review and develop "consensus" standards like those being developed by ISO/TC 176 (ISO 9000) for quality management systems.

In 1993 the International Organization for Standardization (ISO) formed the Technical Committee on Environmental Management referred to simply as ISO/TC 207. ISO recognized the need for ISO/TC 207 and ISO/TC 176 to work closely together "in the areas of management systems, auditing, and related terminology." The results of this close cooperation can be seen today with the release of the third edition of the ISO 9000 standards, introduced in December 2000, along with the compatibility of the wording and several of the requirements common to both standards (ISO 9001:2000 and ISO 14001:1996). Another example of the cooperation between the two committees is the joint standard for auditing, ISO 19011:2002, *Guidelines for quality and/or environmental management systems auditing*. With the release of ISO 19011, it has canceled and replaced the auditing standards originally published by the two committees separately: ISO 10011-1:1990, ISO 10011-2:1991, ISO 10011-3:1991, published by ISO/TC 176; and ISO 14010:1996, ISO 14011:1996, and ISO 14012:1996, published by ISO/TC 207.

ISO/TC 207—Its Scope and Committees

ISO/TC 207's scope is: "standardization in the field of environmental management tools and systems." Excluded from its scope were test methods for pollutants that fall within the responsibility of the following four technical committees: ISO/TC 146 "Air Quality," ISO/TC 147 "Water Quality," ISO/TC 190 "Soil Quality," and ISO/TC 43 "Acoustics." Also excluded from its scope are the setting of limit values regarding pollutants or effluents, the setting of environmental performance levels, and the standardization of products.

Within the structure of ISO/TC 207 there are numerous subcommittees (SC) and working groups (WG) who have been charged with the responsibility for developing the family of ISO 14000 standards and guidance documents.

Main Points of ISO 14001

The ISO 14000 family of standards is viewed as having two focuses, the first being "organization-oriented," and the second "product-oriented." The organization-oriented group's focus is on giving guidance for "establishing, maintaining, and evaluating an environmental management system." The second group is focused on "determining the environmental impacts of products and services over their lifecycles, and with environmental labels and declarations." Both hopefully assist organizations in gathering the data it needs for its planning and decision-making processes, as well as keeping consumers and other interested parties informed on specific environmental information.

As one reviews the requirements of ISO 14001, you quickly begin to see the key points of the standard. They are the requirement for the organization to define its environmental policy, the requirement for planning, the issues of implementation and operation, the requirement for checking and corrective action, management review, and the emphasis on a commitment to continual improvement.

Clause 4.2, Environmental Policy, stresses that the organization must define its environmental policy and make a commitment to prevention of pollution, and continual improvement. It also emphasizes that the organization must set objectives and targets that relate to its environmental policy. Clause 4.3 on planning focuses the organization on developing procedures that identify the aspects and impacts of its processes, products, or services that it can control. In Clause 4.4, the focus is on implementation and operation. Here the standard details the requirements for establishing the competence of the employees, assignment of roles and responsibilities for the management system, and for communicating with all interested parties, internally and externally. Clause 4.5 addresses the requirements for checking (monitoring) the management system, for taking timely corrective action on nonconformities, as well as initiating preventive actions to identify and eliminate potentials for nonconformities and conducting self-evaluations via the internal audit process. Management Review is the title of clause 4.6, and stresses that "top management" must review the environmental management system at defined intervals in order to "ensure its continuing suitability, adequacy, and effectiveness."

Finally, the results of effectively implementing these key points hopefully provide organizations with the objective evidence that they are continually improving.

The ISO 14000 Family of Standards

Unlike the three standards that are the heart of the ISO 9000 family, the ISO 14000 family has over 20 family members covering a wide and diverse range of topics and issues. After reviewing the 14000 family of standards, one hopefully gains a respect for the magnitude of the task undertaken by the members of ISO/TC 207 worldwide since its inception in 1993. Additionally, one must keep in mind that all of the standards that make up the ISO 14000 family of standards are "consensus" standards—each member nation casting one vote to either accept or reject a standard. See Table 10.1 for a complete listing of the ISO 14000 family of standards.

Table 10.1   The ISO 14000 family of standards.

Document Title	Description
ISO Guide 64:1997: *A guide for the inclusion of environmental aspects in product standards*	Helps the writers of product standards address environmental aspects in those standards
ISO 14001:1996 (currently in the final stages of revision, release expected in 2003): *Environmental Management Systems— Specifications with guidance for use*	Specifies the requirements for an EMS that may be objectively audited for self-declaration or third-party certification/registration purposes
ISO 14004:1996 (currently in the final stages of revision, release expected in 2003): *Environmental Management Systems— General Guidelines on Principles, Systems and Supporting Techniques*	Provides guidance to help an organization establish and implement an EMS, including guidance that goes beyond the requirements of ISO 14001
ISO 14010:1996 (replaced by ISO 19011:2002): *Guidelines for Environmental Auditing—General Principles on Environmental Auditing*	Provides the general principles common to the conduct of any environmental audit
ISO 14011:1996 (replaced by ISO 19011:2002): *Guidelines for Environmental Auditing—Audit Procedures—Auditing of Environmental Management Systems*	Provides the procedures for the conduct of an EMS audit, including the criteria for selection and composition of audit teams
ISO 14012:1996 (replaced by ISO 19011:2002): *Guidelines for Environmental Auditing— Qualification Criteria for Environmental Auditors*	Provides guidance on the qualifications of internal or external environmental auditors and lead auditors
ISO 14015:2001: *Environmental Management— Environmental Assessment of Sites and Organizations*	Helps an organization identify and assess the environmental aspects of sites and entities to support the transfer of properties, responsibilities, and obligations from one party to another
ISO 19011:2002: *Guidelines for Quality and/or Environmental Management Systems Auditing*	A joint effort between ISO/TC 176 and ISO/TC 207 to develop one ISO standard for auditing either quality and/or environmental management systems
ISO 14020:2000: *Environmental labels and declarations—General principles*	Provides general principles, which serve as a basis for the development of ISO guidelines and standards on environmental claims and declarations

continued

continued

Document Title	Description
ISO 14021:1999: *Environmental labels and declarations—Self-declared environmental claims (Type II environmental labeling)*	Provides guidance on the terminology, symbols, and testing and verification methodologies an organization should use for self-declaration of the environmental aspects of its products and services (Type II Environmental Labeling)
ISO 14024:1999: *Environmental labels and declarations—Type I environmental labeling—Principles and procedures*	Provides the guiding principles and procedures for third-party environmental labeling certification programs (Type I Environmental Labeling)
ISO/TR 14025:2000: *Environmental labels and declarations—Type III environmental declarations*	Provides guidance and procedures on a specialized form of third-party environmental labeling certification using quantified product information labels and preset indices (Type III Environmental Labeling)
ISO 14031:1999: *Environmental management—Environmental performance*	Provides guidance on the selection and use of indicators to evaluate an organization's environmental performance
ISO/TR 14032:1999: *Environmental management—Examples of environmental performance evaluation (EPE)*	Provides examples from real organizations to illustrate the use of the guidance in ISO 14031
ISO 14040:1997: *Environmental management—Life cycle assessment—Principles and framework*	Provides the general principles, framework, and methodological requirements for the LCA of products and services
ISO 14041:1998: *Environmental management—Life cycle assessment—Goal and scope definition and inventory analysis*	Provides guidance for determining the goal and scope of an LCA study, and for conducting a lifecycle inventory
ISO 14042:2000: *Environmental management—Life cycle assessment—Life cycle impact assessment*	Provides guidance for conducting the lifecycle impact assessment phase of an LCA study
ISO 14043:2000: *Environmental management—Life cycle assessment—Life cycle interpretation*	Provides guidance for the interpretation of results from an LCA study
ISO/WD TR 14047: *Environmental management—Life cycle assessment—Examples of application of ISO 14042*	Provides examples of how to apply the lifecycle impact assessment
ISO/TS 14048:2002: *Environmental management—Life cycle assessment—Data documentation format*	Provides information regarding the formatting of data to support lifecycle assessment
ISO/TR 14049: *Environmental management—Life cycle assessment—Examples of application of ISO 14041 to goal and scope definition and inventory analysis*	Provides examples that illustrate how to apply the guidance of ISO 14041
ISO 14050:2002: *Environmental management—Vocabulary*	Helps an organization understand the terms used in the ISO 14000 family of standards
ISO/TR 14061:1998: *Information to assist forestry organizations in the use of Environmental Management Systems standards ISO 14001 and ISO 14004*	Provides information to the forestry organizations on the use of ISO 14001 and ISO 14004
ISO/CD TR 14062 (in committee draft phase as of 2002): *Environmental management—Integrating environmental aspects into product design and development*	Will address the environmental aspects of a product from design and development through its useful life to recycling
ISO/AWI 14063 (an approved work item as of 2002): *Environmental management—Environmental communications—Guidelines and examples*	Will provide principles for external environmental communications

Since its inception in 1993, ISO/TC 207 has endeavored to develop international standards that are not only practical, but are useful for businesses of every size, purpose, and structure regardless of where their operation(s) may be located in the world. The family of standards is going to be of increased strategic importance to businesses given today's competitive business environment. By establishing the framework for "improved environmental performance" the family of standards will address one of the key purposes of environmental management standards, that of supporting "sustainable development."

REFERENCES

Abstract of chapter 14, ISO 14000—International Environmental Compliance, by David Gillum. Amherst, MA: University of Massachusetts on-line reference materials, 2002. www.unix.oit.umass.edu .

ASTM's Web site—www.astm.org ; a paper titled: *ASTM: Technical Committees: ISO/TC 207.* West Conshohocken, PA: 2003.

ISO 14001:1996, *Environmental management—Specification with guidance for use.* Geneva, Switzerland: ISO Central Secretariat, 1996.

ISO 14004:1996, *Environmental management—General guidelines on principles, systems and supporting techniques.* Geneva, Switzerland: ISO Central Secretariat, 1996.

ISO FDIS 19011:2002, (E) *Guidelines for quality and/or environmental management systems auditing.* Geneva, Switzerland: ISO Copyright Office, 2002.

ISO's Web site—www.iso.ch/ and www.iso.org . Geneva, Switzerland: International Organization for Standardization, 2003.

ISO/TC 207 Web site—www.tc207.org ; Document development, international standards of the ISO 14000 series. Toronto, ON: Standards Council of Canada, 2002.

11

Lean Enterprise

George Alukal and Anthony Manos

In the last ten years or so, a new term has entered our vocabulary: "lean." Those of us working as senior leaders, especially in executive management, quality, human resource, operations, and engineering have been hearing of lean *recently in a context other than dieting.*

WHAT IS LEAN?

It is a manufacturing philosophy that shortens the lead time between a customer order and the shipment of the parts ordered by the elimination of all forms of waste. Lean helps firms in the reduction of costs, cycle times, and non-value-added activities, thus resulting in a more competitive, agile, and market-responsive company.

Lean concepts are applicable beyond just the shop floor. Companies have realized great benefit by implementing lean techniques in the office functions of manufacturing firms, as well as in purely service firms such as banks, hospitals, restaurants, and so on. Lean manufacturing in this context is known as *lean enterprise.*

A definition of *lean,* used by the Manufacturing Extension Partnership (of NIST/MEP, a part of the U.S. Department of Commerce) is "a systematic approach in identifying and eliminating waste (non-value-added activities) through continuous improvement by flowing the product at the pull of the customer in pursuit of perfection." Lean focuses on value-added expenditure of resources from the customers' viewpoint. Another way of putting it would be to give the customers:

- What they want

- When they want it

- Where they want it

- In the quantities and varieties they want

A planned, systematic implementation of lean leads to improved quality, better cash flow, increased sales, greater productivity and throughput, improved morale, and higher profits.

Many of the concepts in total quality management (TQM) and team-based continuous improvement are also common to the implementation of lean strategies.

WHY THE EMPHASIS ON LEAN NOW?

Some of the reasons why lean is especially important today as a winning strategy are (1) to compete effectively in the global economy, (2) pressures from customers for price reductions, (3) fast-paced technological changes, (4) continued focus by the marketplace on quality, cost, and on-time delivery, (5) quality standards such as QS-9000 and the new ISO 9001:2000, (6) Internet auctions, (7) OEMs holding on to their core competencies and outsourcing the rest, and (8) higher and higher expectations from customers.

To compete successfully in today's economy, we need to be at least as good as any of our global competitors, if not better.

BRIEF HISTORY OF LEAN

Lean emphasizes teamwork, continuous training/learning, make-to-demand ("pull"), mass customization and batch size reduction, cellular production, quick changeover, total productive maintenance, and so on. Not surprisingly lean implementation utilizes improvement approaches that are both incremental and breakthrough.

Presented in Table 11.1 is a summary of some of the changes that have occurred since the industrial revolution.

Most of the lean concepts are not new. Many of them were being practiced at Ford during the 1920s, or are familiar to most industrial engineers.

A few years after the Second World War, Eiji Toyoda of Japan's Toyota Motor Company visited the American car manufacturers to learn from them, and to transplant U.S. automobile production practices to the Toyota plants. With the eventual assistance of Toyota's Taiichi Ohno and Shigeo Shingo, he introduced and continuously refined a system of manufacturing whose goal was the reduction or elimination of non-value-added tasks (for which the customer was not willing to pay). The concepts and techniques that go into this system are now known as TPS or Toyota Production System, and James Womack reintroduced and popularized many of these concepts back into America under the umbrella of "lean manufacturing."

American Society for Quality (ASQ) has seen a steady increase in the demand among its members about lean, as evidenced by the attendance and interest in lean presentations

Table 11.1 Evolution of manufacturing.

	Craftsman Circa 1890	Mass Production Circa 1920	Lean Manufacturing Circa 2000
People	• Perform all work • Self-taught or apprenticeship training	• Employees contribute minimally to total product • Training for limited skills • Management makes decisions (Taylor system)	• Clusters of employees working in teams • Extensive continuing training and cross-training
Product	• Customized nonstandard products • Variation in quality	• Standardized, focused on volume, not quality or variety • Assembly line • Economies of scale	• Focus on internal/external customer needor demand • Variety; mass customization
Work environment	• Independence, discretion • Variety of skills • Responsibility	• Obey management • Repetitive work • Limited skills, knowledge little discretion, simplified tasks	• Some discretion, group effectiveness, empowerment, team accountability, work cells, job rotation

This Table is based on a NIST/MEP model.

• Eliminate waste by identifying and purging all non-value-added activities:

  ◆ Waste is any activity that does not add value to the final product for the customer.

  ◆ Value-adding activity is an activity that transforms or shapes raw material or information to meet customer requirements. Approximately 5% of total work/time.

  ◆ Non-value-adding activity is an activity that takes time, resources or space, but does not add to the value of the product itself. Approximately 70% of total work/time.

  ◆ Non-value-adding but necessary—For example, accounting, governmental regulations, and so on. Approximately 25% of total work/time.

Figure 11.1 Value-added versus non-value-added activities.

at the Annual Quality Congress, the new two-day workshop on lean being offered by ASQ, and the recent formation of a new interest group titled "Advanced Manufacturing Interest Group" (AMIG) for members to participate in lean-based activities.

THE "WASTES" OF LEAN

Waste of resources has direct impact on our costs, quality, and delivery. Conversely, the elimination of wastes results in higher customer satisfaction, profitability, throughput, and efficiency. Excess inventory, unnecessary movement, untapped human potential, unplanned downtime, and suboptimal changeover time are all symptoms of waste.

There are eight "wastes" (*muda* in Japanese) associated with lean:

1. *Overproduction.* Making more, earlier, or faster than is required by the next process.

2. *Inventory waste.* Any supply in excess of a one-piece flow through the manufacturing process, whether it is raw materials, work-in-process (WIP) or finished goods.

3. *Defective product.* Product requiring inspection, sorting, scrapping, downgrading, replacement, or repair.

4. *Over-processing.* Extra effort that adds no value to the product (or service) from the customer's point of view.

5. *Waiting waste.* Idle time created waiting for manpower, materials, machinery, measurement, information, and so on.

6. *People waste.* The waste of not fully using people's abilities (mental, creative, skills, experience, and so on).

7. *Motion waste.* Any movement of people (or tooling/equipment) that does not add value to the product (or service).

8. *Transportation waste.* Transporting parts or materials around the plant.

The continuous elimination of these eight wastes results in surprisingly high reductions in costs and cycle times. If we were to do a root cause analysis of each of the eight wastes, we could come up with the appropriate lean tool to tackle the causes identified. If, for instance, long lead times and missed delivery dates are major bottlenecks, identifying the underlying reasons might lead us to focus in on setup times, machine downtime, absenteeism, missed supplier shipments, quality problems, overproduction resulting in excess WIP, and so on.

Let us look at one example in detail: the primary reason for overproduction and carrying excess inventory might be due to long process changeover times, in which case the correct tool (or "lean building block") to use will most likely be SMED (single minute exchange of dies) or quick changeover techniques.

Changeover time is defined as "the time between the last good piece off the current run and the first good piece off the next run." The traditional changeover assumption is that long runs are necessary to offset the cost of lengthy changeovers. This is not valid if the changeover time can be reduced as far as possible (under 10 minutes if the SMED technique is applicable), and standardized at that level so that we are confident that a good piece from the next run can be made in a certain time period. The changeover improvement process typically includes the following steps:

- Identify and form the changeover improvement team (operators, manufacturing/quality engineers, setup specialists, material handlers, tool/jig/fixture makers, maintenance technicians, supervisors/team leaders, and so on).

- Document the current changeover (videotape where possible).

• Poor layout	• Not following procedures
• Long setup time	• Instructions/information not clear
• Poor workplace organization	• Poor planning
• Poor equipment maintenance	• Supplier quality problems
• Inadequate training	• Inaccurate gages
• Use of improper methods	• Poor work environment (for example, light, heat, humidity, cleanliness, clutter, and so on)
• Statistically incapable processes	

Figure 11.2 Variation and waste.

- Through brainstorming, analyze the changeover and identify ways to reduce, eliminate, consolidate or mistake-proof steps, and convert from internal to external time/tasks. "Internal" time is when the machine is stopped, whereas "external" time is when the machine is running, producing the previous part.

- Implement improvements and monitor results.

- Streamline all aspects of setup operations.

- Now standardize the improved changeover.

Another example for quick changeover is in a hospital. Changeover can be how quickly an operating room and be readied after an operation for the next patient.

Besides attacking overproduction/inventory wastes, quick changeover can result in the reduction of lead time, defective product, and space requirements, while improving productivity, flexibility, and variety (mass customization).

Many of the wastes could be associated with variations in processes (see Figure 11.2); statistical tools, including the currently popular Six Sigma DMAIC (define–measure–analyze–improve–control) methodology might be appropriate to attack such wastes. Lean and Six Sigma, thus, are not mutually exclusive—rather they are complementary. Some firms use the appropriate combination of lean, Six Sigma, theory of constraints, and elements of TQM in their constant strive for continuous improvement and competitive advantage. See chapter 15 for more information on Six Sigma and the DMAIC methodology.

THE "BUILDING BLOCKS" OF LEAN

The tools and techniques used in the introduction, sustaining, and improvement of the lean system are sometimes referred to as the *lean building blocks*. These building blocks (as shown in Figure 11.3) make up the "house of lean." Many of these building blocks are interconnected, and can be implemented in tandem: for example, 5S (workplace

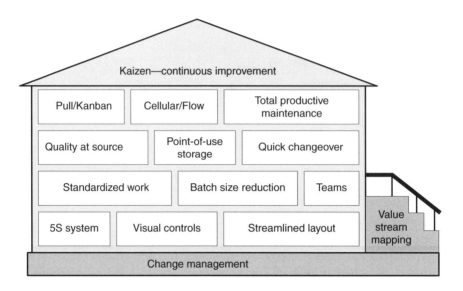

Figure 11.3   House of lean.

Based on an NIST/MEP model.

organization and standardization), visual controls, point-of-use-storage, standardized work, streamlined layout, and autonomous maintenance (part of total productive maintenance) can all be constituents of a planned implementation effort.

The building blocks include:

1. *5S.* A system for workplace organization and standardization. The five steps that go into this technique all start with the letter S in Japanese (seiri, seiton, seison, seiketsu, and shitsuke). These five terms are loosely translated as sort, set in order, shine, standardize, and sustain in English.

2. *Visual controls.* The placement in plain view of all tooling, parts, production activities, and indicators so everyone involved can understand the status of the system at a glance.

3. *Streamlined layout.* Plant layout designed according to optimum operational sequence.

4. *Standardized work.* Consistent performance of a task, according to prescribed methods, without waste, and focused on human movement (ergonomics).

5. *Batch size reduction.* The best batch size is one-piece flow, or make one and move one! If one-piece flow is not appropriate, reduce the batch to the smallest size possible.

6. *Teams.* In the lean environment, the emphasis is on working in teams, whether it is improvement teams or daily work teams.

7. *Quality at the source.* Inspection and process control by the operators so that they are certain that the product that is passed on to the next process is of acceptable quality.

8. *Point of use storage.* Raw material, parts, information, tooling, work standards, procedures, and so on, are stored where needed.

9. *Quick changeover.* The ability to change tooling and fixtures rapidly (usually in minutes) so multiple products in smaller batches can be run on the same equipment.

10. *Pull/kanban.* A system of cascading production and delivery instructions from downstream to upstream activities in which the upstream supplier does not produce until the downstream customer signals a need (using a "kanban" system).

11. *Cellular/flow.* Physically linking and arranging manual and machine process steps into the most efficient combination to maximize value-added content while minimizing waste; the aim is single-piece flow.

12. *Total productive maintenance.* A lean equipment maintenance strategy for maximizing overall equipment effectiveness.

Besides the building blocks mentioned above, there are other concepts or techniques that are equally important in lean: value stream mapping (VSM), just-in-time (JIT), error-proofing (*poka-yoke*), autonomation (*jidoka*), continuous improvement (*kaizen*), kaizen blitz for breakthrough improvements, change management, and so on. Since lean is a never-ending journey, there is always room for continuously improving.

Lean will not work if it is viewed as merely a project, or as point solutions, or as a vehicle for downsizing. It works best if deployed as a never-ending philosophy of continuous improvement. Many firms have appointed and empowered lean "champions" for successfully implementing their lean transformations; these champions help others as mentors, trainers, group facilitators, and communicators, and act as the drivers of continuous improvements, planners, evaluators, and cheerleaders celebrating each success. They also help in standardizing at the higher levels of performance as lean is implemented, so as not to slip back.

HOW TO START THE LEAN JOURNEY

The starting point of lean initiatives could be any one of the following:

1. Value stream mapping (VSM). A set of specific actions required to bring a product family from raw material to finished goods per customer demand, concentrating on information management and physical transformation tasks. The outputs of VSM are a *current state map*, a *future state map,* and an *implementation plan* to get from the current to the

future state. Using VSM, we can drastically reduce the lead time closer and closer to the actual value-added processing time, typically in a short duration such as 12 months, by attacking the identified bottlenecks and constraints. The implementation plan acts as the guide for doing so. Bottlenecks addressed could be long setup times, unreliable equipment, unacceptable first-pass yield, high work-in-process inventories, and so on. A typical current state map (see Figure 11.4) and future state map (see Figure 11.5), drawn using different icons, are presented here.

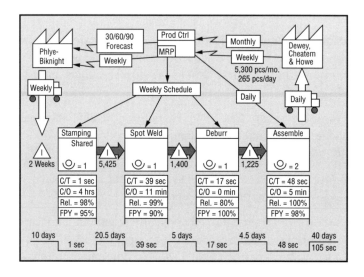

Figure 11.4 Current state map.

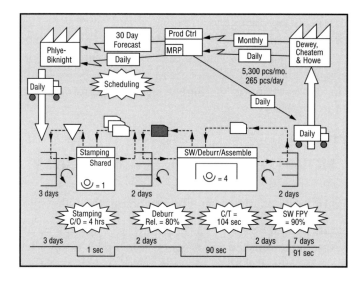

Figure 11.5 Future state map.

In the map in Figure 11.4, the requirements from the customer and the requirements to the supplier, plus internal scheduling communications are drawn at the top: "the information flow." In the middle are the material flows from purchased product to finished goods. And, at the bottom are data boxes with the lead time (40 days in this example) and the actual processing time (only 105 seconds).

In the future state map in Figure 11.5, we were able to plan on reducing the lead time to seven days, and the processing time by a few seconds to 91 seconds. The road map (or implementation plan) to get to the future state is not shown, but it can be as simple a project management tool as a Gantt chart; and the duration of the project is in months, not in years. The timely implementation of the kaizens (represented by starbursts) identified on the future state map is the key.

2. Lean baseline assessment. Using interviews, informal flowcharting, process observations, and analysis of reliable data, an "as-is" situational report can be generated from which would flow the lean improvement plan based on the identified "gaps."

3. Start by providing "massive" training in lean to a critical mass of employees in "teach–do" cycles. Lean implementation should continue immediately after the training.

4. Begin by implementing the "basic" building blocks first: 5S, visual controls, streamlined layout, point-of-use storage, standardized work, and so on. Then build on with the higher-level tools and techniques, finally achieving production flow based on customer "pull."

5. Pilot project. Choose a bottleneck or constraint area to do breakthrough lean improvement (use the kaizen blitz approach); then with the lessons learned, migrate lean implementation to other areas.

6. Change management. Align the company's strategies and employees' goals, then change the culture from the traditional "push" production to lean "pull." This should result eventually in a philosophical change in peoples' daily work life.

7. Start by analyzing the internal overall equipment effectiveness (OEE) and the OEE losses; a Pareto chart of these losses will identify the "biggest bang for the buck" to indicate where to start the lean journey.

LEAN ENTERPRISE

Enterprisewide lean implementation has slightly different challenges compared to deploying lean in manufacturing. On the shop floor, there is a tangible product that is being transformed; so the utility of the tools and techniques described in this chapter for cost and cycle time reduction in the processing of raw materials into usable finished goods is fairly evident. In the office functions in a manufacturing firm, or in a service firm, many of the same tools and techniques are applicable, be it in a slightly modified form—instead of hardware one looks at value-adding processing and/or use of information (or software). For example, one can visualize the usefulness of lean in a hospital setting where many processes could be improved from the point of view of cycle time reduction strategies, through proceduralization, team training, standardized work, point-of-use storage, visual systems, quality at the source, and so on. The concept of streamlining and purging of non-value-added steps in the "order to cash" cycle (or RFP-to-cash cycle) is currently in vogue. Bottlenecks are attacked using the P–D–C–A model and the appropriate lean building blocks.

BARRIERS TO IMPROVEMENT

As managers, we know that we can not stand still in the face of global competition because our rivals are not standing pat, but improving their processes and systems to catch up with us. If we do not improve also, sooner or later they will overtake us. We lose market share, our margins deteriorate, sales revenue and profitability suffer. So if we know that we need to improve, the question then becomes: Why don't we?

Proper planning and implementation management is the key in obtaining enduring success with lean deployment. Lean is not a quick fix; we are kidding ourselves if we think that lean implementation is easy. Success requires not only good change management practices, but also the integration of lean into the overall business strategy. "Flavor-of-the-week" syndrome should be avoided.

Complete implementation of lean might not be for everybody; so a well-thought-out master plan based on cost–benefit analysis is a useful preliminary step. Great benefits from lean implementation are derived by first focusing on what processes we have, the product families we make, the environment we operate in, the competitive situation we face, and using the right technique at the right time. For example, a firm producing parts to customer orders rather than to stock will face different challenges.

Some of the factors in the success of lean implementation are due to the senior executives' active role in:

- A planned approach to lean implementation, rather than point solutions

- Providing the needed resources

- Appointing lean champions

- Empowered and involved employees; emphasis on teamwork and cooperation

- Good communication channels—both top-down as well as bottom-up

- Managing expectations: for example, fear of loss of jobs

- Everybody understanding the need for change, as well as their new roles as change is implemented

- Creating an atmosphere of experimentation: risk-taking environment, safety net for trial and error

- Good rewards and recognition programs, suggestion systems, gain sharing

• Internalize into daily work	• Communication channels
• It is a never-ending process or philosophy	• Standardize so as not to slip back
• Discipline/motivation/incentives	• Role of lean champions
• Continued, visible management commitment	• Job rotation

Figure 11.6 How to sustain lean.

- Making everybody understand the competitive reasons why, and benefits of, lean for the company as well as for themselves personally

- Creating a "vision" of the future state after the change

- Introducing a performance measurement system based on meeting company goals

- Analysis and sharing of costs versus benefits

- Emphasizing accountability of everyone

In many cases, implementing pilot projects first, perhaps in a kaizen blitz mode, gets immediate buy-in from skeptics. The success achieved from these quick hitters can then be migrated to other areas in a planned approach. Ultimately, lean has to become the daily work habit or operating philosophy of the whole firm to be sustainable.

Starting the lean process is comparatively easy; but sustaining it over the long haul takes robust planning, discipline, commitment, patience, an environment of tolerating some risks/mistakes, a good reward and recognition program, and peoples' receptivity to change and grow (see Figure 11.6). Many managers have found that the three essential ingredients for successful lean implementation are: (1) sustained, hands-on, long-term commitment from senior management, (2) training in the lean building blocks for all employees, and (3) good "cultural" change management in the transformation from the traditional "push" to the lean "pull" mentality.

CORE CONCEPTS OF LEAN

Following are some important concepts that will be useful to keep in mind while preparing for the lean transformation:

- Creativity before capital. In lean, instead of spending large sums of money on capital expenditures, team brainstorming of ideas and solutions is emphasized. People working in the process are brought together to tap into their experiences, skills, and brainpower to generate the plan for reducing wastes and for process improvements.

- A solution that is not so perfect implemented today is better than a perfect solution that is late. "Just do it *now*!"

- Inventory is not an asset, but a cost/waste.

- Use the proven plan–do–check–act methodology for deploying improvements—both incremental and breakthrough.

- Once started, lean is a philosophy on a never-ending journey.

- Typically, 95 percent of lead time is not value-added. Collapsing the lead time closer to the actual processing time by squeezing out non-value-added time and tasks results in both cost and cycle time reductions. Henry Ford knew this in 1926, when he said, "One of the most noteworthy accomplishments in keeping the price of Ford products low is the gradual shortening of the production cycle. The longer an article is in the process of manufacture and the more it is moved about, the greater is its ultimate cost."

PULL/KANBAN SYSTEMS

Push System

The traditional *push system* is based on forecasts and schedules and usually is managed through an ERP/MRP (enterprise resource planning/manufacturing resource planning) production control system in most companies. By definition, a forecast is a prediction. The accuracy of the prediction can be improved with correct information, but it will never be perfect since some assumptions are always part of any prediction. The push system is normally made up of schedules for different departments all trying to prioritize and utilize the firm's resources to make and deliver products. This production is based not on whether the next operation is ready for the output from this process or whether the next process currently has the capacity to work on it, but on anticipated needs. And it is not based on whether the end customer has placed an order for the product.

Pull System

A *pull system* is also a form of scheduling system, but a much more reliable one than traditional scheduling. Production is based on actual consumption and not a predetermined forecast. To move from a push to a pull system, there is more than just creating kanban cards or setting up controlled inventory through "supermarkets." The first step is to determine if the organization is going to build to shipping (for immediate delivery) or to a supermarket. Next, determine the size and location of supermarkets. And, finally, determine the appropriate signal to move/withdraw and/or produce/replenish material. Make sure that the signal to produce only comes into the process at one point, called the "pacemaker." Use of a pull system will automatically remove the need for expediting where MRP cannot. Other terms used in, or associated with, pull systems include: two-bin system, min/max levels, just-in-time or JIT, supermarkets, and kanban.

"Pull," therefore, is a system of cascading production and delivery instructions from downstream to upstream activities in which the upstream supplier does not produce until the downstream customer signals a need.

Kanban

Kanban is a visual signal to move product or to produce product inside our company; supplier kanbans are used to purchase parts or material from suppliers. There are several types of signals that can trigger these events. These signals can be as simple as a two-bin system, kanban cards, specially marked floor space, or more sophisticated electronic kanban or even virtual kanban. The key to the kanban signal is to make it simple and visual. If workers do not follow the rules set up for kanban systems, the system can fail like any other. This is why it is important to build discipline into your organization and to prevent errors from occurring.

Pull/kanban system benefits—as material and information flows improve:

- Inventory levels decrease.

- Productivity goes up.

- Various wastes are decreased or eliminated.

- "Hot lists," "bumping," and expediting become unnecessary.

- Operating expenses decrease.

- Delivery and service levels improve.

- Order-to-cash cycle time is reduced.

- Cash flow improves.

CELLULAR/FLOW MANUFACTURING

The ideal goal of cellular manufacturing is line-balanced single-piece flow. "Flow" can be regarded as using a series of processes where continuous value-adding takes place, from raw material to finished goods, through a production sequence in one linked man–machine system. Normally a five-step process is used in designing the lean cells:

1. Group all the parts we want made in the flexible cell we are designing; products with similar processing requirements (which use the same equipment, machinery, and so on) are grouped into "product families."

2. Establish "takt" time. *Takt time* is the "work time available" divided by the "customer demand" (or the number of units to be made within the available time). The goal is to produce to demand.

3. Review work sequence by analyzing the value-added work content each worker performs.

4. Combine the work content to balance the line, keeping in mind the takt time and the staffing requirements.

5. Now, using the above analysis, design the cell layout. Fine-tune, as needed, during the cell implementation.

TOTAL PRODUCTIVE MAINTENANCE

As a lean implementation strategy, total productive maintenance (TPM) focuses on the elimination of equipment-related wastes, using in part the concept of shared responsibility for equipment reliability. Management, engineers, maintenance technicians, and the machine operators work as a team to realize the benefits of TPM. Autonomous maintenance, whereby the operators themselves perform routine cleaning, lubrication, inspection of their equipment, adjustments, minor repairs, record keeping, and so on, go hand in hand with 5S efforts.

Maximizing the overall equipment effectiveness (OEE) to as close to 100 percent is the TPM goal. OEE is the combination of (1) equipment availability, (2) equipment performance, and (3) quality of the parts being produced on the equipment, measured in first-pass yield.

Some of the major benefits of TPM are:

- Equipment always available when needed

- Reduced equipment breakdowns; fewer maintenance emergencies or unplanned downtime

- Increased productive life of equipment

- Improved throughput

- Equipment operating at rated/designed capacity

- Improved product quality

- Reduced overall lead time

- Lower operating costs

- Multiskilled workforce; better teamwork

- Lower inventory and safety stock (supermarkets)

KAIZEN BLITZ EXAMPLES

Kaizen (loosely translated as continuous improvement) and kaizen blitz (breakthrough improvement) pave the road on our lean journey. Kaizen blitzes (also called quick kaizen, kaizen events, rapid kaizen, and so on) are very popular in America since substantial improvement results are typically achieved in a short duration, normally three to five days. These team-based projects use the axiom: *creativity before capital.* Three examples of the great benefits of kaizen blitz breakthrough improvements are presented in Figure 11.7. It is important to note the amount of time and money saved.

Universal Joint Kaizen Blitz Project

Category	Changeover	Tool Change
Target hours to be saved	4.9 hours (75%)	14.8 hours (75%)
Actual hours saved	4.5 hours	13.8 hours
Percentage	*69%*	*70%*
$ Target savings/day	$291	$879
Actual savings/day	*$268*	*$820*
$ Target savings/year	$72,802	$ 219,823
Actual savings/year	*$67,007*	*$ 205,034*
Total Savings	$272,041 per year	

Tube Mill Changeover Kaizen Blitz Project

Changeover savings/year: $510,000 on two mills

Reduced changeover time from 4 hours, 40 minutes to 2 hours, 11 minutes

Employees happier—bonuses based on changeovers

Management happier—more changeovers, more production, more cash in the door

Trailer Truck Shipping Kaizen Blitz Project

Goal: Reduce loading time from 8 hours to 4 hours per trailer, with no errors

Through kaizen blitz, lead time reduced 87%

Resulting in savings of $702,624 per year

Figure 11.7   Benefits of kaizen blitz breakthrough improvements.

SUMMARY

"Lean" is a planned approach to cost/waste/time reduction, necessary for us to remain profitable and competitive in the global marketplace. The different tools and techniques, called "building blocks" are applied systematically on the journey from traditional production to "lean" manufacturing. "Lean" needs a change in mind-set or philosophy for maximum results and for it to be sustainable over the long term.

REFERENCES

The lean concept is expanding rapidly. The reader is encouraged to access the following Web sites for periodically updated descriptions of lean and related approaches.

www.lean.org
www.mep.nist.gov
www.productivityinc.com

Part III

Measuring and Evaluating Improvement

Chapter 12 Customer Satisfaction As a Driver for Improvement and Change

Chapter 13 Performance Enhancement through Management Audits

Chapter 14 Measurement—The Balanced Scorecard

Chapter 15 Six Sigma

Chapter 16 How to Get Results: Setting Goals and Hitting Targets

12

Customer Satisfaction As a Driver for Improvement and Change

Grace L. Duffy

WHY ARE CUSTOMERS IMPORTANT?

Without customers, your business does not exist. You create products and services for customers to buy so that money flows into your organization. Without a reliable core of customers, the business is not sustainable.

The above statements may sound intuitively obvious, and yet it is easy to forget where your revenue comes from. Current literature is replete with advice on being customer focused. How do you get there; and once there, how do you maintain and improve your relationship with the customer?

Customer focus is a journey, not a discrete action item. Customers must feel confident in the organization's ability to consistently meet their requirements for products and services. Unless the organization builds an integrated management system dedicated to the customer, there is always the risk of becoming focused on short-term production rather than long-term relationships with your end users. The organization must institute a constant program of self-assessment and adjustment to maintain this imperative long-term vision.

VEHICLES AVAILABLE FOR SELF-ASSESSMENT AND ADJUSTMENT

Two major approaches for organizational self-assessment are the Baldrige National Quality Program and the ISO 9001:2000 standard. Both approaches identify customer and market focus as critical to successful results for the organization. Executive leaders who prefer to begin with the strategic concepts of the organization usually find the

Baldrige program to be most appropriate. Those leaders more comfortable with tangible and structured action plans generally start with the ISO 9001:2000 approach. If used in the spirit of excellence and improvement, either one will help the organization identify valuable areas for improvement and change.

The Baldrige National Quality Program, developed in the United States, identifies customer and market focus as to how an organization determines requirements, expectations, and preferences of customers and markets. It examines how the organization builds relationships with customers and determines the key factors that lead to customer acquisition, satisfaction, retention and, subsequently, to business expansion. Customer and market focus is only one of seven categories that comprise the Baldrige Criteria for Performance Excellence. The Baldrige National Quality Program is a nationally and internationally accepted standard, available in three versions: business, education, and healthcare. The Malcolm Baldrige National Quality Award is the centerpiece of the program and since 1988 has been presented annually by the president to recognize performance excellence. The program's Web site at www.quality.nist.gov provides current information about the award, the performance criteria, award winners, and a variety of other information. See chapter 5 for more information on assessment and recognition programs.

The ISO 9001:2000 standard provides a more definitive structure for assessment. One of the eight quality management principles identified by the standard is customer focus. The standard states:

> Organizations depend on their customers and therefore should understand current and future customer needs, should meet customer requirements and strive to exceed customer expectations.[1]

Section 5 of the standard, Management responsibility, further identifies customer focus in which "top management shall ensure that customer requirements are determined and are met with the aim of enhancing customer satisfaction"[2] See chapter 9 for more information on how to use the ISO family of standards for organizational improvement.

Customer satisfaction has been defined as the degree to which the customer believes their requirements have been met. The Kano model, developed by the Japanese professor Noriaki Kano, identifies three levels of customer response: dissatisfaction, satisfaction, and delight. The customer compares a service or product with his or her own expectations of that experience and then assesses the difference between reality and perception. Dissatisfaction results if the reality of the experience is less than that expected. Satisfaction results when the customer experience is equal to or moderately greater than that expected. Only when the service or product is significantly greater than expected will the customer reach a stage of delight. Your role as a supplier is to anticipate the customer's expectation and to meet or exceed that expectation on a consistent basis.

Many measurement and tracking systems measure dissatisfaction rather than satisfaction, thus becoming customer *dissatisfaction* programs. A note of caution is due here. Just eliminating dissatisfaction on the part of your customers is not tantamount to increasing satisfaction. A customer may be totally neutral about your service or product, rather than being satisfied. It is critical that customers not only be satisfied, but very satisfied to delighted before they will brag about that satisfaction to others.

The concept of meeting and exceeding customer expectation is a major driver for improvement and change within the organization. It is human nature to become accustomed to the current state. What delights a customer today will become ordinary in the short term. Once the product or service is ordinary, competitive offerings prompt the customer to view your original item as only a satisfier, or worse yet, a dissatisfier.

Ongoing customer research is required to determine dissatisfiers, satisfiers, and potential delighters. Difficulties occur when an organization assumes it knows what customers need or want. Systematic testing within existing and potential market segments provides a basis for improving your current customer offerings. Wider research into future trends and technologies gives you the opportunity for significant change and advancement into customer delight.

Satisfied customers may or may not return to do business with you again. Equally importantly, they tend to tell other potential customers. A percentage of these potential customers will not purchase based on the bad experience of your existing customers. Not only do you need to maintain satisfied or delighted customers, you need to create and expand your base of loyal customers. One of the key tasks is to identify the components of customer satisfaction. The challenge is in measuring customer satisfaction and tying it directly to profitability. This is a complex undertaking. Once you identify areas of continued customer satisfaction, you must create processes that allow you to anticipate changes in customer requirements and modify your offerings in a way that delights your existing customers. A loyal customer is the best advertising a company can have. If you can maintain a solid base of visibly and vocally loyal customers, new customers are only a conversation away.

WHO ARE YOUR CUSTOMERS?

Sometimes you choose your customers. Most often, customers choose you. Rarely is it possible to filter or select customers meeting the exact profiles that match your product or service designs. Usually it happens the other way around.

The customer defines what they consider acceptable, often without even knowing it. There are several different approaches customers take in deciding what best meets their needs in a product or service. Dr. Joseph Juran has defined three different approaches customers take in establishing expectations:

1. Emphasize initial purchase price as equal to or more important than performance.

2. Evaluate alternative products or services on both initial price and performance simultaneously.

3. Emphasize obtaining "the best."[3]

The first approach defines acceptability on the basis of *value*, or the relationship of usefulness or satisfaction to price. From this perspective, a valuable product is one that is as useful as competing products and is sold at a lower price, or one that offers greater usefulness or satisfaction at a comparable price.

The second approach is more user-based. Individuals have different wants and needs and view performance from a changing perspective. Performance is defined as *fitness for use*, or how well the product performs its intended function, given the price paid to obtain it.

The third approach is the most difficult to measure. Often called the *transcendent* definition, acceptability is considered both absolute and universally recognizable. This is the approach of "I'll know it when I see it." Unfortunately, the customer does not always see the product or service from the same perspective and this approach becomes a moving target.

The most effective way to find out your customer's preference is to ask. The concept of quality function deployment (QFD), often called "the voice of the customer," is a useful tool in identifying customers and focusing on their needs and wants as a basis for the design and improvement of our offerings. Since customers often cannot exactly articulate their expectations, you must be clever in what questions you ask or observations you make.

Quality function deployment is a complex and detailed methodology that translates customer requirements, correlates them with technical requirements, and cascades them down through each stage of development or production. The matrix format used in QFD is also referred to as a "house of quality" because of its resemblance to a house. See Figure 12.1 for a summary of the QFD model. Specific vehicles for gathering data on customer wants and needs are presented later in this chapter.

FOCUSING ON THE EXTERNAL CUSTOMER

There is much in current business literature making the distinction between external and internal customers. This chapter focuses first on the external customer as a critical basis for organizational success. The internal customer is just as critical and will be addressed later in the chapter.

External customers are those who use a product or service supplied by the organization but are not members of the organization that produces the product or service. Internal customers are those who are impacted by the product or service and are also members of the organization that produces the product or service. Both are critical to the effectiveness of the business. The attitude of one is intimately connected to the attitude of the other. You start with external customers, since that is the source of most revenue coming into the organization.

There are many types of external customers, and most organizations segment their customer base to better serve the needs of different types of customers. It is critical to develop a system by which customer satisfaction can be assessed and improved. Linking this system to the company's financial success encourages you to focus on high-margin or high-potential customers.

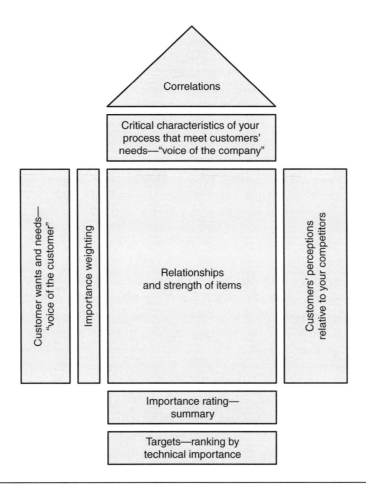

Figure 12.1 Quality function deployment matrix—"house of quality."

How do you identify customer segments worth going after? With constant pressure to improve margins and contain costs, businesses need to ensure that scarce resources are applied to attracting and growing the "right" customers. All customers are not equal in terms of their profitability to a supplier, or in their reasons for selecting a company's products and services. Therefore, a company must determine the lifetime values of their current and potential customer base and then make choices about whom they want to serve. Identifying customers that find more value in doing business with the company, and understanding the reasons why, will help in growing that segment.

A good place to start is your existing financial system. What customers that you now serve bring in the most profit (not necessarily the most revenue)? It is as important to understand what your customers demand from you on the expense side as it is to understand how much they pay you for providing goods and services. A solid activity-based costing system is helpful in identifying revenue and expense flows by customer, process, or product line within the organization.

Activity-based costing is an accounting procedure for allocating the cost of indirect and overhead expenses to specific activities in proportion to the use of a given resource by that activity.[4] This is in contrast to conventional accounting practice, which allocates indirect and overhead expenses in proportion to direct costs incurred by an activity. Once an organization decides to identify, collect, and monitor its indirect customer-related expenses, it can then scan the existing accounting categories to identify those accounts that represent or contain costs related to specific customers or customer segments.[5]

An organization must decide whether it merely wants more customers or to focus on acquiring more of the right customers. By analyzing their customers, an organization often finds it is not economically feasible to continue serving a particular segment. An organization may also find it is uniquely able to expand a particular market or even discover a niche not presently served by competitors. In this area, the economic concept of "relative opportunity costs" is a very good one to employ in making decisions and setting improvement priorities.

Tracking, measuring, and reporting on a real dollar basis is usually more meaningful than percentages or quantities alone. Knowing what it costs to lose a customer is a good place to start. Lost-customer research may take the form of interviews with customers who have stopped buying your product or service or significantly reduced their usage. These surveys are generally administered by phone so the interviewer can probe areas of dissatisfaction. Another approach is to ask lost customers to join a focus group for open discussion of issues surrounding customer withdrawal. See chapter 3 for more information on linking quality and profits.

Improving customer retention is generally a better strategy than new customer attraction. Studies have shown that it costs anywhere from five to 10 times as much to attract new customers as keep the ones we already have. These figures have a direct impact on the profit or expense management goals of the organization. Refer to chapter 3 on cost of quality for an excellent approach to tying customer activity to direct financial status of the organization.

HOW DO WE KNOW WHAT THE CUSTOMER WANTS?

Customer relationship management (CRM) is a relatively new term for having a good, solid working relationship with your external customers. CRM relates less to the product or service provided and more to improving sales, marketing, customer service, and support. In a customer-focused organization, the issue is more the nurturing of existing customers than the search for new customers. A key principle of good customer relations is determining and improving customer satisfaction. Additionally, CRM takes advantage of technology and information systems to provide real-time customer satisfaction.

The basic elements of customer relationship management are:

- Customer identification

- Differentiation of customers by value to the organization

- Differentiation by customer needs, attitudes, and behaviors

- Interpreting and disseminating the differentiated information throughout the value chain

- Establishing a strong alignment between company activities and the customer needs

- Creating long-term ties to the customer through product or service customization

CRM drives an increase in average revenue per customer. Increased customer loyalty and retention improves sales per customer, enhances cross-selling of additional products and services, and reduces selling costs. Organizing the business around customers rather than functional silos reduces workflow, shortens production cycle times, and improves flow of information.

It is important that the organization adopt a CRM focus in its strategy before trying to implement it through technology. Technology is only the tool with which human relationships are enhanced. CRM is an essential component of the total supply chain management concept. Establishing good relationships with external customers is only part of the complete customer satisfaction system. Establishing a culture of trust and communication among suppliers, employees, partners, and end users is imperative to guarantee a consistently high level of reliability and performance in delivering products and services. Maintaining this complex interrelationship is a full-time job of the organization. See chapter 4 for more information on supply chain management and its importance to customer satisfaction and organizational improvement.

Perceptions of customer satisfaction must be validated through collecting, analyzing, and acting upon customer feedback. Effective systems for using customer feedback involve several elements:

- Formal processes for collecting, measuring, and analyzing customer data

- Channels for communicating results to the appropriate business functions for action

- A feedback mechanism to determine how well an organization is meeting customer requirements

Once customer satisfaction data has been gathered, sophisticated techniques can be used to analyze the data and target areas for improvement. Customer information must be designed, formatted, and stored appropriately and made available to those who need it.

Example sources of customer data used in determining customer satisfaction are:

- Customer satisfaction surveys

- Advisory groups

- Warranty registrations

- Customer complaint tracking

- Action logs from service activities

- Focus groups and interviews

- Subscription services on customer trends

- Lost-customer analysis

An excellent text for more detailed information on the specifics of data sources is *Measuring and Managing Customer Satisfaction* by Sheila Kessler. See the reference section at the end of this chapter for more information.

Customer satisfaction surveys are so commonly used that they deserve some coverage within the body of this chapter. Many organizations solicit feedback with formal customer surveys. The goal of most surveys is to get as high a response rate as possible for the most representative sampling of the customer population surveyed and to get as much useful data as possible. Designing surveys and analyzing the subsequent data requires extensive skill and knowledge. Survey administration is expensive. It is even more expensive to misinterpret or misuse the data.

Kessler recommends the following steps in designing any survey for measuring customer satisfaction:

- Determine objectives and how you will use the survey

- Determine performance requirements

- Determine format

- Determine sampling procedure

- Develop questions

- Test questions and refine[6]

Surveys should be administered at least yearly, if not more frequently. Most people will not accurately remember an experience with a product, service, or employee for longer than a year. Current experience also shows that after only a quarter many customers have either moved or are no longer accessible for survey purposes. In addition, rapidly changing customer needs and perceptions make input highly time-dependent. If surveys are to be given more frequently than quarterly, however, use a personal approach. Filling out forms is not a favored practice for most customers.

There are several methods already well established for administering customer surveys. The rise of electronic communication has greatly reduced the expense of hardcopy survey mailings, although response rates are still low for these less personal avenues of communication. Focus groups and one-on-one conversation, are most effective. They also are generally the most expensive.

Some methods of administering surveys are:

- Mail

- Electronic (e-mail or Web site)

- Telephone

- Face-to-face

- Group

- Panels

Figure 12.2 is a suggested starting point for asking customers about their needs and expectations.

Each survey method has its useful and less desirable characteristics. Relative effectiveness of one over another also depends on the purpose of the survey, the population to be surveyed, and the benefit-to-cost ratio of conducting the survey. The mailed survey has its costs, but can reach unlimited numbers of potential respondents. The response rate can be low; the types of customers responding may not represent a reliable sample but it is far less expensive than face-to-face surveys. Electronic surveys are also less expensive when used in conjunction with an already established Web site, but usually yield very low response rates. Often, surveys not directly targeted to specific customers generate responses from only very delighted or highly dissatisfied customers, thus skewing the subsequent analysis.

CRM and supply-chain management techniques can be helpful in establishing relationships with high priority customers and suppliers who are willing to share their ideas and concerns on an ongoing basis. Using existing relationships greatly reduces the expense of surveying less targeted audiences.

Targeting existing audiences is not enough, however. It is important to gather information from potential customer markets, customers who have chosen to stop doing business with our organization, or those customers who have become dissatisfied, but have not yet made their concerns known to us. It takes special effort to communicate

---

1. Ask customers to list their requirements.

2. Identify what measurements the customer uses to determine if their requirements are being met.

3. Find out your customer's highest priority. Ask customers to rank requirements.

4. What is your customer's biggest complaint?

5. What process of yours that is not governed by specifications would cause the most problems for your customers?

6. What improvement would give your customer a competitive edge?

7. Are your customer's requirements possible?

8. Discuss and try to agree on targets, specifications, limits, and measurement systems.

Figure 12.2   Identifying customer requirements.

effectively with these market groups. Very focused survey or data-gathering techniques are required to secure reliable information in these cases.

TRACKING, MEASURING, AND REPORTING CUSTOMER SATISFACTION

Producing tabulations of customer satisfaction data, trend charts, and so on, is of minimal value unless there is an established objective against which to compare. To make sense of the time and energy involved in collecting the data, there must be a target. To justify the preventive action that may be indicated by the analyzed data there needs to be a basis for estimating the anticipated gain to be achieved by the action, a means for tracking progress toward achieving the objective, and the basis for evaluating the effectiveness of the action taken.

Industry-specific analysis firms exist for many product and service types. Professional societies also offer data gathering and reporting services either for subscription fees or on a contract basis to help the organization get a benchmark for comparison and further improvement. Companies such as The Gallup Organization or the American Customer Satisfaction Index regularly publish generic studies of customer opinion by select industries as well as work individually with organizations for specific research. Much information of a generic level is available through Web site searches.

Tracking customer satisfaction by product, service, and customer segment over time provides an excellent vehicle for identifying areas for improvement and change. Graphing customer satisfaction on a scheduled basis using a bar chart or control chart is a quick and effective visual way to focus attention on the areas of highest concern or payback.

Graphs are visual representations of data, including bar charts, pie charts, histograms, or scatter diagrams, which make data analysis and decision making easier for most people. See Figure 12.3 for a sample of these visual tools.

A control chart is used to monitor a process to see whether that process is in statistical control. Control charts help identify what the current practices and systems can predictably yield. Once targets and customer response expectations are established, the control chart will show quickly whether our products and services are meeting established targets or whether we need to refine our efforts. See Figure 12.4 for an example of a control chart. More information on a series of effective management tools is available in *The Quality Improvement Handbook* by Bauer, Duffy, and Westcott. See suggested readings at the end of this chapter for more information.

Revenue and profit analysis are more familiar tracking and reporting vehicles for executives. More recently, executives have been using these reports in an integrated way that combines financial, customer, and employee performance characteristics. The integrated measurement systems now being developed in many organizations combine data into knowledge-management structures that can be studied from different perspectives. Customer satisfaction processes are a significant part of these integrated database analysis and reporting systems.

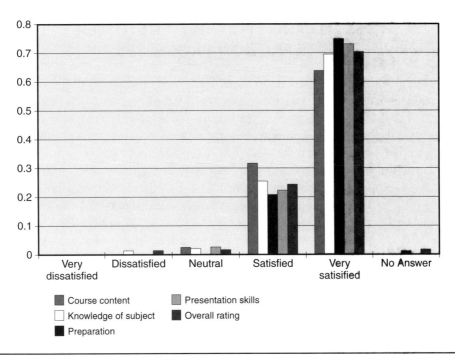

Figure 12.3 Customer service training, January–May 2002.

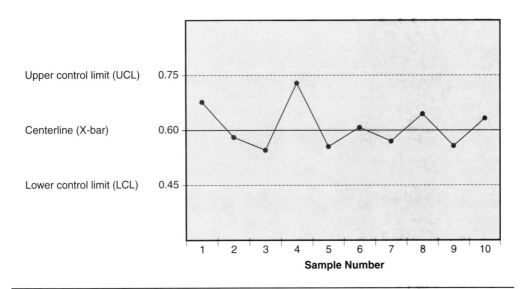

Figure 12.4 Control chart (process in control).

DEVELOPING EFFECTIVE CUSTOMER SATISFACTION PROCESSES

This chapter began with a focus on external customer satisfaction. Equally critical to organizational success is the satisfaction of the internal customer. The culture of the organization will affect the attitude of the employee who interfaces with our external customers and suppliers. If the employee is not customer-focused, the organization will not be customer-focused. As identified in chapter 4, Supply Chain Management, the relationship between customers and suppliers is really nothing more than a cycle of internal and external customers. See Figure 12.5 for an illustration of suppliers feeding resources into the organization from one side, while customers provide requirements from the other. Inside the organization is a series of customer/supplier relationships performing the actions to transform the supplied resources into products and services to meet customer requirements.

Internal customers are those within the organization. Who are they? How can an organization work with internal customers to effectively improve processes and services? How does an organization's treatment of its internal customers influence its approach to external customers?

Every function and work group in an organization is both a receiver of services or products from internal or external sources as well as a provider of services and/or products to internal or external customers. Each receiver has needs and requirements. Whether

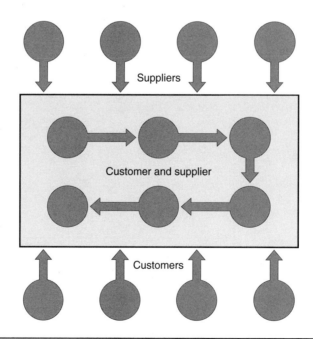

Figure 12.5 Contemporary view of suppliers and customers.

the delivered service or product meets these needs or requirements impacts the customers' effectiveness and performance of that service or product to their customers, and so on.

If we are to establish and maintain an excellent relationship with our external customers, we must likewise maintain an equally effective relationship with our internal customers and suppliers. Employee satisfaction thus becomes as important as customer satisfaction. Russ Westcott identifies a sound process for establishing an internal customer improvement system that addresses both employees and the processes with which they work.

Steps to improve processes and services:

- Identify internal customer interfaces (providers of services/products and receivers of their service/products)

- Establish internal customers' service/product needs/requirements

- Ensure that the internal customer requirements are consistent with and supportive of external customer requirements

- Document service-level agreements between provider and receivers

- Establish improvement goals and measurements

- Implement systems for tracking and reporting performance and for supporting the continuous improvement of the process.[7]

If the steps above sound familiar, they should. The process for establishing and maintaining good internal customer and supplier relationships is basically the same as that for external suppliers and customers. We are all people. We have many of the same expectations for products, services, and personal attention.

HOW INTERNAL CUSTOMERS ARE TREATED AFFECTS EXTERNAL CUSTOMERS

Careless behavior of management or management systems toward internal customers (for example, poor tools and equipment, unhealthy work environment, disinterest in internal complaints, and so on) may encourage careless treatment of external customers. This attitude by those who work with our external customers can generate an environment that will adversely affect the organization's business results. Ignoring the needs of internal customers makes it difficult to instill a desire to care for the needs of external customers.

So many organizations fail to learn, or ignore, the internal customers' needs and wonder why their internal customers no longer care about how and what they do for external customers. The poor attitude of the sales representative, environmental service employee, healthcare provider, or customer service representative often exemplifies lack of caring for internal customers.

USING CUSTOMER SATISFACTION FOR IMPROVEMENT AND CHANGE

Using approaches such as those described in chapter 4, Supply Chain Management, will go a long way toward improving our overall customer satisfaction results. The best management systems fail because of a lack of true commitment and demonstrated leadership, and a misalignment of organizational practices that engage the workforce. Therefore, strong leadership is necessary to instill a clear sense of mission based on customer value throughout the total organizational system. This strong sense of direction must guide daily decision making and all members of the organization must share the same mission and values. Engaging the workforce by instilling this sense of purpose, and appropriately aligning employee practices, will enhance employee loyalty. This will lead to improved customer retention and profit.

Once we have established an effective cycle of external and internal customer satisfaction measurement, analysis, and reporting, we are able to focus on areas of improvement. By choosing those areas that provide the greatest long-term results, we can institute a cycle of improvement and change that should consistently delight our existing customers and attract new customers to our expanding business.

ENDNOTES

1. ANSI/ISO/ASQ Q9001:2000 American National Standard. Milwaukee: ASQ Quality Press, 2000.
2. Ibid.
3. F. Gryna, *Quality Planning and Analysis*, 4th ed. (New York: McGraw Hill, 2001).
4. R. Cooper and R. S. Kaplan, *The Design of Cost Management Systems: Text, Cases, and Readings* (New York: Prentice Hall, 1991).
5. ASQ Quality Costs Committee, *Principles of Quality Costs*, 3rd ed. (Milwaukee: ASQ Quality Press, 1999): 61.
6. S. Kessler, *Measuring and Managing Customer Satisfaction* (Milwaukee: ASQC Quality Press, 1996): 146.
7. J. E. Bauer, G. L. Duffy, R. L. Westcott, *The Quality Improvement Handbook* (Milwaukee: ASQ Quality Press, 2002): 124–25.

SUGGESTED READING

ASQ Quality Costs Committee. *Principles of Quality Costs*, 3rd ed. Milwaukee: ASQ Quality Press, 1999.

Bauer, J. E., G. L. Duffy, and R. L. Westcott. *The Quality Improvement Handbook*. Milwaukee: ASQ Quality Press, 2002.

Kessler, S. *Measuring and Managing Customer Satisfaction*. Milwaukee: ASQC Quality Press, 1996.

13

Performance Enhancement through Management Audits

Terry L. Regel

The implementation of quality management systems based on ISO and other industry standards has been both positive and negative. While organizations have developed and implemented quality management systems, optimal results have not been achieved. One reason is the applicable standards' requirements have not been linked to the organizations' goals but rather have been implemented as an end unto themselves without true integration into the organizations' practices and manner of doing business. Another reason is the belief by implementers in the multitude of "ISO myths" that make the quality management system rigidly "ISO" rather than satisfying the needs of the organization. More often than not, such standards are implemented as a customer pacifier rather than a tool to enhance business performance.

Implementation of an effective quality management system requires skill and experience, but is not, as the saying goes, rocket science. One thing that should be understood is that the ISO standards, or any other industry standard, should be transparent to the organization's business management system. Each policy, procedure, or practice should be implemented because doing so improves performance or addresses a customer requirement, not simply because of an ISO requirement.

The organization's audit function is a critical component, determining not only the effectiveness of your quality management system, but also the success of your business. In this chapter, the elements of an effective audit function are presented. None of these elements is discussed in terms of any specific standard, but rather in consideration of an organization's needs for continual performance improvement.

AUDIT MANAGEMENT PLANNING

The audit function, whether an independent function or a component of another function, must be well defined, with a specific purpose and objectives. While one may think this so fundamental that it deserves little consideration, organizations rarely consider the audit function's purpose to be anything more than to evaluate the effectiveness of the implementation and maintenance of the quality management system. Yet, based on our experience, an organization will not realize one-fourth of the potential benefit from the audit function if this is the only purpose served. In order to correct this deficiency, the audit function should be utilized to aid the organization in achieving its strategic plan objectives.

Senior management should evaluate the audit function's role during the operational planning process just as is done with other functions. Operational planning is frequently performed as illustrated in Figure 13.1.

Senior management evaluates the strategic plan and current customer expectations in order to determine resources, priorities, and expenditures necessary for success. With consideration of the organization's mission and values, specific goals and objectives are defined. Middle management determines the critical processes directly related to the achievement of these goals with input from supervisors and associates involved in these processes on a daily basis. Supervisors and associates identify key measures for monitoring the performance of these processes. Throughout the fiscal year, associates monitor, measure, and gather information regarding critical process performance. Supervisors and managers summarize, evaluate, and report the overall performance against the stated goals to senior management in regular performance review meetings.

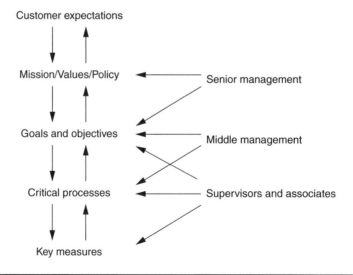

Figure 13.1 Operational planning.

These management reviews evaluate key operational performance measures to identify gaps requiring attention. The questions to be answered during this review include:

- Are strategic goals and objectives being met?

- Is the management system adequate to achieve these goals and objectives?

- Are improvement projects achieving the expected results?

- Are products and processes performing at required capability levels?

When the answers to these questions are unsatisfactory, an independent audit needs to be conducted to provide unbiased information to management so that the gaps in performance may be addressed effectively.

As with any other function, management must determine the audit function's role in achieving the stated goals and objectives. Consideration should include:

- Capability to achieve goals and objectives

- Identification of hidden costs

- Effectiveness of measurement systems

- Effectiveness and efficiency of systems, policies, and procedures

- Risks associated with new projects and products

- New product or service launches

- Customer satisfaction ratings

- Identification of improvement opportunities

- Capability of suppliers to satisfy requirements

- Implementing national quality award criteria

Beginning with a review of historical performance, management may identify activities, products, or projects that have resulted in high cost, customer complaints, performance concerns, chronic failures, unsatisfactory production levels, and delivery issues. The areas having the greatest impact on achieving the operational goals and objectives are the highest priority for the audit function to evaluate. The result of this evaluation will provide the basis for scheduling the types and frequency of the audits to be conducted. If the audit function is not involved in this manner, it will need to be to achieve compliance to the requirements of ISO 9001:2000, ISO/TS 16949:2000, and other management system standards.

If there is none, an audit manager, with the management experience, audit credentials, and audit experience to develop and manage the audit program effectively, must be identified. The audit manager is responsible for determining the resources required, including the work space, equipment, budget, and personnel necessary to achieve the audit function's objectives. This does not mean, necessarily, that the organization has to have a dedicated staff of auditors. In fact, organizations benefit most when the audit function is composed of representatives from the various functions within the organization. These cross-functional members of the audit function may include managers, engineers, supervisors, group leaders, and specialists.

The selection and training of auditors from within the organization is to be considered neither a simple task nor one requiring little thought or effort. Since these auditors will be evaluating every aspect of the organization, they should be the most experienced people available. Candidates should include the associates with direct responsibility for achieving the defined goals and objectives as they are the most motivated to ensure that the management system is implemented effectively and efficiently.

AUDITOR CREDENTIALS

Many managers are confused about auditor credentials with regard to a "certified" auditor. The confusion arises from the belief that having sent a person to a Registrar Accreditation Board (RAB)–accredited 36-hour lead auditor course, the candidate must be a certified auditor. Most auditors attend such a course for any of the following reasons:

- Their company is implementing an "ISO-like" industry standard.

- They are seeking certification as an RAB QMS auditor or lead auditor.

- They need verification of their understanding of the standard.

- They need additional recertification units.

- They have not attained ASQ certified quality auditor status.

The fact of the matter is that the successful completion of a 36-hour lead auditor course is the first step in achieving RAB certification as quality management systems auditor. The certificate received on the successful completion of this course attests to the candidate's understanding of the ISO standard and basic audit principles, but does not attest to the candidate's auditing ability. From your organization's viewpoint, this step should be initiated for only a very few, proven members of the organization after they have successfully completed other formal training and attained other certifications or credentials.

THE IMPORTANCE OF ASQ CERTIFICATIONS

The ASQ offers certifications that are essential to the effectiveness of an auditor, including the ASQ Certified Quality Engineer (CQE), ASQ Certified Quality Manager (CQMgr), and the ASQ Certified Quality Auditor (CQA). In combination, these are to the Audit Manager what the Certified Public Accountant (CPA) is to the Accounting Manager. Of course, there is no direct comparison between the CPA and the ASQ CQE, the ASQ CQMgr or the ASQ

Table 13.1 Exam success rates.

Credential	Exam	Success Rate
Certified public accountant	16 hours	36–45%/part[*]
ASQ certified quality engineer	5 hours	38%[†]
ASQ certified quality manager	4 hours	44%[†]
ASQ certified quality auditor	4 hours	50%[†]
36-hour lead auditor course	2 hours	95%[‡]

[*] Utah State University Web site citing the National Association of State Boards of Accountancy (www.usu.edu/account/assessment/pass_cpa.htm).
[†] American Society for Quality. These percentages were calculated from the total number of candidates who have sat for each exam and the total number of candidates who passed the exam since first offered.
[‡] The RAB did not have a success rate at the time this was being prepared. The number above was provided by averaging the responses from different course providers who asked not to be cited by name.

CQA, yet the combination of the ASQ CQE, ASQ CQMgr, and the CQA is the equivalent for the quality professional. Consider the information in Table 13.1.

Comparing the "success rate" column, the relative difficulty of the ASQ exams versus the 36-hour lead auditor course is apparent. The success rates for the individual ASQ exams are similar to those for each part of the CPA exam, and candidates for the ASQ exams must also meet the minimum education and work experience requirements as well as be sponsored by a quality professional. See appendix A for an abbreviated outline of each of the ASQ exams' bodies of knowledge or, for additional information about these exams, visit the ASQ Web site (www.asq.org).

The ASQ does not require that candidates for certification take the ASQ exams in any order, nor is there special recognition for attaining these three certifications. Yet a candidate that has successfully completed these exams has demonstrated competence in every area required of a quality assurance professional.

The RAB does not require an individual to hold any of the ASQ certifications. However, the RAB does require that candidates for the RAB's QMS auditor certification meet minimum education, work experience, training, and audit experience criteria. The primary difference in the RAB's QMS auditor certification and the ASQ's certifications is that the RAB's certification attests to a candidate's understanding of an ISO standard and ability to audit to that standard, but not the candidate's ability to perform effectively as a quality assurance professional.

With this in mind, candidates under consideration to manage your audit function should have a proven performance history as a quality professional. The criteria that you should consider essential are the following:

- Quality management system implementation experience

- ASQ certifications in one of the following combinations:

- ASQ CQE and ASQ CQA certifications

- ASQ CQMgr and ASQ CQA certifications

- ASQ CQE, ASQ CQMgr, and ASQ CQA certifications

- RAB QMS auditor or QMS lead auditor certification

- Audit experience

You both expect and demand that your accounting professional have appropriate credentials and experience to perform effectively. You should expect no less of the auditors responsible for the evaluation of your system's performance.

INTERNAL AUDITOR CREDENTIALS

Your audit manager must have the skills and experience to effectively manage the audit function. However, your organization may not have the resources required to sustain a staff of auditors with similar credentials. If yours is a large multisite organization, there may be advantages to having a dedicated staff of experienced auditors. However, there is also an inherent disadvantage in that the audits may be viewed as adversarial. Both management and the auditors will have to diligently guard against this happening within your organization.

If yours is a small organization or one that does not have the budget to sustain a dedicated staff of auditors, then you should identify people from within the organization to be trained as auditors. These candidates must be the "best and brightest," selected from each management level and function of the organization. Selecting candidates without technical expertise in the areas they will be auditing is a formula for failure.

The training and preparation of internal auditors is time-consuming. However, the organization cannot afford to skimp on auditor training and development. The use of untrained, poorly prepared auditors will cause the audit function to fall into disfavor, and the organization will not recognize the expected performance improvement. As a result, the greatest management challenge is to ensure that the audits are conducted to assess the effectiveness and efficiency of performance, not people.

You also need to define and document your requirements for internal auditor certification. Generally, companies require internal auditors to:

- Complete a basic audit course

- Complete a course on the required standard, if applicable

- Complete a course in corrective action

- Complete a course in quality tools

- Participate in at least two supervised audits

- Demonstrate the ability to perform as an auditor

- Participate in at least one audit every 18 months

The list of training requirements varies by company, but the above list contains the most common requirements for an internal auditor. However, auditor training should also include Sayle's 12 Golden Rules:[1]

1. Never challenge a person.

2. Always present a true and fair view.

3. Go fact-finding, not fault finding.

4. Use systematic methods.

5. Never lose sight of the product.

6. Find out the auditee's interpretation, not yours.

7. Always be properly prepared.

8. Always help the auditee.

9. Always define the audit objectives.

10. Communicate effectively with the auditee.

11. Find and address the real cause of problems found.

12. Always follow up corrective action requests.

Auditor evaluations should include an assessment of their ability to incorporate these rules in order for the auditee and the organization to realize benefit from the audits.

Before initiating audits, provide training for your management and supervisory staff as well. This training will not only provide the foundation for the audit function to interact effectively with your staff but will also provide an understanding of:

- The organization's purpose for conducting audits

- The audit process

- The standards to which they will be audited

- How they should interact with the auditors

- How they should respond to questions

- The types of evidence they should provide

- What is expected of them when responding to corrective action requests

- How the effectiveness of the actions implemented will be determined

This training does not need to be more than a few hours long, and, for best results, you or another senior manager should provide a brief introduction to the session. These sessions, if more than one is required, will provide the opportunity for management to communicate the expectation of the benefit to be derived from the performance of the audits. Your management staff will also be provided the opportunity to ask questions in order to better understand the process. You and the Audit Manager should be able to provide the assurance the objective is to improve the effectiveness and efficiency of the management system.

PARTNERSHIP AUDITS

Organizations with limited resources might also consider partnering with suppliers, other noncompeting companies in your area, or with other sites within the company to participate in training and conducting audits at each other's facilities. Partnership audits provide mutual benefits to the parties involved, including[2]:

- Reducing training costs as each facility will share the training expense

- Reducing the strain on limited resources

- Ensuring independence of the auditors

- Learning new methods and techniques

- Helping your suppliers to understand your needs

- Helping you to understand your supplier's needs

However, partnering in this way with another organization or facility within your own company requires coordination and the services of an experienced lead auditor. Training needs to be coordinated so that members of each partnering group attend training sessions together. You may also find the training more effective when conducted by a neutral party; this avoids sending the message that your group has all the answers. Senior managers from each location should also introduce the training session stating their expectations, including the fact that:

- The audit report will only be distributed to the auditee.

- Good practices may be shared freely.

- Specific details of the audit will not be divulged to others.

Even though your customers may require supplier audits, partnering with them in this way will be more productive than the typical supplier quality audit. These audits also address one of ISO 9000:2000's eight quality management principles,[3] "mutually beneficial supplier relationships," which many companies struggle to address. Remember, the objective is to achieve mutual benefit for all parties concerned. However, unless the managers and auditors of each organization maintain their agreement regarding audit confidentiality, the partnership will not succeed.

AUDIT PERFORMANCE

Internal audits tend to be less formal than those performed by customers or registrars. Internal audit or not, the audit manager needs to prepare an annual audit schedule for your review and approval based on the prioritized list developed during operation planning. The audit manager should also prepare a draft audit plan for each of the scheduled audits planned so that the auditors and their supervisors may be prepared.

Audit team size is dependent upon the scope of the audit and available resources. However, the audit manager will assign a minimum of two auditors to each audit to reduce the duration of the audit and to provide for corroboration of evidence. The practice may seem excessive, but the confirmation of an issue by evidence from two independent sources provides greater assurance for the auditee. In addition, two auditors will not report an issue that cannot be verified by both, reducing the probability of reporting issues of no consequence for the organization.

Even though the auditee will receive a final audit plan, the lead auditor should review it during the opening meeting. The meeting will be brief, but will provide the opportunity for minor adjustments to be made in the order the interviews take place. During the audit, the auditors will:

- Conduct interviews

- Review documentation and records

- Observe activities

- Inform the auditee of any issues or concerns

If the audit is a full system audit, the audit team will hold daily briefings to provide updates on the progress of the audit, review issues identified, review additional information related to the issues, and adjust the audit timetable as necessary.

Managers often question the need to conduct a full system audit when an audit is conducted on each process or each clause of the applicable standard throughout the fiscal year. Experience has shown that no matter how well these partial audits have been conducted, critical interactions between processes or subsystems are missed. Frequently, the limiting factors are the audit scope and the time allotted for the audit. To ensure that the management system is functioning effectively, a full system audit should be conducted at least once each year.

The closing meeting is to provide a summary of the audit results and the conclusion of the audit team. The importance of this meeting is evidenced by the attendees and, if senior management wants to emphasize the importance of these audits, they must attend the closing meetings for the following reasons:

- To support the management and staff

- To support the audit team

- To provide positive feedback, as appropriate

- To assign responsibility for corrective action

The latter of these is very important since issues are frequently identified in a process audit that are beyond the control of the auditee. Assigning corrective action to the manager of the process audited will not result in effective corrective action. Instead, the corrective action must be addressed by a cross-functional team for resolution.

SCORED CHECKLISTS

Some companies utilize a scoring system for conducting internal audits so that they may monitor management system improvement. However, the scored results of an internal management system audit often are more dependent upon the skill of the audit team and the time allowed for the audit than the organization's performance. In addition, some of the scoring methods require minor nonconformities to be escalated to major nonconformities if a minimum number of "minors" is exceeded in a given area. These checklists are frequently biased in that questions for one key area address high-level issues while another is addressed in extreme detail. For scored checklists to work, each area of the system should be weighted the same or should include a factor to facilitate the comparison of each of the subsystems. Even then, an audit by the same audit team auditing the same system will not score the system the same way each time because the auditors:

- Have different assignments

- Ask questions differently each time

- Interview different people

- Follow evidence trails differently

- Have different levels of experience

- Encounter different situations in each audit

- Review evidence not previously seen by the audit team

This list is not all-inclusive, but provides a few of the reasons to avoid scored checklists for internal audits. Scored checklists require balance and standardization in their development and application, and may better serve as an evaluation of higher-level functions. Instead, management should focus their attention on performance improvement rather than a score that may provide a false sense of security one day, only to demoralize all concerned on another.

REPORTING RESULTS

No matter how skilled the audit team, if the audit results are not reported in a manner that facilitates management decisions for corrective action, the audit is a failure. The audit team should avoid the temptation to report the audit results in the same manner as their customers or their registrar. Instead of reporting a list of nonconformities, each with its own corrective action request (CAR), the audit team should be allowed the time to evaluate the results of the audit so that the systems issues may be identified. Lists of nonconformities:

- Are merely lists of individual symptoms of problems

- Overwhelm the corrective action system

- Result in uncoordinated corrective actions

- Do not identify problems within the system

The audit team must evaluate the issues identified to report the system deficiencies that caused these issues to occur, and report findings with supporting evidence (the individual nonconformities).

Writing findings, which are the statements describing the system failures, is not easy for the audit team. Patience and practice are required for auditors to become proficient in their preparation. They also require more time during the audit to prepare, but result in a better understanding of the system issues. As a guide, relate findings to "FACCT." Findings must be:

Factual: Based on fact.

Accurate: Free from error and emotion.

Concise: Brief and free from superfluous detail.

Complete: Having all the detail necessary for understanding.

Traceable: Verifiable and repeatable.

As the audit is conducted, nonconformances are recorded and verified in the usual manner. When the audit is complete, all the nonconformances are reviewed by the audit team to ensure that they are valid and clearly stated. Similar concerns (nonconformances) are then grouped. Each group is then analyzed to state the system concern. The following is an example of a finding statement with supporting evidence (nonconformances):

Finding: Process controls in the warehouse area do not include the small-packaging line, allowing poor-quality product to be shipped to key customers.

Supporting evidence:

- There is no procedure for packaging of specialty containers.

- The partly filled drums used to fill small containers are not controlled.

- A top is missing from one of the partially filled drums.

- The scales used for can weighing were either beyond the calibration date or were never calibrated.

- Product is left in the canning machine between runs. The current product has been in the machine for two days.

- The small filled containers stored in the area were rusty and dirty, requiring area personnel to repackage any damaged or deteriorated containers prior to shipment.

- Rusty drums have been shipped to customers, resulting in five complaints last quarter.

- Contaminated product was found in three of seven drums inspected.

This finding satisfies the criteria stated previously. The effect, the shipment of poor-quality product to key customers, is clearly stated as the system issue. The supporting evidence (nonconformance statements), provide the basis for corrective action.

The corrective action team will use this information to initiate effective corrective action by putting the finding in the "effect" box of a cause-and-effect diagram and the nonconformances in the appropriate slots in the backbone of the diagram. Further investigation by the team will identify related issues that contribute to the effect (the finding) identified.

While a list of nonconformances fragments the corrective action process, finding statements focus corrective action activities on the system issue. When presented to management, the auditor should describe not only the system issue, but also the reason resources should be devoted to the resolution of the finding. Not only will this method provide focus for the corrective action team, it also provides a starting point for the problem-solving process.

MAJOR AND MINOR NONCONFORMITIES

Neither the audit team nor the auditee should be concerned about the classification of audit findings as major or minor. The definitions used by customers and registrars for these are:

Major   The absence, breakdown, or total failure of a system to meet the requirements of the applicable standard; any nonconformance that would probably result in the shipment of nonconforming product, such as a condition that may result in the failure of or materially reduce the usability of the product or service.

Minor   Random and isolated indications of control weaknesses but such that would not result in a system breakdown, reduce its ability to assure controlled processes, or in the shipment of nonconforming product.

Frequently, a major nonconformity is addressed by the auditee by writing a procedure and verifying that the action is effective. A minor nonconformity, on the other hand, requires more time and resources since processes and procedures may have to be modified and the corrective action team has to verify that neither the product nor the interrelated process have been adversely affected by the changes. For this reason, a "minor" nonconformity is frequently more difficult to resolve than a so-called "major" nonconformity. Neither classification is of importance for internal audits since the audit team will identify and report any issue that affects performance. Any issue reducing the effectiveness and efficiency of the system must be addressed no matter how they may be classified.

RECOMMENDATIONS OR ALTERNATIVES?

The audit team may be asked for recommendations for corrective action. Making specific recommendations may relieve the auditee of the responsibility of investigating the finding thoroughly. The audit team may avoid the necessity of making recommendations by providing at least two "alternatives for consideration" for the corrective action team to consider based on the conditions observed during the audit. The auditee then has additional information for brainstorming alternatives for corrective action.

TIMELINESS

Audit reports should be provided to management as soon as possible following the completion of the audit. If at all possible, this should be at the closing meeting. Of course, the audit team may need to amend the audit report based on the discussion in the closing meeting, but such occurrences are rare. Even then, with today's technology, the corrections should be, and often can be, made the same day. In any case, a draft report, with the changes indicated by the audit team leader may be distributed immediately.

Delaying the distribution of the audit report diminishes the effectiveness of the audit and the credibility of the audit team. Any delay in issuing the report also delays the initiation of corrective action of the issues that the audit team indicated require urgent attention by management. Of course, there can be extenuating circumstances in which the final audit report cannot be issued in less than five days, but they are rare. However, if under normal conditions the audit reports cannot be issued in less than 48 hours following the audit, reevaluate the audit process.

CORRECTIVE ACTION

The corrective action teams need to verify that the finding is understood. Yet once the audit report is issued, interaction between the audit team leader and the auditee normally ceases. Rather than waste time and resources that may be dedicated to a corrective action activity for days, weeks, or even months, the corrective action team may utilize the *Audit Function Improvement Process*[2] (see Figure 13.2). This process provides a mechanism to ensure that findings are understood by the auditee through interaction with the audit team leader. In addition, the audit team leader is provided regular updates of the corrective action investigation to:

- Ensure the corrective action is appropriate for the finding
- Provide evidence that corrective action is progressing as it should
- Avoid wasting resources addressing the wrong issue
- Provide an independent review of data
- Reduce the necessity of a follow-up audit
- Provide evidence for closure of the finding

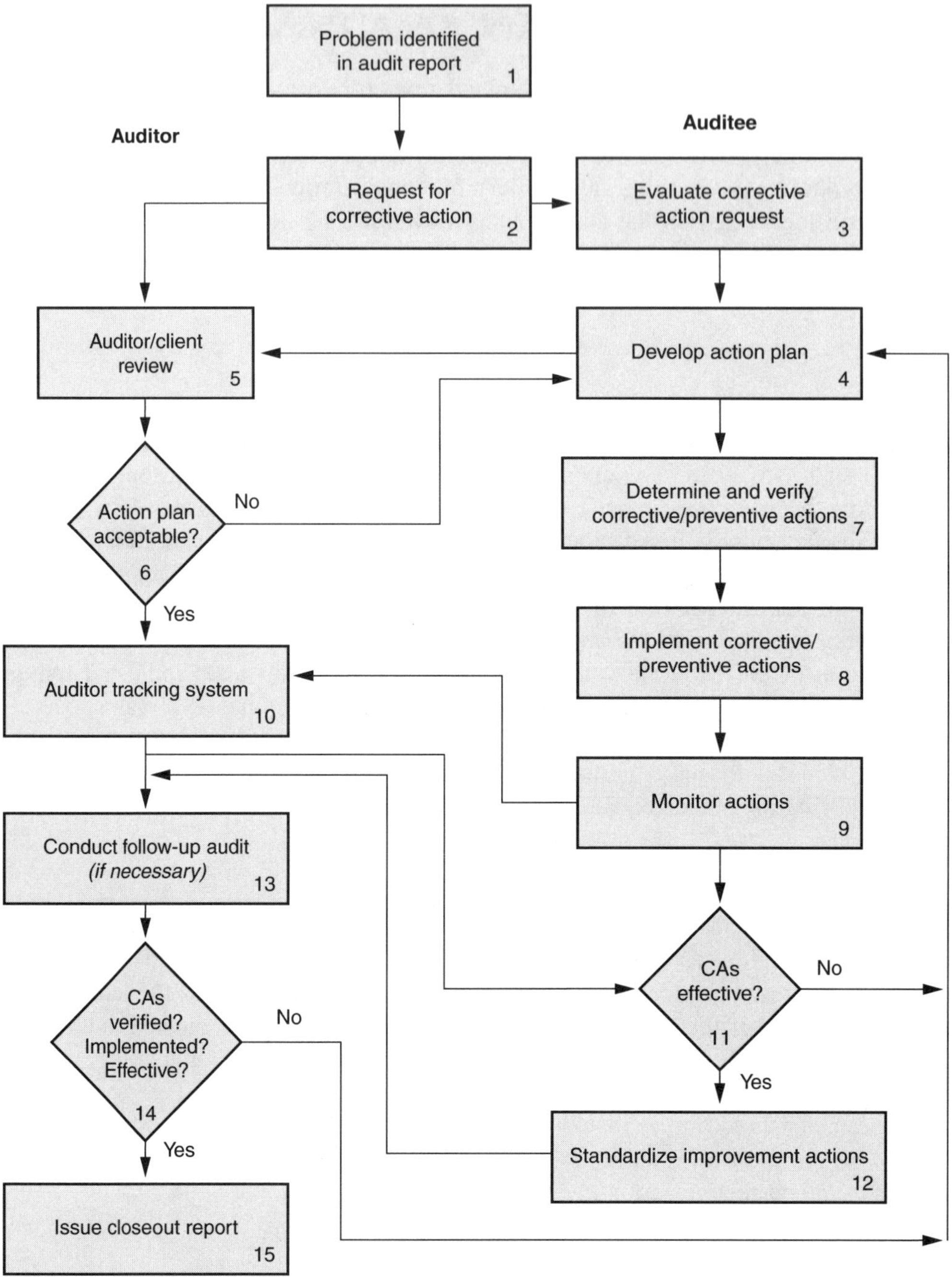

Figure 13.2   The audit function improvement process.

Source: J. P. Russell and T. L. Regel, *After the Quality Audit: Closing the Loop on the Audit Process,* Second Edition. Milwaukee: ASQ Quality Press, 2000. © 2000 Terry L. Regel and J. P. Russell. Used by permission.

The corrective action teams may not include a resource with the experience to analyze and interpret the charts and other data gathered through the corrective action process.

Routing the information gathered to the audit manager on a regular basis for review resolves this deficiency. The audit manager will be able to provide independent confirmation that the corrective action team's activities are achieving the desired results. With this information in hand, the audit manager may also provide a positive status report of the corrective actions to management during management review meetings.

AUDIT CLOSURE

Audit closure may require a brief follow-up audit even though evidence is provided throughout the corrective action process. The necessity for a follow-up audit depends upon the nature of the finding and will have to be determined on a case-by-case basis. However, the necessity of a formal follow-up audit by the audit team leader is reduced when the audit function improvement process is utilized. With multisite organizations, this can result in significant savings while ensuring effective corrective actions. Once the corrective action is verified as having been implemented and effective, the audit team leader should issue a notice of closure of the finding to the auditee and management.

MONITORING PERFORMANCE OF AUDIT FUNCTION

Most audit functions report things that have little to do with the organization's success, such as the number of nonconformities reported, the number of issues open, the number of audits conducted, the number of auditors trained, and so on. Instead, the audit manager should use the audit reports to track issues that affect the company's overall performance, including:

- Cost savings identified

- Process improvements identified and implemented

- Vendor improvements identified and implemented

- Risks identified and avoided (included safety, environmental, and product/customer) and so on

- Other goals and objectives of the audit function

Using the audit reports to capture this information, the audit manager will be able to monitor and report the effectiveness of the audit function. This process requires the audit manager to work with the audit team during the preparation of each report and assign each issue identified to one of three categories: cost, opportunity, or risk.[3] These categories will aid the audit team in the preparation of their report and to make a more effective presentation to management on the effect of the finding. They are also the basis of the audit manager's data for tracking and trending the audit function's performance.

SUMMARY

The audit function is often considered a necessary evil rather than a value-added function. This may be because audits have been dictated by customers or standards. As a result, people with minimal industry experience have been assigned responsibility for the audit function rather than individuals with the skills necessary to achieve the intended objectives.

Senior management must make the decision to choose an audit manager with both industry experience and professional credentials for the audit function to succeed. In addition, the budget and the resources necessary for conducting effective audits must be allocated. These resources include the auditors who will be trained in the performance of audits. They must not be selected from the lowest ranks of the organization. As a general rule, the lowest level in the organization that should be considered as candidates for auditors is the supervisory level. Even then, not all those selected will perform satisfactorily as auditors, but they will gain valuable experience through their participation that will benefit the company.

Management has to use every tool available to enhance performance. Audits have proven to be an effective tool when provided the appropriate resources and support. Management will achieve the results expected when:

- The goals and objectives are clearly stated.

- Organizational needs are communicated to all associates.

- Resources are allocated.

- People with the appropriate skill are identified.

- Training is provided.

- Progress is monitored.

- Management ensures corrective actions are implemented and effective.

Utilizing the Audit Function effectively requires planning and coordination. However, management will recognize and overcome stubborn performance barriers through the performance of effective management audits.

ENDNOTES

1. A. J. Sayle, *Management Audits,* Third Edition (Brighton, MI: Allan Sayle Associates, 1997).
2. J. P. Russell and T. L. Regel, *After the Quality Audit: Closing the Loop on the Audit Process,* Second Edition (Milwaukee: ASQ Quality Press, 2000).
3. Ibid., p. 27ff.

SUGGESTED READINGS

Dew, J. R. *Quality-Centered Strategic Planning: A Step-by-Step Guide.* New York: Quality Resources, 1997.

Edelson, N. M., and C. L. Bennett. *Process Discipline: How to Maximize Profitability and Quality through Manufacturing Consistency.* New York: Quality Resources, 1998.

Mizuno, S., ed. *Management for Quality Improvement: The 7 New QC Tools.* Cambridge, MA: Productivity Press, 1988.

14

Measurement—The Balanced Scorecard

Kevin Sharlow

Why is performance measurement important? Imagine waking up and finding yourself driving in a car along a highway. You don't know where you are, let alone where you are going. You have no idea how long you have been on the road and have no way of estimating how much longer your journey will take. In essence, this is analogous to a company operating on a daily basis without any sense of the progress it has made (or lost) or the strategic direction in which it is headed. In other words, a company that does not measure and report its performance on a routine and meaningful basis in order to drive the daily operations toward a defined set of objectives.

As the previous analogy implies, measuring and monitoring operational performance is of critical importance to an organization's strategic and fiscal well-being. When designed and implemented effectively, performance measurement provides the following benefits:

- It supports the organization's strategic plan by providing management with tangible indicators and goals that are relevant to their daily activities.

- It provides executive management with sufficient and timely information regarding the effectiveness and efficiency of operations before significant financial impacts are experienced.

- It creates a work environment that supports and rewards coordination and cooperation among and between departments and key functional areas to attain desired results.

- It clarifies management and staff roles and responsibilities as they relate to driving expected performance and outcomes.

- It drives change by focusing resources and shaping behaviors toward specific and tangible expectations and results.

- It establishes a mechanism for assigning and enforcing accountability, as well as for recognizing and rewarding outstanding performance.

Many companies have started to implement various performance measurement tools in order to enhance their ability to effectively manage the complex business environment that we all operate in today. A common term utilized to define such a measurement tool is the *balanced scorecard* (BSC). The remainder of this chapter outlines the process for designing and implementing a BSC, and defines some of the critical success factors of such initiatives.

My professional experience has been focused on the financial operations of the healthcare industry, hence, most of the examples included are based on my experiences within this industry. However, the key processes and concepts related to BSC design and implementation initiatives are applicable to all industries and business sectors.

THE BALANCED SCORECARD: A DEFINITION

All companies are familiar with the most common form of performance reporting through the creation of annual budgets and the production and review of periodic income statements and balance sheets, or financial statements. However, these traditional tools are not sufficient to monitor progress, identify issues, and drive behavioral change in a timely and effective manner. These are produced at a very high level and are not, for the most part, relevant to middle management or daily departmental staff activities. As a result, organizations require a second-level information source that synthesizes and summarizes the myriad of information that is available in today's business environment into a format that provides a "snapshot" view of the key departmental and functional trends and results which can then, in turn, be utilized to address deficiencies and develop action plans in order to stop or mitigate adverse operational impacts.

This second-level information source has taken on many names and formats, such as the balanced scorecard, key performance indicators, and dashboard report card. Regardless of the name, they all serve to satisfy an organization's need and desire for enhanced reporting, increased control and accountability, and improved financial results. So what is a balanced scorecard? Whatever the format or name you choose to use, it is basically a report card on the core business processes and functions that includes three key components, or perspectives, on performance:

- Historical-state performance information (baseline/trends)

- Current-state performance level

- Future-state performance goals/targets

Recalling the car-driving analogy at the beginning of the chapter, the historical, or baseline information is important because it provides a sense of "beginning" from which future progress and results will be evaluated. The current-state performance-level information is critical in that it tells people where we are in the "journey," how far we have come from our starting point, or historical level, and allows for an assessment of how far we have to go in order to arrive at our desired, or future-state goals. The future-state goals and targets are arguably the most critical piece of information included in any report card in that they provide incentive and drive actions and behaviors that support the organization's strategic plan and fiscal performance goals.

In order to be effective, a BSC has to be simple and brief in its format and presentation. Most of the report cards that I have encountered have been one to two pages in length and contained sufficient information to satisfy the reporting needs from the board of directors down to the line staff. A simple analogy would be the report cards you used to get in school. At the end of the year, you had a trend of quarterly performance information (grades) that indicated both your historical and current-state performance for all of your "core scholastic functions" (subjects). The only item missing was the future-state goals, which I believe were implied to be 100 percent, or A+, for everybody in every subject.

Before proceeding, it is important to note what a report card is and what it is not. A report card is a management tool, intended to provide all levels of management and staff with an enhanced ability to monitor performance and progress, establish and maintain accountability and responsibility, reward superior results, identify operational deficiencies, and provide incentives for appropriate behavior and actions towards common goals. It is not a replacement for other meaningful and necessary reporting mechanisms, such as monthly financial statements or departmental-level operating reports. It is also not a panacea for a company's fiscal problems. A report card, in and of itself, will not be effective unless it is designed, implemented, and supported in an effective and consistent manner.

The focus of a report card varies depending upon the organization's needs at the time. It can be financial, operational, satisfaction, continual quality improvement, marketing, and so on. For the purposes of this chapter, I have focused on a financial/fiscal performance-based report card design and implementation effort. Again, the primary concepts and tenets apply irrespective of the focus of the report card.

A sample report card that I designed and implemented in the healthcare setting is shown in Figure 14.1. This is not an organizationwide BSC. Rather, it is a report card for a single, albeit extremely important, department—patient accounting. By combining summary financial information with key indicator benchmarking, this report card provides sufficient information to allow the organization to maintain a timely and accurate pulse on the performance of the patient accounting department. It also facilitates the identification of negative trends and performance deficiencies which, in turn, allows for timely corrective action planning and implementation. This report was designed to be used at all levels of the organization, from the board of directors, to management and staff.

XYZ Hospital
Patient Accounting Report Card
Key Indicators Report Card

A: A/R Activity

A/R Activity	Current Month	Year to Date
Starting A/R	$36,710,666	$34,111,964
Charges	15,828,394	90,558,000
Payments	(6,899,267)	(40,639,115)
Adjustments	(8,606,825)	(43,533,315)
Denial write-offs	(193,130)	(1,342,714)
Bad debt W/Os	(466,293)	(2,781,275)
Ending A/R	$36,373,545	$36,373,545
Dollar change	$ (337,121)	$ 2,261,581
Percent change	-0.92%	6.63%

B: Key Indicators Analysis

Key Indicator	Current Month	Prior Month	Prior F/Y End	Goal	Benchmark
Gross days revenue—billed A/R	59.8	61.6	68.4	57.5	58.2
Net days revenue—net A/R	78.7	82.5	88.9	75.0	79.5
% billed A/R > 90 days	34.1%	36.7%	39.6%	30.0%	27.5%
Gross days in credit balances	0.9	1.1	1.3	1.0	1.2
Gross days in medical records	6.8	6.9	7.9	7.0	7.1

Key Indicator	Current Month	Year to Date	Prior F/Y End	Goal	Benchmark
Gross collection percent	43.6%	44.9%	45.5%	46.0%	N/A
Denials & bad debt % of revenue	4.2%	4.6%	4.3%	4.0%	3.5%

C: Aging of Accounts Receivable by Dollar Amount

	Unbilled	0–30	31–60	61–90	91–120	121–180	181–360	> 360	Credit Balances	Total
Current month	$ 4,668,016	$ 10,512,199	$ 8,807,626	$ 4,450,749	$ 2,031,278	$ 2,016,690	$ 3,385,447	$ 3,387,386	$ (2,869,846)	$ 36,373,545
Prior month	$ 5,437,963	$ 10,967,660	$ 7,854,939	$ 3,720,133	$ 2,009,780	$ 2,118,474	$ 4,143,898	$ 3,195,549	$ (2,737,730)	$ 36,710,666
Variance	$ (769,947)	$ (455,461)	$ 952,687	$ 730,616	$ 21,498	$ (101,784)	$ (758,451)	$ 175,837	$ (132,116)	$ (337,121)
Prior F/Y end	$ 4,234,423	$ 8,836,959	$ 8,197,536	$ 4,178,681	$ 2,340,199	$ 2,394,089	$ 4,100,414	$ 2,998,410	$ (3,168,747)	$ 34,111,964
Variance	$ 433,593	$ 1,675,240	$ 610,090	$ 272,068	$ (308,921)	$ (377,399)	$ (714,967)	$ 372,976	$ 298,901	$ 2,261,581

D: Aging of Accounts Receivable by Percentage

	Unbilled	0–30	31–60	61–90	91–120	121–180	181–360	> 360	Credit Balances	Total
Current month	12.83%	28.90%	24.21%	12.24%	5.58%	5.54%	9.31%	9.27%	-7.89%	100.00%
Prior month	14.81%	29.88%	21.40%	10.13%	5.47%	5.77%	11.29%	8.70%	-7.46%	100.00%
Variance	-1.98%	-0.98%	2.82%	2.10%	0.11%	-0.23%	-1.98%	0.56%	-0.43%	0.00%
Prior F/Y end	12.41%	25.91%	24.03%	12.25%	6.86%	7.02%	12.02%	8.79%	-9.29%	100.00%
Variance	0.42%	2.99%	0.18%	-0.01%	-1.28%	-1.47%	-2.71%	0.48%	1.40%	0.00%

Note: Information is for illustrative purposes only and does not reflect the actual performance or results of any specific hospital or healthcare provider.

Figure 14.1   Key indicators report card sample.

DESIGNING A BALANCED SCORECARD/REPORT CARD

Where Do I Start?

Most of the balanced scorecard/report card initiatives I have been involved with have been born out of a larger, organizationwide fiscal performance improvement effort. These are typically the result of deteriorating fiscal performance over the course of several months or even years. At this stage, the focus has usually digressed to the bottom-line financial results, with a heavy emphasis on one or two key functional areas or indicators (in healthcare, it is invariably the accounts receivable area).

The key first step to designing any report card is to raise your sights above the income statement bottom line and look at your business as a whole. What needs to be done here is to identify and define the core business functions, units, or processes that have a critical impact on the organization's overall operations and fiscal performance. Most organizations have a number of departments and functions that play a prominent role in their overall fiscal performance. It's important to note that we are not talking merely about issues like cost controls or staffing levels. Rather, we are concerned here with processes and functions that, when performed and managed effectively, play a critical role in driving positive financial results (and vice versa). These will vary from industry to industry, but they should be consistent from company to company within the same industry. I have yet to find an organization that is so unique within its industry that the core set of business functions and processes did not apply to them.

With respect to financial performance, there is a unique aspect in the healthcare industry as it relates to what is called the "revenue cycle". This term involves all of the departments and functions that impact the timely and accurate capture, processing, billing, and collecting of patient service revenues associated with providing medical care to patients. The revenue cycle is, in essence, the lifeblood of a healthcare provider organization in that it controls and impacts cash flow. For obvious reasons, many BSC initiatives are focused on the revenue cycle. With respect to the healthcare industry revenue cycle, the following core business functions and processes are typically identified and included in a BSC initiative:

- *Patient access.* Also known as *admissions* or *registration;* controls the capture and flow of patient information required for billing and reimbursement, including insurance coverage and related benefits.

- *Charge capture.* Departmental-level information flow related to services provided, focused on timely and accurate capture and flow of information.

- *Health information management.* Also known as *medical records;* controls the documentation, clinical coding, and flow of related information of medical services provided.

- *Reimbursement.* Controls the functions related to rates charged for services provided and the net reimbursements received from insurers.

- *Patient accounting.* Manages the functions associated with the processing and collecting of insurance invoices and patient statements for medical services provided. Controls the overall accounts receivable and ultimately responsible for cash flow.

Other industries, such as manufacturing and banking, would have their own core business processes and functions that would need to be identified and defined as part of a BSC initiative. The key aspects of this step are:

1. The identification of those areas of your business that play a critical role in your success (be it financial, operational, satisfaction, or whatever you are focusing on).

2. The inclusion and participation of the departmental and functional managers that control these key areas in the overall BSC design and implementation efforts.

Defining Success Metrics

Once you have identified the key business functions and processes to be included in the BSC, the next step is to define the critical success metrics that will be utilized to measure and track progress and results associated with each function and process. This can be a difficult and onerous task simply due to the fact that many of the people you get involved in the initiative won't be familiar with, or used to dealing with and managing to, the specific performance metrics that will be defined as part of the initiative. While most managers have a solid understanding what it is their department and staff do and are responsible for on a daily basis, they are so close to the activity that their focus becomes too micro in nature. Translating their daily activities and efforts into a set of success metrics will most likely prove to be a challenging, if not threatening, task. As a result, it is important to follow a number of tenets when going through the exercise of metric selection and definition:

1. Remember that the goal is to create a brief and concise report card of pertinent business performance information. As such, it is imperative to keep the number of success metrics to a manageable level, with no more than a few per function or process (on average). You need to fight the urge to continuously drill down to the micro level of a process or function. I have witnessed several occasions where a perfectly good metric became exploded into a more complex set of metrics in a matter of a few minutes' discussion. Too much information, or too many metrics, will not produce the desired end results and will become a burden to manage on an ongoing basis.

2. Metrics need to be directly pertinent to the overall objective(s) that created the need for the BSC initiative in the first place. In other words, remember that one of the goals of implementing any report card is behavior modification. When defining success metrics, you need to be sure that in establishing the metric you will be encouraging the actions and behaviors that will achieve the desired end results.

3. It is easier to edit than to create. In other words, where possible, utilize metrics that are already available and commonly used to track performance in your industry. Chances are that you will find sufficient benchmarking and key indicator information to support the vast majority of your BSC goals and efforts. Try to minimize the number of metrics that are totally unique to your initiatives. As a result, identifying, monitoring and supporting your success metrics will prove to be easier and more effective over time.

4. Success metrics between departments and functions need to be supplementary and complementary. You will find that the departments and functions included in your BSC initiative do not operate in a vacuum. They are most likely all interconnected and interdependent at some level. As a result, it is important that the established success metrics all support the overall objective(s), and that they do not contradict each other.

5. Success metrics need to be relevant to the particular department or function to which they are being applied. The management and staff within a department or function must be able to relate to, and understand, a performance measure in order for them to manage and work toward it. Many financial BSC initiatives are spearheaded by Finance, or the CFO. It is very easy for metrics to start to be defined in terms that the CFO and other finance department staff relate to on a daily basis. However, these may or may not be relevant or pertinent to the department or function staff. If they don't understand the metric, they most likely will not understand how, or even if, they impact it.

6. Success metrics should be defined in terms that continue to be relevant as the business evolves and grows over time. A metric defined today should be relevant a year from now, or five years from now. Mistakes are made in this area when metrics are defined in terms of the current business environment. As an example, defining a metric in terms of dollars of sales, as opposed to a percentage of sales or days of sales outstanding (DSO), will result in an obsolete measurement if the business either grows or contracts to any significant degree. As a result, the metrics will need to be continually reviewed and revised, creating too much effort to maintain a valid and reliable report card.

7. Success metrics should be relatively easy to calculate and understand. And, everyone involved should understand the calculation and rationale behind each metric. Remember, you do not want the outcome of your BSC initiative to include excessive time and effort required to calculate, validate, and produce the report card. In order to be effective, to promote desired actions, and attain desired results, this information needs to be created timely and consistently, and needs to be understood from the board room to the break room.

8. Not all success metrics will lend themselves to a numeric or statistical quantification. In those cases, some sort of metric still needs to be created to establish expectations and be able to effectively manage the process or function. These areas typically lend themselves to measurements related to time frames, frequency of occurrence, or other more qualitative parameters.

Determining Your Historical and Current-State Performance

Once you have defined your success metrics you need to begin creating the "anchor" for your report card by establishing your historical and current-state/baseline performance measurements for each metric defined. Depending on the availability of information sources, this can prove to be a frustrating exercise. Personally, I view a BSC effort as a go-forward initiative more focused on driving future results than on pining over past failures. With respect to historical trends, if you can go back to the prior fiscal year-end and trend forward on a monthly basis up to the current month-end then that should be sufficient. Don't waste time and effort creating custom reports through your information systems department to do this. If you have severe limitations on historical data, then concentrate on establishing your current-state baseline performance and developing your reporting needs going forward. It is likely that your ability to establish historical performance measures will vary by success metric. Again, don't waste time trying to have the same amount of historical trend information for each metric. It is much more productive to concentrate on establishing a consistent current-state baseline for your report card.

One of the more common and significant challenges in creating a reliable report card is defining and/or creating the information sources that will be utilized to establish your baseline performance measurements and calculate your metrics on an ongoing basis. Most organizations have various information systems and software applications that contain large amounts of information. These systems are not always in 100 percent synchronization, resulting in inconsistent information from various sources. Where possible, reports and information to be used for the BSC should be obtained from the same information system, preferably the primary system utilized by the organization to conduct and manage its business. Within healthcare, and the revenue cycle in particular, this would be the patient accounting system that is used to manage the billing and accounts receivable activity. Consistent and reliable information sources that are trusted within the organization are critical for a successful BSC initiative. As such, it is important to take the time necessary to review and analyze information sources to ensure that the information is accurate and consistent, and that it's use will result in a valid and reliable report card.

Accurate and credible information is particularly important at this stage of the development process since this is the first time actual performance measures will be calculated and shared. As a result, you should expect a certain level of challenge and push-back with respect to the accuracy of the information, particularly from those areas that are not performing well according to the metrics. Again, this is to be expected and most easily deflected by ensuring that the information sources are accurate. This also provides a good opportunity to reinforce that the focus of the initiative is to prospectively improve performance, and not to finger-point and assign blame for past deficiencies.

Finally, you may find it necessary to modify some of your metrics or the related calculations based on limitations of the information sources, or based on some unique aspect of your particular operating environment that was identified while establishing your current-state performance measurements. That's OK. As scientific as we'd like it to be, a BSC initiative is still part art form. It does not need to be exact, but it needs to be relevant and, more importantly, it needs to drive actions and behavior towards desired results.

Utilizing Comparative Industry Data and Benchmarks

Up until this point we have focused on the individual company's environment and performance. At this point it is necessary to look outside of your organization to obtain comparative performance information that relates to the success metrics you have developed and will be tracking. Utilizing comparative industry statistics and benchmarking information is important because it helps establish an appropriate perspective related to your organization's performance. In other words, you know how you are doing internally, but how are you doing compared to other similar organizations in your industry? This information also plays a critical role in helping to establish and modify your organization's targets and goals (see next section).

Most industries have a number of primary sources that produce well-established and respected comparative statistics and benchmarking information. For instance, within the healthcare industry, both the Healthcare Financial Management Association and the Medical Group Management Association are commonly relied upon for providing excellent information in the areas of healthcare finance, receivables management, and operations. It should be rather easy to identify the key sources for this type of information within your particular industry. A quick search on the Internet will produce a substantial list of Web sites that offer information, tools, and industry-specific links related to benchmarking. In researching, obtaining, and selecting comparative statistics and benchmarking information for use in your report, you should consider the following points and caveats:

• You should attempt to use comparative information from organizations whose niche or operating environment most closely resembles your own. This may prove difficult depending on how specialized you are in your field or industry. However, remembering that this is part science, part art form, it does not have to be exact. Get the best information you can and make sure everyone involved understands the pros and cons of the information source.

• Different surveys and information sources utilize various data, calculations, and definitions. Make sure you understand what is, and is not, included in the statistics and benchmarks you are considering. If you are going to be comparing your own performance against this data, be sure it's relevant.

• Make sure you understand the sample size, or survey response size that resulted in the information you are reviewing. A small or limited sample size can greatly impact the reliability and validity of the information.

• Be careful of the term "benchmark" in your process. I have found that most information available is what I would term "comparative information," meaning it reflects either an average performance or a range of performance across an industry. The term "benchmark" is usually interpreted to mean the "best in class" performers. If you want to emulate best practices, try to obtain information that is specific to the top performers in your industry.

• It is possible that comparable statistics or benchmark information will not be available for all of the success metrics you have defined. Again, that's OK. Here you will need to be creative in not only determining comparative performance levels, but also in establishing your internal goals and targets. My best advice here is to get on the phone with some of your industry colleagues to see if they are tracking the metrics you want to track. If they are, great, get the information. If not, maybe you can work with them to jointly begin to track and report on this performance information to create your own source of comparative information.

Developing Your Internal Goals and Targets

Now that you have defined your success metrics, established your current-state performance, and obtained comparative industry performance information, you are ready to develop your own internal goals and targets for each metric. This can be another challenging and frustrating stage for departmental and functional managers, especially if their current performance measures are significantly below the comparative or benchmark indicators.

This is also a critical part of the process since the goals you establish now, although not set in stone forever, will be the initial catalyst for modifying behavior and activities directed at operational changes to improve overall performance. Even if all of the work and actions taken up until this point in the process have been carefully and appropriately completed, the establishment of inappropriate or conflicting goals and targets can result in a loss of momentum and buy-in, which can in turn lead to suboptimal or undesirable results. With this in mind, when establishing your goals and targets you should consider and incorporate the following factors and caveats:

• The most basic tenet regarding goals is that they be reasonable and achievable in order to elicit actions necessary to attain the desired results. If goals and targets are set in a way that is perceived as unreasonable and without any consideration for the current environment and industry experience, then the departmental and functional management and staff will not be motivated to strive to reach those goals.

• The second basic tenet of goals and targets is that they need to have input and acceptance from the people who will be held accountable for their ultimate achievement. While the departmental and functional managers should be challenged to accept higher standards of performance, the ultimate approval of goals and targets rests with senior management. Goals and targets cannot be dictated in a unilateral top-down manner.

• It is easy to fall into the trap of establishing the top-percentile "best practice" performance measurements as your targets across all metrics, the argument being "if they can do it, so can we." It is also dangerous. Don't misunderstand me, I certainly support all efforts to strive for excellence. However, the reality is that within most organizations there are certain limitations that are a part of the current state that won't allow for "best practice"–level performance across all core business processes and functions. While these can be addressed over time, they impact an organization's ability to drive results in the near term. Further, you don't have to be "best practice" in order to produce good performance results. Again, goals and targets need to consider all factors, internal and external, and need to be based on sound business rationale. This is why I prefer comparative industry information that is provided in the form of performance "ranges," that is, percentile rankings. First, they offer an easy way to determine where your current-state performance ranks in the industry. Second, they allow you to establish goals and targets along a performance continuum.

• Depending on how your current-state performance indicators compare to the comparative industry statistics, you may want to consider establishing different goals to achieve varying levels of performance improvement:

  • *Intermediate or short-term goals.* Utilized in instances where the current-state performance is so significantly below the comparative industry standards that an intermediate target or goal is deemed necessary in order to provide motivation and incentive for short-term results and success. This may be required for some metrics but not for others.

  • *Standard or ultimate goals.* These are established for every metric and reflect the organization's expected and accepted level of performance. Attaining this level means you have met your goals and satisfied management's expectations.

  • *Stretch goals.* These are performance levels beyond the standard goals and reflect a "best practice" level of accomplishment that is still deemed reasonable and attainable with superior creativity, cooperation, planning, and execution. These are especially useful in situations where the stretch goals are tied to an employee recognition and/or reward plan.

• Although nothing about the report card is intended to be static, goals and targets, once set and made public, are very difficult to modify. Therefore, it is important that you take the time and effort necessary in order to evaluate all of the information available and establish realistic and attainable targets and goals that the entire management team can support and live by. With that said, don't be afraid to modify an established goal if there is a sound and logical business case to do so. It is better to take on the battle with senior management in order to have realistic goals than to try to live with one that is not achievable.

PRODUCING THE BALANCED SCORECARD

Once you have created the report format, defined your success metrics, identified and/or created your information sources, established historical and/or baseline performance levels, incorporated comparative industry standards, and established your set of targets and goals, you are ready to produce your "pilot" version of the report card. While this seems easy, it is harder than it sounds and it is also an important part of the process that should not be overlooked or minimized.

As with anything you do for the first time, there is a learning curve that requires more time and effort in the beginning stages that will diminish over time. In addition, in the production of the initial versions you will invariably encounter issues with either the source information, the metric calculations, or some other component that will force you to go "back to the drawing board" to revisit and resolve before going forward. Again, this is to be expected. The BSC should be viewed as a long-term initiative, so taking a little extra time to "get it right the first time" is time well spent. These initial draft versions of the report card provide the development team the opportunity to discuss the initial output/results, to begin to formulate preliminary corrective actions to address perceived weaknesses or deficient areas, and to start getting accustomed to the idea that they are now going to be held accountable for the information contained in the report card on a routine basis. At this stage you need to be sure that all of your success metrics, related calculations, assumptions, benchmarks, and goals/targets are sufficiently documented and footnoted to ensure consistent understanding and interpretation.

Automation versus Manual Efforts

Regarding the actual production of the BSC, it is common for organizations to want to fully automate the process through the development of a complex computer program to retrieve, analyze, calculate, and format all of the data required to complete the BSC. While this sounds logical on the surface, I have found it to be, more often than not, both an infeasible and undesirable approach. First of all, the information needed to populate the BSC is most likely going to come from many individual systems and sources. Second, there will be a significant amount of analysis and validation required in order to transform the raw data into meaningful information. The goal here should be to automate as much of the raw data and source reports as required for the BSC. In addition, this information should be integrated into a single application and format. Finally, standard formulas and calculations can be preprogrammed. However, the "human element" should not be totally removed from the production process. A certain level of manual efforts will be required in order to ensure the ongoing consistency and integrity of the source information and resulting performance metrics. It is important to maintain accountability and ownership of the routine "intellectual interrogation" of the BSC to ensure its consistency and integrity.

IMPLEMENTING A BALANCED SCORECARD/REPORT CARD

Once you have developed a report card, the next stage of the process is implementation. What we are talking about here is not the mere production and distribution of the report card. In order to attain the desired results and maximize the benefits, the report card needs to become an integral part of the organization's operating culture. It needs to be recognized as *the* center of senior management's attention and evaluation of the performance and level of success attained by the core departments and functions in driving towards the overall corporate financial and operational goals.

If you've reached this point in the process, then you have already accomplished a couple of key tasks needed for successful implementation. Specifically, in the development of the report card you have:

1. Identified the results you want to achieve through the use of a report card

2. Identified the core business functions and processes that have a critical impact on your ultimate financial and/or operational success

3. Engaged the management staff from multidisciplinary departments as the key participants in the process

4. Defined your success metrics, obtained comparative performance measures, and established your goals and targets

However, in order to implement the report card such that it has the desired impact, there are a few more key steps that need to be taken into consideration:

1. Assign the ownership of, and accountability for, the routine production of the report card to a key member of the management team. This is usually assigned to the manager from the department or functional area that is most "vested" in the overall project and ultimate results. For example, in the healthcare revenue cycle example, this is typically the manager of patient accounting or the director of patient financial services. This does not mean that this person has to actually create the entire document. Other staff should be responsible for calculating and providing their metrics information on a routine basis. However, somebody has to "own" the production process—it cannot be fragmented.

2. Utilize the management team you assembled for creating the report card to establish a standing committee or forum charged with routinely monitoring and addressing performance and progress issues related to the areas covered by the report card. In this way, the report card becomes "operationalized," or utilized and accepted by the team as a key management tool that helps them to focus their department's daily work efforts towards established goals and results.

3. Utilize the report card as intended—as a management tool. However, the focus of discussions and actions need to be centered around the processes, systems, and controls

that ultimately drive the metrics. In other words, the report card will help to identify the organization's symptoms (like a thermometer allows a physician to ascertain that you have a fever), but you need to delve into the actual daily operations in order to success-fully diagnose and address the root causes of the deficiencies. This is where the focus needs to be in order to modify behaviors and achieve results.

4. Ensure that the report card is shared both upward and downward in the organiza-tion. Once you have a sufficient comfort level with the information contained in the report card, it should be presented to the board of directors and should become a stan-dard component of the monthly reporting package provided to the board. In addition, the report card should also be explained to and shared with the rank-and-file staff in order to establish their buy-in and to help focus their efforts toward the common goals.

It has been my experience that the acceptance and "adoption" of a balanced scorecard is a process that happens much more quickly than one would expect. On the one hand, it is seen by members of the board as a positive, proactive measure that enhances senior man-agement's (let alone their own) ability to monitor performance and progress, and is aimed at improving the organization's overall performance and bottom line. In addition, the mere focus and attention created during the development process almost invariably has the effect of producing immediate, albeit not necessarily significant, improvements in a majority of the success metrics. As a result, the report card is quickly deemed a "successful project." Further, the middle management team sees value in that it ("finally") clarifies senior management's expectations, it connects their individual department or function to the overall operations and strategic direction of the company, and it provides a mechanism for focusing their work effort and priorities based on established goals and targets.

CRITICAL SUCCESS FACTORS FOR BALANCED SCORECARD INITIATIVES

Like any other type of project, balanced scorecard initiatives experience varying levels of success. Again, like other projects, BSC initiatives need to have core components and follow certain tenets in order to be successful, not only in the short term, but on an ongoing long-term basis. Based on my experiences with such efforts, I have outlined below what I consider to be some of the more critical success factors that must be considered and incorporated in a balanced scorecard development and implementation initiative:

• *Senior management–driven.* These initiatives have to be the product of a top-down focus and pressure from the senior level of management within the organization. Attempts to accomplish these objectives from a grassroots bottom-up approach will not be sustained long enough to attain any long-term, organizationwide operational improvement.

• *Senior management commitment and involvement.* Senior management needs to have a consistent and vested presence and involvement in the initiative, during devel-opment, through implementation, and going forward in order to ensure that the neces-sary time, attention, and resources are committed throughout all phases of the project.

• *Clear and rational objectives.* From the outset, the overall goals and objectives of the initiative need to be clearly defined and must be aligned with and support the organization's overall strategy. It is not enough to start a BSC project driven simply by poor financial results and the desire to "reverse the current trends." Clear and logical objectives provide the basis for all of the phases and efforts of the project to move forward in an efficient and effective manner.

• *Focus on behaviors and processes, not the numbers.* The BSC, like any report card, is just a reflection of the relative level of success being produced by the detailed work required to run a department or function. Therefore, successful BSC initiatives are those that are able to immediately focus efforts on analyzing and managing the core business functions and processes that drive the success metrics, as opposed to trying to "manage the numbers."

• *Long-term vision.* While the initial focus of a BSC project may be a rapid short-term improvement in operations and the financial bottom line, truly successful BSC initiatives are viewed and managed as having long-term impact on the organization's culture, daily operating environment, and financial well-being. A long-term view allows time for the operational and behavioral changes to be translated into measurable performance improvements. It also ensures that the BSC will continue to receive the support and attention necessary for sustained relevance and importance.

• *Merged into corporate culture.* Simply put, if one of the objectives of a BSC is to support the organization's overall strategy, then it must be incorporated into the overall culture in such a way that the management and staff understand how they impact the operating results and, more importantly, how meeting and/or exceeding goals and targets impacts them. The BSC, or the components contained in it, must become part of the routine dialogue and communication that transpires throughout the company. In addition, the BSC success metrics need to be somehow incorporated into the organization's performance appraisal and compensation programs in order to have maximum impact on creating motivation and modifying behaviors.

• *Flexible and adaptable.* While it is important to have a consistent and stable reporting tool that management and staff can rely on, the BSC can not be deemed to be so sacred that it can never be changed or revised once established and implemented. As time goes by, certain metrics will need to be revised, others may lose importance, and yet other new metrics will need to be added in order for the BSC to continue to provide the information and value needed to drive operations and organizational change. Remember, the focus is on improving operational and financial performance.

SUGGESTED READING

Kaplan, R. S., and D. Norton. *The Balanced Scorecard*. Boston: Harvard Business School Press, 1996.

15

Six Sigma

Michael D. Nichols and Richard D. Collins

THE LATEST HEADLINES!

"Six Sigma Saves Money!" "Six Sigma Makes Customers Happy!" "Six Sigma Increases Revenue!" How often have we heard these headlines? The business world is constantly assaulted with new methodology after new methodology that makes these promises. Over the years we have lived through SPC, TQM, ISO, Baldrige, process management, and business process reengineering. Each time the new program brings with it a promotion worthy of a presidential press corps. Each time we are told that this is the one true answer to help fix all our problems, no matter what they are!

So how is Six Sigma truly different? In the last few years Six Sigma has reached almost mythical proportions in some sectors of business. It is hard to find a management bookshelf at the local bookseller without at least a dozen books related to this topic. Not to mention the number of conferences and Web sites that have sprung up seemingly from nowhere. In this brief overview we hope to answer a few simple questions in a straightforward manner. Our objective is to give you an honest working knowledge of the "hows and whys" of this latest quality management trend. The complete details behind these answers are already the subject of many classes and texts. We will provide a reference list of recommended reading at the end of this chapter, if you wish to pursue a deeper understanding.

These are the questions that we hope to answer for you:

1. Why do Six Sigma?

2. What should Six Sigma do for me?

3. What is Six Sigma?

4. How does it work?

5. What are the key roles?

6. How do I deploy Six Sigma?

WHY DO SIX SIGMA?

This is the fundamental question you must answer before embarking on this journey. This question requires you to probe deeper into your organization than you might first assume. We have outlined a subset of questions you need to satisfy to arrive at this answer. By working with your leadership team to answer the following questions, you will arrive at the answer you need and simultaneously develop support for the effort the journey will require:

1. *How well are we meeting our customers' and shareholders' needs?* You need to understand how well your organization is currently performing in meeting your customers' and shareholders' needs. In order to define these needs there is, of course, another lower level set of questions:

   a. Do we understand what our most common defects are? Based on what data?

   b. How do we measure our performance against our customer's expectations?

   c. Have we defined our core processes and established key metrics?

   d. Are our improvement projects linked to these metrics?

   e. What are the most important aspects of our products or service to our customer? (That is, *F*ulfillment, *A*ccuracy, *C*ycle time, *T*reatment)

   f. How do our costs compare to best in class for our industry? This applies not only to the operational costs of your products and services, but also to the costs of your enabling processes such as billing and customer service.

2. *What is the potential of our current processes?* With the demand to constantly implement products and services to stay ahead or abreast of the competition you must understand how capable your processes are. Once you understand the capability of your processes you can predict how well they will perform as you add new products and services. You may also identify new opportunities for competitive offerings by looking at the potential of the process.

3. *How do we measure the results of the first two questions?* We all have been bombarded with information about scorecards and metric development. We often start with the single question, "how will you know if you have been successful when you implement the new XYZ system?" This generally leads to a robust discussion on what should be measured, leading to a discussion on current performance and process failures. It is usually quite enlightening for management to realize the gap between perceived and actual performance. Once again this begs a lower level set of questions:

    a. How do you know if you are tracking the vital few?

    b. How do you know they are linked to your strategy and your customers?

    c. How do you know if the results of changes to your organization will have an impact on those measures?

4. *How do you know that you have the right people working on the right things?* An old mentor often advised that work grows to fill any void whether or not it is the most valuable use of your time.

5. *What has been our ability to change and to implement change?* You need to understand your current culture's ability to accept and handle change. Six Sigma is all about change. Experience has shown us that the use of the statistical tools, the part that scares most people, is only about 10 to 20 percent of any project. The change management issues make up the remainder.

OK, OK, I know these are a lot of questions, and you want to see how the answer to these questions will tell you if you need Six Sigma. If you can honestly answer these questions with hard validated data then you probably don't need Six Sigma. But if you can't . . . then you might want to take advantage of a methodology that has proven it can drive results in both dollars and customers. It is not even a new tool, but a combination of quality and management techniques that have evolved over the last 72 years since Walter A. Shewhart first published his groundbreaking book on the economic control of quality in 1931. These techniques have been tightly packaged in a deployment strategy that drives success. But before we can cover how Six Sigma does this, we need to outline what your expectations for it should be.

WHAT SHOULD SIX SIGMA DO FOR ME?

As you pursue this path you will eventually have to decide how to learn and adopt Six Sigma into your organization. You will more than likely use a combination of outside consultants or vendors to do this, at least until you have built or acquired a sustainable knowledge base within your company. Even though the term Six Sigma itself is a registered trademark and service mark of Motorola, you will find many, many variations in the training offered, content provided, and deployment strategies. We will cover the answer to what Six Sigma is and how to deploy it in the next several sections. That will give you the most commonly accepted framework in use. Right now you need to understand what the program should do for you before you meet with any training group or service provider.

    Six Sigma is both a methodology and a management system. The methodology is the detailed and rigorous process for solving critical business problems using a structured data-driven approach. This is the detailed methodology on which you will train Blackbelts. We will discuss what this methodology is and what Blackbelts are in the next two sections. The management system is the structure used to deploy these highly skilled improvement experts. The management system is as important, if not more important, than the methodology itself. This is what drives you to answer the questions we asked in the first section.

If deployed properly, Six Sigma will create a structure to ensure that you have the right resources working on activities that will meet or exceed your customers' needs, reduce direct expense costs from your organization, and provide a framework for measuring and monitoring those efforts. This is also the answer to the question, "what should Six Sigma do for me?" If done correctly, Six Sigma will:

1. Create an infrastructure for managing improvement efforts and focus your resources on those efforts.

2. Ensure that those improvement efforts are aligned with your customer and shareholder needs.

3. Develop a measurement system to monitor the impact of your improvement efforts.

The one remaining issue you will need to follow up on is how you will manage the change you are introducing into the system. The following are examples of change-related issues we have seen or heard in less than thorough deployments:

• Lack of resource support for the project team

• Lack of support for gathering data for a project

• Failure or resistance to implement a recommended solution

When these occur you will have one very lonely Blackbelt. Someone whom you have spent precious money to train and will eventually leave to another company who is willing to pay a premium for that training.

WHAT IS SIX SIGMA?

Six Sigma is a continuous process improvement methodology that facilitates near-perfection in the processes of your organization. It considers not only the average performance but also the variability of what your business presents to the customer. This variation is often the cause of what is considered the "hidden factory," or the penalty for not getting it right the first time. It consists of rework costs to repair the item before delivery, scrap costs, concessions for late deliveries, and write-offs to retain offended customers, just to name a few.

Let us give you an example. You promised your customer that you could deliver 10,000 precisely machined dowels to be included in their manufacturing of generators in seven business days. On average, the whole shipment arrives on time but 2,500 pieces arrive in 10 business days. Now consider all the impacts: expedited delivery costs due to the shipment being late in the first place; reduced profit due to concessions for missing the contractual deadline; incremental rework costs for fixing any defective parts created in the "rush," (you would probably expedite these as well, which could delay current orders and set the entire defect cycle up again); loss of confidence in your organization, placing future orders from this client at risk; distraction of your leadership team away from value-added activities; potential loss of new customers that associate with the offended client, and so on. And this is only considering cycle time; moreover, can you imagine if we change the focus to the quality of the machined piece, where it becomes scrap if it is defective? As you can guess, this can set up a downward spiral that causes you to raise prices to stay profitable while producing a substandard product in the market. Hmmmm! Is this where you want to be? Let's see, losing market share and charging higher prices for the same defective product. We think you would agree that this is not an enviable position to operate from.

When your Six Sigma resources have improved the processes to the point that you have very little variation in your operation and it presents less than 3.4 defects to your customer in a million attempts, then you have achieved the elusive goal of Six Sigma.[1] In the machining example, this would equate to only three defects in every 100 shipments of 10,000 units. Conversely, let's explore the impacts of higher quality product that can command a higher price; unblemished reputation in the marketplace, which stimulates more business; unparalleled efficiency resulting in lower operating costs; maximum utilization of strategic resources on value-added activities; and so on. If you imagined both of these scenarios, we know your pulse rate is now on a much more even keel and the sweat on your forehead is evaporating!

Again, we must warn you that this does not happen overnight, and the Six Sigma management system must have all the elements in place before you will see these type of business transformation results. We will address these issues and more in the following section on how the methodology goes about achieving this level of performance and the key roles that must be played.

HOW DOES IT WORK?

As mentioned before, the methodology is a tight linkage of quality tools that facilitates making the best business decisions based on data-driven analysis. The Six Sigma resources use these tools much like an attorney uses logic and reasoning regarding the facts to build his or her case prior to presenting it in court. Each step feeds the next, and skipping one or more of the phases or tools will severely weaken the results and increase the risk of failure of the program.

The system is laid out in phases to ensure that nothing is overlooked and the defect is fixed permanently. The phases are define, measure, analyze, improve, and control. Let's look at each of these more closely:

1. *Define.* Just as the name implies, this where the defect, and moreover, the scope of the effort is determined. Most often, you should expect your Project Champions to partner with your Master Blackbelts (MBBs) to develop the parameters under which the Blackbelt will operate. They should work closely to define the defect, determine the customer and business impact, assign target dates, assign resources, and set goals for the

project, all of which is documented in a *project charter,* which becomes the "contract" with the Blackbelt. Moreover, they must ensure that this contract aligns with the business strategy to avoid any incongruence in the goals of the project and the business. Once this is complete, a Blackbelt can begin using the tools, such as the process map and cause-and-effect diagram, to uncover the mystery and get to the root cause of the defects.

Due to the importance of this phase, you want to be involved heavily in validating the benefit to the customer and the business, ensuring the strategic linkage to the company's vision, and visibly demonstrating that you sanction this project.[2] Without this, your change agents will not gain the traction that you expect and your Six Sigma program will miss the mark!

2. *Measure.* In this phase, the Six Sigma resource determines the baseline performance of the process, validates that the measurement system in place is accurate, verifies the *cost of poor quality* (COPQ)—the aforementioned cost of not doing it right the first time—and makes an assessment of *capability.* This is the sigma level of the process and is the measure of process performance against the customer's expectation.

In other words, how *capable* is my process in meeting my customers' needs. To give you a frame of reference, if a process is at a sigma level of six, it produces very few defects. Consequently, if you have a sigma level of zero, 50 percent of what you produce is a defect in the eyes of the consumer. This is the first checkpoint, or tollgate, where the determination to continue the effort is made. Some of the tools you should expect to be employed are the gage R & R, the cost–benefit analysis, and the capability analysis.

3. *Analyze.* This is the phase where the technical expert, the Blackbelt, "tortures" the data collected to uncover the root cause(s) of the defect. Once they have isolated the potential factors, they use statistical, or hypothesis, testing to prove conclusively that the factors are indeed causing or contributing to the problem. You should expect to see graphical analysis completed before any statistical testing is undertaken and question any analysis that does not have the statistical rigor backing it up. Expect all of these results to be documented in an *FMEA* alongside the current risk mitigation measures for each of those factors.

4. *Improve.* Now that the Blackbelt knows what is causing the problem, you should expect them to predict what the performance of the process would be if they fixed the issues they have uncovered. This is achieved through a *design of experiments,* and allows them to build an equation called the *transfer function.* This is crucial as it facilitates the evaluation of the multiple solution sets, which should be documented in a *solutions design matrix,* by allowing side-by-side comparisons of the proposed solutions and the performance of the competition. This is the final opportunity for you to halt the project prior to further investment and irreversible, at least without great cost, changes to the process.

5. *Control.* After implementation in the improve phase, the final phase is ensuring that the solution is integrated into the operational environment and that it indeed improved the process. Some tools you can expect to see employed are *control charts,*

dashboards or *balanced scorecards*, and *updated process capability*. You must demand statistical proof that post-implementation performance is better than it was and that it is in *statistical process control* (SPC). This ensures that if the process ever breaks again, the process owner knows when and how to react to the situation. Another element that is important for you to be involved in is the sanctioning of the "standardization" of the solution across other areas of the organization. In other words, if a solution is found in one center and your organization has three others, then you need to ensure that the others gain the benefit of the project as well.

This section outlined the DMAIC methodology at a high level and several of the critical tools required in each phase. This is by no means the sum total of all the tools used. Tools such as QFD or simulation are also found in many different training programs. A trained Blackbelt will be able to apply the right tool at the right time.

Again, we stress that the entire infrastructure has to be in place for this to produce the results you have read about in the headlines. If any one of the elements is lacking, the Blackbelts will fight the good fight but miss the mark on your expectations. So let's discuss the different roles and expectations for each of the players in the system.

WHAT ARE THE KEY ROLES?

Blackbelt

This is the resource that applies most of the Six Sigma tools and is the technical process expert on the project. They are often the project manager and facilitate the project team to solve the assigned problem. Blackbelt training is most commonly four weeks in length, although some variation exists. We have seen both three-week and five-week versions.

Master Blackbelt

This individual is responsible for training all roles in Six Sigma and providing ongoing support to the infrastructure of the program. That activity is comprised primarily of partnering with the project and deployment champion to develop and prioritize the business transformation plan, aligning those projects, along with the appropriate resources, and coaching Blackbelts on tools and techniques in those projects. They also help to identify the next generation of Six Sigma resources. Master Blackbelt training normally runs two to three weeks over and above the Blackbelt training. There is usually a period of time from 12 to 18 months between trainings to allow the Blackbelt to demonstrate their skills.

Greenbelt

Greenbelts often receive less training than Blackbelts and use their skills only in the activities of the current role. They have also been known to support Blackbelt projects as subject matter experts and the "keepers" of the control phase. This is where we see the greatest variation in training, from two days to four weeks. The difference will be based on your decision as to how many of the tools you want them to be able to apply in support of Blackbelts and how autonomous you want them to be.

Executive Sponsor

As the name implies, this key player is responsible for ensuring open dialogue between impacted parties, removing roadblocks, securing funding, providing resources, and rewarding the project team, if successful. This training normally runs from one-half to two days.

Deployment Champion

Often a high-ranking individual, this role is responsible for coordinating the efforts of the Six Sigma management system, ensuring the strategic linkages are made for the continuous process improvements, setting the operational vision, and preventing conflicts with other business transformation efforts presently underway. This training normally runs two to three days.

Project Champion

Often the process owner, this is often the weakest link in the Six Sigma infrastructure. These individuals are in the business units and are usually responding to the very issues that utilizing Six Sigma effectively would prevent. They are responsible for tollgate reviews, providing additional resources, approving solutions, and maintaining ownership once the project is complete. They also act as source for the next generation of Greenbelts, Blackbelts, and Master Blackbelts. This training normally runs one to two days.

Each deployment we've seen uses these roles in a slightly different way. Even within an organization we have seen these roles shift slightly between business units based on the capability of the different individuals. The key point is to define these roles on the front end for your organization. This will drive much of your training requirements and more importantly your deployment strategy.

HOW DO I DEPLOY SIX SIGMA?

As we stated earlier in this chapter, the key to success with Six Sigma is in the management system. While this sounds pretty simple, merging the demands of any new initiative with the existing demands of the workplace will cause friction. After all, do you have anyone working in your organization that has an excessive amount of free time on his or her schedule? If so, they are probably not the type of person you would want involved. While there are several strategies available, our recommendation is to cover as much ground as quickly as possible. This might mean engaging an entire business unit or even the entire company. What it does not mean is "let's send a few people to Blackbelt training and see how they do." Without creating the support infrastructure, they will fail.

Let's take the example where you are deploying Six Sigma within a specific business unit. Division XX is critical to your company's long-term strategy in the market. They have been a strong contributor to the bottom line, however competition is eroding that position based on price and quality. Your deployment must first begin at the top. Leadership commitment and enthusiasm must be visible. The initial leadership sessions must focus on identifying and prioritizing key processes to be attacked, setting goals, and aligning resources. Executive sponsors for each process must be identified and measurable goals included in their reward system. Executive training must be given, and all employee communications prepared. Critical thought must be given to which resources will be selected for the champion and Blackbelt roles. The company with the most successful implementation to date communicated that the people who filled these roles would become the future leaders of the company.

Next you engage the middle management and operational layers of the organization and then expand to fill the gaps in between. One strategy would be to select your first wave of deployment champions and Blackbelts. As these resources begin to close projects and achieve certification you begin to fill in the deployment gaps by adding project champions and Master Blackbelts. As the Master Blackbelts gain experience, you may want to create either lead MBBs and/or design MBBs. A lead MBB is an experienced MBB who works with the business leaders to help further refine and enhance their deployment strategy. At this point you are making a strong statement as to the emphasis your leadership team is placing on Six Sigma and the value of learning the tools of the trade. A design MBB is an MBB who is specially trained to lead design for Six Sigma (DFSS) projects. DFSS is a special variation of Six Sigma and we have added a brief section following the chapter summary to discuss it.

One critical hurdle you are going to face at the start, middle, and throughout your entire deployment will be successful project selection. Face the fact that there will be a certain amount of 'churning' necessary to identify strong high-value projects. As a leader you will need to reward those who were successful and those who took risks. The challenge will be differentiating those who took appropriate risks and selected difficult but significant projects from those who did not show results but should have succeeded. Project selection is a critical decision activity and requires detailed training on the part of those making the selection.

Depending on who your initial training provider is, you should expect your deployment champions to learn different portfolio development approaches. The deployment champion should lead project portfolio creation and project prioritization. As your MBBs and BBs gain experience in their respective process areas, they will provide valuable input on potential opportunities. Make no mistake about it, the define phase should be owned by the deployment champion with input from the MBB. The Blackbelts, or probably by now the Greenbelts, should be handed a tightly scoped project that includes the initial COPQ, customer impact, and the names of the team members he or she will be working with.

You will also face a number of human resources and certification issues in your deployment. Define your strategy to deal with these issues on the front end, knowing that change happens! Most HR issues will center on pay, recognition, and retention for the professional you have trained. You want to provide incentives for your best people to take part in this program and to retain them once they are trained and certified. The benefits of requiring your Blackbelts and Master Blackbelts to be certified are:

- They must demonstrate knowledge and experience with the tools they are to apply.

- Allows you to see who has the talent and capability to apply the Six Sigma methodology.

- Aligns with your incentive program.

- Maintains the rigor of the program.

The rigor is the crucial aspect. All too many times you have seen a previous quality program that was implemented and then immediately watered down. They taught people how to apply basic tools but never required them to apply them. All you had left was a structured method for gut-based decisions. The drawback of a certification program is often the extra effort required from the Blackbelt and Master Blackbelt. If you have someone who was able to close a half million dollars in projects but not completed their certification then you need to look closer at the program.

Another common source of friction in your deployment will be the role of the corporate quality department. You want your Blackbelts and Greenbelts to come out of the process area you are working on. This provides you with a high level of subject matter expertise and demonstrates that you are interested in using this as a path for leadership growth. This often leaves the former quality group on the sidelines. What should their role be? There are several critical activities that should occur in addition to the MBB/BB training. The following four activities are necessary to your deployment:

- Center of excellence. Depending on the technical level of the employees who are being trained on the DMAIC model, additional support may be needed. The center of excellence model allows you to provide a centralized resource for more technical statistical and experimental support.

- Consulting team. In the early deployment phases it is important to have a central group of consultants to assist business leaders and deployment champions with problem identification, portfolio development, and strategy deployment.

- Training staff. It is important to look at any outside consultants as a temporary fix until you can develop your own materials and people to fill their roles. Your corporate quality group can then assume the role of providing the training.

- Customer satisfaction, benchmarking, and measurement. This critical requirement of Six Sigma needs to be created unless you already have an existing function that supports it.

The extent to which you choose to do each of these activities will depend on the size, capability, and structure of your specific company. The same person can actually perform the first three activities. One deployment model we have seen goes as follows: Use an outside vendor to train Blackbelts in the operation. Once the internal Blackbelts are certified, create a 12- to 18-month assignment to the corporate group as an MBB-in-training. This person provides training and consulting while developing their own skills. They can also support the development of your own in-house course materials. At the end of their apprenticeship, they are returned to the operations as an MBB. While the benefits of this deployment strategy are obvious, there is one drawback. The further removed from the operation you are, the less able you will be to influence results. This is the weakness of all internal consulting groups. Trying to influence others without straight-line responsibility. It can be overcome if addressed through your change management plan up front.

The role of technology is the final road block to remove before your deployment can begin. Six Sigma is a very data-driven methodology. Implementing Six Sigma will cause significant demands for data collection and reporting. This will create friction between your existing technology plans and the new needs being created to support projects (low-level data needs), control plans (low- and mid-level measures) and scorecards (high-level measures). Plan on having a way to prioritize these data needs. It should be a balance between the more strategic or structural needs for your high-level scorecards for your management system and the low- to mid-level needs of the DMAIC methodology.

SUMMARY

So why should we do Six Sigma? It is obviously a detailed and thorough methodology with a highly effective management system; but is it worth the effort? The answer is yes! Unequivocally! Over and over again we have seen dramatic examples of process and customer satisfaction improvement when properly deployed. The five-phase DMAIC methodology uses tried and proven quality and statistical tools in a rigorous process. The methodology is data-driven. The methodology is linked to the customer and drives costs associated with poor quality out of the business. The methodology is embedded within an infrastructure that requires specific roles with specific goals to be successful. In summary, the methodology works.

DESIGN FOR SIX SIGMA

Design for Six Sigma (DFSS) is a variation of Six Sigma that is used for designing new products or services or redesigning an end-to-end process for existing products or services. For new processes, it is focused on building a process that delivers at a near defect-free rate from the start. For redesigning processes, it is used when you have reached entitlement with the existing process using the DMAIC model and the only way you are going to take it to the next level is through a total redesign. Unlike DMAIC, there is no one consistent model being used in the marketplace. This area of Six Sigma is most likely to be the next area of growth as quality practitioners look to incorporate many new and existing techniques such as lean manufacturing and theory of inventive problem solving (TRIZ).

ENDNOTES

1. This term is derived from the fact that six standard deviations (σ) can be added to the average process performance without creating a defect in the eyes of the customer. If you are interested in understanding more around the statistics behind the Six Sigma term, please see your Master Blackbelt.
2. For a list of questions that you can ask during these sessions or phases, again contact your Master Blackbelt. They can explain the why and the importance of the answers. For instance, in a cause-and-effect diagram, the Blackbelt should "question to the void" or ask the question "why" until the root cause is revealed. For more on this topic, please refer to Ford Motor Company's TOPS-8D methodology.

SUGGESTED READING

Chowdhury, S. *Design for Six Sigma*. Chicago: Dearborn Trade Publishing, 2002.

Harry, M., and R. Schroeder. *Six Sigma*. New York: Currency Doubleday, 2000.

Lawton, R. L. *Creating a Customer Centered Culture*. Milwaukee: ASQ Quality Press, 1993.

Pande, P. S., R. P. Neuman, and R. R. Cavanagh. *The Six Sigma Way*. New York: McGraw-Hill, 2000.

Pyzdek, T. *The Six-Sigma Handbook*. New York: McGraw-Hill, 2002.

For a summary of how the Malcolm Baldrige National Quality Program, Six Sigma, and ISO can be used together to ensure overall success in any organization, see: www.quality.nist.gov/Issue_Sheet_Options.htm .

16

How to Get Results: Setting Goals and Hitting Targets

Mary Thornley

This success story was first presented to the Quality Management Division of ASQ at the 2000 Quality Management Conference in Orlando, Florida. I was honored that such a group of quality professionals wanted to hear from me—a practitioner of quality, not a professional in the quality field—about my perspective on how quality can affect the bottom line. I serve as president of Trident Technical College, a two-year public college in Charleston, South Carolina. Over 11,000 credit students and over 30,000 continuing education registrants attend classes on our three Charleston-area campuses, making us the fifth largest college in South Carolina. We serve a diverse population using dwindling resources, so we must focus on quality of service and the bottom line. My experiences as president of Trident Technical College provide the context for this chapter on setting goals and hitting targets. This is a true story of executive leadership for improvement and change.

I was appointed president of Trident in 1991. Less than a year later, in August 1992, I made an announcement that would have a major impact on the way we did business. With one simple sentence, "Today I am alerting you that we will initiate Trident's quality management (TQM) approach this year," I committed the college to a quality journey that continues to this day. Armed with experiences I gained in my 15 years in various roles at the college, I realized that a transformation to participative or "quality" management would require top-level commitment. Given that commitment, I knew that the college would welcome the notion of participative management driven by quality principles. Additionally, the college faced the prospect of serving more students as our percentage of state funding declined, enhancing our need for quality management that affected the bottom line. Therefore, I had given our college a quality call to arms—it was now time to act.

In the fall of 1992, we began the implementation of Trident's quality management. As we worked to define our training program, we drew heavily on W. Edwards Deming's 14 points. As you are no doubt well aware, Deming outlined his core quality concepts through these 14 points. We adapted his 14 points to fit higher education, specifically Trident Technical College. Then we went one step further by examining everything we had adapted or created, and we simplified our program into five elements of total quality that any employee that works for the college can internalize (see Figure 16.1). The minute we had our training program, we began training using our "Introduction to Quality" course. In 1992, I taught this course to all employees (in groups of 25), and I continue to teach the seminar for all new employees. I want all of our employees to have a common foundation using our idea of what quality is all about.

Once we had provided every employee with a foundation in quality, we initiated process improvement teams (PITs). To date, we have had 13 PITs that have examined those aspects of college operations that our faculty and staff suggested most needed review. Today, almost nine years after we started our journey, we do have some substantial results to show for our efforts.

Each year, we administer a graduate follow-up survey, which is a customer satisfaction survey. It asks graduates to indicate whether they were pleased with a wide range of college operations. In the 1998 survey, the college asked graduates to evaluate sixteen processes or services. Overall, there was an average increase of 20 percent in satisfaction rates for these processes and services in 1998 over the same processes and services in the 1993 survey. A sampling of the results is in the Table 16.1. These are significant gains in satisfaction rates, but we realize that there is room for improvement.

The second significant result stems from a problem we had in the early '90s with unanswered phone calls during peak registration periods. For example, during one

- Focus on internal/external customer
- Product/service excellence
- Employee involvement
- Data-based decision making
- Continuous improvement

Figure 16.1 Trident's five elements of quality.

Table 16.1 Graduate follow-up survey results.

Process or Service	1993	1998	Increase
Academic advising	62%	81%	+19%
Bookstore	48%	69%	+21%
Financial aid services	51%	75%	+24%
Food services	43%	70%	+27%
Library facilities/services	65%	85%	+20%
Preadmissions advising and testing	55%	77%	+22%
Registration process	42%	66%	+24%

month, we documented some 3,000 calls for which students or potential students received an "all lines busy, please call again" message. Through changes resulting from the efforts of one of our PITs, these 3,000 calls were reduced to five during a recent period. That's not quite zero defects, but we are getting there.

I am especially proud of the third significant result. The 1993 graduate survey referenced earlier showed that 62 percent of graduates expressed satisfaction with the academic advising process. A PIT team assigned to study this area and make improvements answered the call. In addition to making significant improvements to the advising process for students, this group was recognized nationally as a finalist for the coveted RIT/USA Today Quality Cup Award. While Ohio State University won the award, we were proud to come in second place. The impact of the improvements this team made continues to resonate as more and more students report satisfaction with our advising process.

I provide this background on Trident Technical College and our successes only as a means of expressing appreciation for the many giants in the world of quality who contributed to our program. We did not purchase a training program or hire a consultant—we created our program ourselves. In order to develop our program, we studied and borrowed shamelessly from the likes of Crosby and Juran, but we found Deming most adaptable to higher education. And as I reviewed Deming's enormous accomplishments over the years, I was struck again by his idea that management had walked away from the job of managing, away from the ideals of quality, of constant improvement, of concern for customer and worker that alone can keep a company in business today. I looked at how he worked with post-WWII Japanese industry to revolutionize their processes and helped turn the Japanese economy into a powerhouse. Finally, I saw how, in the 1980s, American management finally heeded his call and shifted their focus from products to processes and from quantity to quality.

Fast-forward to the booming economy of the late 1990s, a time of unparalleled economic prosperity in the United States. Is it possible that the incredible economic boom has sent management back in time to the 1950s, where they can only focus on quantity, not quality? A quick trip from the factory floor to cyberspace may reasonably suggest to you that Deming's lessons and the quality movement are both gasping for breath. Try to access the British Deming Association's Web site and you'll find that as of April 2000 the Association no longer exists. Take a quick look at the declining number of applications for the Baldrige Award for another suggestion that the once-strong quality movement is in trouble.

Why the perceived decline? Academicians point to the movement's weak theoretical foundation and say that TQM is inflexible and autocratic. The guy in the office next door is more likely to say that it's just another passing management fad like MBO. No doubt, many quality initiatives failed or did not achieve the desired results. However, others have achieved remarkable results, begging the question, "Have the failures resulted more from flaws in the philosophy, or more from flawed application of the philosophy?" In my opinion, it's the latter.

In the 1995 book *The Death and Life of the American Quality Movement*,[1] Robert Cole and 14 other contributors remind us that the doomsayers have been predicting the death of the American quality movement almost from the outset. However, to paraphrase

Mark Twain, the rumors of the death of the quality movement have been greatly exaggerated. The contributors point out that quality is more important for an organization's competitive success than it has ever been. *The Death and Life of the American Quality Movement* shows us examples of TQM in action and provides lessons from companies with successful programs. The contributors provide us with seven key elements of a successful quality program:

1. Provide leadership from top management.

2. Focus intensively on meeting customer needs.

3. Emphasize the quality of business processes from both an internal and external (customer) perspective.

4. Decentralize decision making.

5. Replace barriers between departments with cross-functional management.

6. Combine continuous improvement with breakthrough strategies.

7. Create supportive reward systems.

Take a minute and compare these elements of success to the five elements of total quality that Trident decided to focus on when we implemented our program in 1992. I think it suggests that the foundation we laid in 1992 for our quality program prepared us for success.

In 1999, another on-target analysis of the current state of the quality movement made its way onto bookshelves when Lori Silverman released *Critical Shift: The Future of Quality in Organizational Performance*.[2] In the book, Silverman argues that the terminology associated with quality fell into disfavor largely because of negative associations and because of the perceived need for both "quick fixes" and "the latest" solutions. The reality, she maintains, is that many organizations are still using the same quality ideas; they are just calling them something different. She adds that while some quality departments have been disbanded, the more positive trend shows that organizations are integrating quality principles into all position descriptions and organizational activities, leading to a broader use of quality principles organizationwide. Finally, Silverman cites statistics showing that the quality movement is more "far-flung" than ever, with individual memberships in ASQ's international chapter rising from 1,100 in 1990 to more than 6,400 in 1998 and the number of countries represented increasing from 50 to more than 80 over the same period. Those numbers do not suggest the death of the quality movement.

Therefore, while the focus remains on quality initiatives that failed, organizations and departments that disbanded, and language that has become passé, interest in and adherence to quality principles continues to abound worldwide. What seems most evident is that if you step back and look at the big picture, the quality movement is alive and really quite well, though its emphases have matured and its language has evolved. I believe it will continue to evolve as organizations race to meet the changing needs of customers.

Clearly, some companies do adapt to change better than others, and this agility gives them a significant advantage over their competitors. I believe that organizations well versed in quality principles are indeed more agile, and this will serve them well in the face of five economic trends:

1. *Rising expectations.* Each generation seems to have higher expectations about the quality of goods and services they consume. For proof, just play a song on a record player for your MP3-savvy high-schooler.

2. *Increased globalization.* Globalized quality standards, such as ISO 9001, will thrive in the new global economy.

3. *Increased competition.* Aside from price and delivery time, two of the most important differentiators of products will be the quality of the product and the quality of support service.

4. *Burgeoning e-commerce.* With instantaneous pricing and quality comparisons of products and services available via the Web, will this not accentuate the increasing need for quality brought on by increasing globalization and competition?

5. *Increased technical ability.* As technology and our ability to use it for measurement and documentation improves, higher quality will be in demand because we can produce it, can measure it, and can afford it.

As I concluded my speech in February, I told the group that I came not to bury Deming, Juran, and others, but to praise these quality giants by suggesting that the quality movement is alive and well. The need for companies to apply quality principles will only increase in the years ahead, even if the names and terminology change. I took my speech title from the British proclamation issued on the death of a monarch: "The King is dead. Long live the King!" This proclamation reassures the public that the transition from ruler to ruler is instantaneous. Indeed, Deming is dead. Long live Deming!

ENDNOTES

1. R. E. Cole, *The Death and Life of the American Quality Movement* (New York: Oxford University Press, 1995).
2. L. L. Silverman, with A. Probst, *Critical Shift: The Future of Quality in Organizational Performance* (Milwaukee: ASQ Quality Press, 1999).

BIBLIOGRAPHY

Cole, R. E. *The Death and Life of the American Quality Movement.* New York: Oxford University Press, 1995.

Silverman, L. L., with A. Probst. *Critical Shift: The Future of Quality in Organizational Performance.* Milwaukee: ASQ Quality Press, 1999.

Part IV

Appendixes

Appendix A Audit-Related Certifications

Appendix B ASQ Quality Awards Listing 2002

Appendix A

Audit-Related Certifications

ASQ CERTIFIED QUALITY ENGINEER (CQE)

Body of Knowledge

Note: The body of knowledge for certification is affected by new technologies, policies, and the changing dynamics of manufacturing and service industries. Updated versions of the examination based on the current body of knowledge are used at each offering.

The following is an abbreviated outline of the topics that constitute the body of knowledge for quality engineering:

I. Management and Leadership in Quality Engineering (19 Questions)
   A. Professional Conduct and ASQ Code of Ethics
   B. Management Systems for Improving Quality
   C. Leadership Principles and Techniques
   D. Facilitation Principles and Techniques
   E. Training
   F. Cost of Quality
   G. Quality Philosophies and Approaches (e.g., Juran, Deming, Taguchi, Ishikawa)
      1. Benefits of quality
      2. History of quality
      3. Definitions of quality
   H. Customer Relations, Expectations, Needs, and Satisfaction
   I. Supplier Relations and Management Methodologies

II. Quality Systems Development, Implementation, and Verification
    (19 Questions)
    A. Elements of a Quality System
    B. Documentation Systems
    C. Domestic and International Standards and Specifications
    D. Quality Audits
        1. Types and purpose of quality audits
        2. Roles and responsibilities of individuals involved in the audit process
        3. Quality audit planning, preparation, and execution
        4. Audit reporting and follow-up

III. Planning, Controlling, and Assuring Product and Process Quality
     (33 Questions)
     A. Processes for Planning Product and Service Development
        1. Classification of quality characteristics
        2. Design inputs and design review
        3. Validation and qualification methods
        4. Interpretation of technical drawings and specifications
        5. Determining product and process control methods
     B. Material Control
        1. Material identification, status, and traceability
        2. Sample integrity
        3. Material segregation
        4. Material review board (MRB)
     C. Acceptance Sampling
        1. General concepts
        2. Definitions of AQL, LTPD, AOQ, AOQL
        3. ANSI/ASQC Z1.4, ANSI/ASQC Z1.9 Standards
        4. Acceptance sampling plans
     D. Measurement Systems
        1. Terms and definitions
        2. Destructive and nondestructive measurement and test methods
        3. Selection of measurement tools, gages, and instruments
        4. Measurement system analysis
        5. Metrology

IV. Reliability and Risk Management (11 Questions)
    A. Terms and Definitions
    B. Reliability Life Characteristic Concepts
    C. Design of Systems for Reliability

    D. Reliability and Maintainability
       1. Prediction
       2. Prevention
       3. Maintenance scheduling
    E. Reliability Failure Analysis and Reporting
    F. Reliability/Safety/Hazard Assessment Tools
       1. Failure mode and effects analysis (FMEA)
       2. Failure mode and effects criticality analysis (FMECA)
       3. Fault-tree analysis (FTA)

V. Problem Solving and Quality Improvement (25 Questions)
    A. Approaches
    B. Management and Planning Tools
    C. Quality Tools
    D. Corrective Action
    E. Preventive Action
    F. Overcoming Barriers to Quality Improvement

VI. Quantitative Methods (53 Questions)
    A. Concepts of Probability and Statistics
       1. Terms
       2. Drawing valid statistical conclusions
       3. Central limit theorem and sampling distribution of the mean
       4. Basic probability concepts
    B. Collecting and Summarizing Data
       1. Types of data
       2. Measurement scales
       3. Methods for collecting data
       4. Techniques for assuring data accuracy and integrity
       5. Descriptive statistics
       6. Graphical methods
    C. Properties and Applications of Probability Distributions
       1. Discrete distributions
       2. Continuous distributions
    D. Statistical Decision-Making
       1. Point and interval estimation
       2. Hypothesis testing (NOTE: Nonparametric tests will not be included.)
       3. Paired comparison tests
          Dcfine, determine applicability, and apply paired comparison
          parametric hypothesis tests, and interpret the results. (Analysis)

4. Goodness-of-fit tests

    Define, determine applicability, and apply Chi-square tests, and interpret the results. (Analysis)

5. Analysis of variance (ANOVA)

    Define, determine applicability, and apply analysis of variance, and interpret the results. (Analysis)

6. Contingency tables

    Define, determine applicability, and construct a contingency table, and use it to determine statistical significance. (Analysis)

E. Measuring and Modeling Relationships between Variables

1. Simple and multiple least-squares linear regression

2. Simple linear correlation

3. Basic time-series analysis

F. Designing Experiments

Note: Mixture designs, data transformations, nested designs, and response surface methods will not be included.

1. Terminology

2. Planning and organizing experiments

3. Design principles

4. Design and analysis of one-factor experiments

5. Design and analysis of full-factorial experiments

6. Design and analysis of two-level fractional factorial experiments

7. Taguchi robustness concepts

G. Statistical Process Control (SPC)

1. Objectives and benefits

2. Selection of variable

3. Rational subgrouping

4. Selection and application of control charts

5. Analysis of control charts

6. PRE-control

7. Short-run SPC

H. Analyzing Process Capability

1. Designing and conducting process capability studies

2. Calculating process performance versus specification

3. Process capability indices

4. Process performance indices

ASQ CERTIFIED QUALITY MANAGER (CQMgr)

Body of Knowledge

The following is an abbreviated outline of the topics that constitute the body of knowledge for quality management:

I. Leadership (30 questions)
    A. Organizational Leadership
        1. Organizational development
        2. Organizational culture
        3. ASQ Code of Ethics
        4. Techniques for facilitating or managing organizational change
        5. Organizational roadblocks
        6. Constraint management
        7. Negotiation techniques
        8. Motivation techniques
        9. Conflict resolution techniques
        10. Employee empowerment
    B. Team Processes
        1. Types of teams
        2. Team formation and evolution
        3. Team-building techniques
        4. Team facilitation techniques
        5. Team leadership techniques
        6. Team performance evaluation
        7. Team reward and recognition
II. Strategy Development and Deployment (30 questions)
    A. Environmental Analysis
        1. Legal and regulatory factors
        2. Market forces, industry trends, competitive analysis
        3. Stakeholder groups
        4. Technology trends and internal capabilities
        5. S.W.O.T. (strengths, weaknesses, opportunities, and threats) analysis
        6. Customer/employee surveys and feedback
        7. Internal capability analysis

    B. Strategic planning and assessment
- 1. Strategic planning techniques and models
- 2. Competitive comparisons and benchmarks
- 3. Formulating quality policies

    C. Deployment
- 1. Assure integration between strategic and other plans
- 2. Deploy strategic goals and objectives into operational plans and improvement projects
- 3. Resource allocation planning activities
- 4. Metrics and goals that drive organizational performance

III. Quality Management Tools (20 questions)

    A. Problem-solving tools
- 1. The seven quality control tools
- 2. The seven management and planning tools
- 3. Root cause analysis, plan–do–check–act (PDCA) and other, like models
- 4. Tools for innovation and creativity
- 5. Cost of quality

    B. Process management approaches
- 1. Process goals
- 2. Cycle time reduction
- 3. Process analysis and documentation
- 4. Theory of constraints
- 5. Theory of variation

    C. Measurement: Assessment and Metrics
- 1. Statistical analysis
- 2. Trend analysis
- 3. Process capability
- 4. Reliability and validity
- 5. Qualitative assessment
- 6. Analysis and use of survey results
- 7. Benchmarking: internal and external

IV. Customer-Focused Organizations (20 questions)

    A. Customer identification and segmentation
- 1. Internal customers
- 2. External customers

B. Customer relationship management and commitment
   1. Determining and assuring customer satisfaction
   2. Customer service principles
   3. Multiple-customer management
   4. Customer retention/loyalty
   5. Anticipate customer expectations, priorities, needs
   6. Deploy the voice of the customer through QFD

V. Supplier Performance (10 questions)
   A. Supplier selection strategies and criteria
   B. Techniques for communicating requirements to suppliers
   C. Techniques for assessment and feedback of supplier performance
   D. Supplier improvement strategies
   E. Supplier certification programs
   F. Partnerships and alliances with suppliers
   G. Logistics and supply chain management

VI. Management (30 questions)
   A. Principles of Management
      1. Principles of management
      2. Total quality management (TQM)
      3. Management styles
      4. Organizational structures
      5. Business systems and interdependence of functions
      6. Staffing
   B. Communications
      1. Communication techniques
      2. Information systems
      3. Knowledge management
   C. Projects
      1. Project justification and prioritization techniques
      2. Project planning and estimation
      3. Monitor and measure project activity
      4. Project documentation and related procedures
   D. The Quality System
      1. The quality function mission
      2. Quality plan deployment in the organization
      3. Review the effectiveness of the quality system

    E. Quality Models

        1. Malcolm Baldrige National Quality Award (MBNQA) Criteria for Performance Excellence

        2. ISO 9000

        3. Major industry and other international standards

VII. Training and Development (10 questions)

    A. Alignment with strategic planning and business needs

    B. Training needs analysis

    C. Training materials and curriculum development

    D. Methods of training delivery

    E. Techniques for evaluating training effectiveness

BODY OF KNOWLEDGE FOR THE CONSTRUCTED-RESPONSE PORTION OF THE CERTIFIED QUALITY MANAGER EXAM

Candidates will be presented with two open-ended questions selected from the following areas and will have 45 minutes in which to write responses to both situations presented. Candidates may split their time spent on the problems as they like. Their responses will be graded on their knowledge of quality management as it relates to the content areas listed below, and in the following skills and abilities: communication, critical thinking (including the ability to analyze and synthesize information) personnel management, and general management.

    A. Contribute to the Strategic Planning and Deployment Process

    Represent the quality system in the strategic planning process; facilitate and train leaders in planning strategies; assure that the voice of the customer is heard; provide structure and methodology for the strategic planning process

        1. Participate in formulating the organization's overall strategic plan.

        2. Develop quality strategies to help the organization achieve its strategic goals.

        3. Develop and maintain an organizational focus on the importance of performance excellence.

        4. Formulate quality-related policies and procedures that support the strategic plan.

        5. Collaborate with other departments on the development of methods for strategic plan deployment throughout the organization.

        6. Develop and implement performance improvement plans that support organization's goals, including developing short- and long-term plans and their impact on various stakeholders.

      7. Identify and obtain the resources necessary for implementing performance improvement plans within the context of organizational constraints.

      8. Collaborate on the development and delivery of training programs for improved performance.

B. Develop and Maintain a Customer Focus (Internal and External Customers)

      1. Use customer expectations as a basis for product and service design and delivery.

      2. Establish and use communication channels (listening posts, feedback mechanisms, etc.) with customers as a resource for quality system requirements.

      3. Evaluate customer feedback for continuous improvement opportunities.

      4. Involve customers in the design and implementation of product, service, and process improvements.

C. Manage the Quality Organization/Department

      1. Define the mission of the quality organization/department, including linking it to the larger organization's mission.

      2. Establish the goals and objectives of the quality organization/department.

      3. Manage the budget and resource requirements of the quality organization/department.

      4. Develop the quality staff, including selection, evaluation, and professional growth.

D. Assess Performance Information

      1. Develop and implement plans to evaluate the effectiveness of the quality system.

      2. Assess the effectiveness and efficiency of organizational performance.

      3. Design and implement feedback loops to provide performance information to the organization for continuous improvement.

      4. Use results of assessments to continuously improve systems and processes.

E. Develop Systems for Managing Supplier Performance

      1. Develop and implement an overall supplier management program, including supplier assessments and monitoring follow-up actions.

      2. Use supplier performance information to continuously improve effectiveness of the value chain, including audits, performance data, JIT, dock-to-stock, etc.

      3. Partner with suppliers, including information-sharing, involving suppliers in design, providing training, collaborating, etc.

ASQ CERTIFIED QUALITY AUDITOR (CQA)

Body of Knowledge

The following is an abbreviated outline of the topics that constitute the body of knowledge for quality auditing:

I. Ethics, Professional Conduct, & Liability Issues (5 questions)
   A. ASQ Code of Ethics
      1. Conflict of interest
      2. Confidentiality
   B. Professional Conduct and Responsibilities
      1. Auditor conduct
      2. Auditor responsibilities
      3. Discovery of illegal or unsafe conditions or activities
   C. Liability Issues
      1. Personal and corporate
      2. Audit record disclosure

II. Audit Preparation (32 questions)
   A. Audit Definition and Plan
      1. Identification of authority (internal and external)
      2. Determination of audit purpose
      3. Determination of audit type and scope
      4. Determination of resources required
      5. Team selection and identification of roles
      6. Requirements to audit against (e.g., standards, contracts, specifications, policy, quality award criteria)
   B. Audit Design
      1. Strategy (e.g., tracing, discovery)
      2. Data collection plan
      3. Sampling plan
      4. Logistics planning
   C. Document Review and Preparation
      1. Audit-related document review
      2. Auditee's performance history review
      3. Preparation of audit checklists, guidelines, log sheets
   D. Communication and Distribution of Audit Plan

III. Audit Performance (32 questions)
    A. Audit Management
        1. Audit team management
        2. Communication of audit status to auditee
        3. Audit plan changes (e.g., schedule, priorities)
    B. Opening Meeting
        1. Presentation and review of the audit plan
        2. Confirmation of audit logistics
        3. Discussion of auditee concerns
    C. Data Collection
        1. Document/record examination
        2. Interviews
        3. Physical examination
        4. Observation of work activities
    D. Audit Working Papers
        1. Documentation of audit trail (e.g., checklists, supporting evidence)
        2. Record of observations
    E. Audit Analysis
        1. Corroboration and objectivity of evidence
        2. Data patterns and trends (e.g., repeat observations, systemic problems)
        3. Classification of observations
        4. Classification of nonconformances
        5. Conclusions
    F. Exit Meeting
        1. Presentation of audit results
        2. Discussion of follow-up actions
        3. Expectations of auditees, auditors, client
IV. Audit Reporting (10 questions)
    A. Review and Finalize Audit Results
    B. Written Report Format and Content
        1. Audit details (e.g., purpose, team members)
        2. Compliance
        3. System effectiveness
        4. Conclusions to be reported
        5. Request for corrective actions

    C. Issue Written Report
        1. Obtain approvals
        2. Distribute report
    D. Audit Records Retention

V. Corrective Action Follow-Up and Closure (12 questions)
    A. Corrective Action Follow-up
        1. Criteria for acceptable corrective action plans (e.g., preventive, assigned responsibilities, time line)
        2. Acceptability of proposed corrective action
        3. Negotiation of corrective action plans
        4. Methods for verifying corrective action
        5. Follow-up audit schedule, as required
        6. Verification of corrective action completion
        7. Effectiveness of corrective action
        8. Strategies when corrective action is not implemented or is not effective
    B. Closure
        1. Criteria for closure
        2. Timeliness

VI. Audit Program Management (10 questions)
    A. Administration
        1. Audit program objectives
        2. Identification and justification of resource requirements
        3. Management's relationship to the audit function
        4. Credibility of audit function
        5. Linkage to business performance
        6. Linkage to continuous improvement
        7. Evaluation of audit program effectiveness
        8. Summary of audit program results for review
        9. Long-term audit planning
    B. Process
        1. Development and implementation of audit program procedures
        2. Development and implementation of audit program schedule
        3. Audit record-keeping requirements

    C. Audit Personnel
        1. Qualifications
        2. Selection
        3. Training
        4. Performance evaluation

VII. General Knowledge and Skills (49 questions)
    A. Auditing Basics
        1. Quality concepts, terms, and definitions
        2. Theories and practices in quality auditing
        3. Benefits and consequences of audits
        4. Roles and responsibilities of client, auditor, auditee
        5. Characteristics of system, process, and product audits
        6. Characteristics of internal and external audits
        7. Characteristics of 1st-, 2nd-, and 3rd-party audits
        8. Characteristics of qualitative and quantitative analysis

    B. Basic Skills
        1. Time management techniques
        2. Conflict resolution
        3. Effective communication techniques
        4. Presentation methods and techniques

    C. Tools and Techniques
        1. Checklists, guidelines, log sheets
        2. Sampling theory, procedures and applications
        3. Flowcharts and process mapping
        4. Pattern and trend analysis
        5. Root cause analysis
        6. Cause-and-effect diagrams
        7. Pareto charts
        8. Histograms
        9. Descriptive statistics
      10. Control chart interpretation
      11. Process capability (C_p, C_{pk}) interpretation

Appendix B

ASQ Quality Awards Listing 2002

compiled by Corinne N. Johnson

The annual Quality Awards Listing is *Quality Progress'* guide to automotive, government, international, national, regional, and state quality-related awards and awards programs.

Awards in the listing are organized by type (national or international, for example), the award's name and sponsor, criteria, contact information, and notes (interesting facts and additional information about the award).

The state quality awards can be found on our Web sites: www.asq.org and www.asqnet.org.

To be included in the list, awards have to meet specific criteria. They must be quality related, eligibility cannot be limited to members of a sponsoring organization, and they have to be based on past achievements. Awards in the form of grants and scholarships for future works are not included.

If you know of any quality-related awards you would like to have considered for inclusion in the 2003 listing, please contact Corinne N. Johnson, *Quality Progress* editorial assistant, at cjohnson@asq.org.

U.S. National Awards	Criteria	Contact Information	Notes
Acclaim Award: American Medical Group Association.	Recognizes quality improvement efforts led by physician-directed organizations that measurably improve health outcomes and the quality of life for patients.	Call Clese Erikson at 703-838-0033, x347; e-mail cerikson@amga.org .	Recipients must demonstrate a serious commitment to continuous improvement. Also sponsors the Models of Excellence in High Risk Patient Management Award. www.amga.org

continued

continued

U.S. National Awards	Criteria	Contact Information	Notes
Akao Prize: Administered by the Quality Function Deployment (QFD) Institute.	Follows the processes used for the Deming Prize. Awarded to individuals for expertise in practice and dissemination of the QFD method.	Call Glenn Mazur at 734-995-0847; e-mail qfdi@qfdi.org .	Named for Yoji Akao, the codeveloper of the QFD method. www.qfdi.org/akao prize.htm
Malcolm Baldrige National Quality Award: National Institute of Standards and Technology (NIST) in a partnership with ASQ.	Award criteria are built on seven core values: leadership, strategic planning, customer and market focus, information analysis, human resource focus, process management, and business results.	Call NIST at 301-975-2036; e-mail nqp@nist.gov .	Three awards may be given in each category every year. Categories include small business, manufacturing, service, education and healthcare. www.quality.nist.gov
Brumbaugh Medal: ASQ.	Presented for the paper published in an ASQ journal that made the largest contribution to the development of the industrial application of quality control.	Call Geoff Vining at 540-231-5657.	No nomination form for this award. The award committee decides independently which paper should receive the award. www.asq.org/join/about/awards
Philip B. Crosby Medal: ASQ.		Currently being developed.	To first be awarded at AQC in 2003.
Deming Medal: ASQ.	Awarded to the leader who combined statistical thinking and management to achieve outstanding quality in product or services.	Call Joyce Orsini at 212-636-6219; e-mail jorsini@mary. fordham.edu .	www.asq.org/join/about/awards
Deming Prize: The Union of Japanese Scientists and Engineers (JUSE).	Awarded to individuals or teams that have contributed significantly to the development and dissemination of total quality control. The prize has three categories: Application Prize, Prize for Individuals, and Quality Control Award for Operations Business Units.	Call the International Relations Section of JUSE at 81-3-5378-9812 (Japan) or e-mail juse@juse.or.jp .	Award was established in 1951 to commemorate Deming's distinguished service. www.juse.or.jp
Design News Engineering Achievement Awards: *Design News.*	Presented to individuals, teams, and organizations whose work greatly improved function, lowered costs, increased reliability, or offered other benefits to the customer.	Call Dena Colucci at 617-558-4660.	Awards include Excellence in Design, the Engineering Quality Award, and the Global Innovation Award.

continued

U.S. National Awards	Criteria	Contact Information	Notes
Distinguished Service Medal: ASQ.	Recognizes the lifetime contribution of a person as a long-term enabler, catalyst, or prime mover in the quality movement. Granted only to those who have driven progress by promulgation of quality principles, methods, or science for the good of society.	Petitions should be submitted to the chairman of the board (c/o Catherine Valentine, executive assistant) for deliberation by the board of directors. Call her at 414-272-8575 or read Policy G-60 on www.asqnet.org .	This gold medal is the highest distinction that can be accorded by ASQ. www.asq.org/join/about/awards
Edwards Medal: ASQ.	Presented to the person who has demonstrated the most outstanding leadership in the application of modern quality control methods. Candidates are evaluated in technical competence, management creativity, and development.	Call Mary Rowzee at 248-512-0598; e-mail mr69@daimlerchrysler.com .	Candidates are also evaluated on innovation in product or service quality control, outstanding leadership, publications, association management, and contributions to society. www.asq.org/join/about/awards
Armand V. Feigenbaum Medal: ASQ.	Recognizes the achievement of professionals under the age of 36 who have displayed outstanding characteristics of leadership, professionalism, and potential in the quality field.	Call Pedro Saraiva at 351-239-798700 (Portugal); e-mail eq1pas@eq.uc.pt .	Accepts only electronic applications. www.asq.org/join/about/awards
Freund-Marquardt Medal: ASQ.	Awarded to nominees who have applied quality principles to the development, implementation, and literature of management standards.	Call Craig Johnson at 850-656-9683; e-mail cjohnson@lsi.fsu.edu .	www.asq.org/join/about/awards
Golden Torch Awards: National Society of Black Engineers.	Recognizes excellence among African-American engineers, scientists, and technologists, as well as organizations that have demonstrated a commitment to the recruitment, retention, and promotion of minorities.	Call Ayoka Blandford at 703-549-2207, x351; e-mail ablandford@nsbe.org .	Categories include engineer of the year, woman in technology, lifetime achievement in industry, and diversity leadership in industry. www.nsbe.org
E. L. Grant Medal: ASQ.	Presented to an individual who has demonstrated exceptional leadership regarding the development and implementation of educational programs in quality control.	Call David McClaskey at 423-229-2684; e-mail Davidqm@preferred.com .	

continued

U.S. National Awards	Criteria	Contact Information	Notes
Hispanic Engineer National Achievement Awards: Hispanic Engineer Achievement Awards Conference.	Seeks, identifies, honors, and documents Hispanic excellence in science and technology nationwide.	Call the Hispanic Engineer National Achievement Awards Conference at 323-262-0997 or 323-262-5545; e-mail adm9@mellcom.com .	Categories include engineer of the year, executive excellence, and outstanding technical achievement. www.henaac.org
Ishikawa Medal: ASQ.	Presented to the individual or team whose work has had a major impact on the human environment in the workplace and the quality of goods or services delivered to customers.	Call Paula Sommer at 817-461-5341; e-mail TexasPaula@aol.com .	www.asq.org/join/about/awards
Juran Medal: ASQ.	Recognizes organizational leaders who exhibit distinguished performance, maintain a sustained role, personally practice key quality principles, and demonstrate breakthrough management.	Call James Buckman at 612-626-7113; e-mail jbuckman@csom.umn.edu .	Medal commemorates J. M. Juran's 75-year career in quality.
E. Jack Lancaster Medal: ASQ.	Awarded to an individual who has demonstrated exceptional leadership and contributions when promoting quality on an international front.	Call Jad Jadunath at 303-757-0187; e-mail jad93908@sprynet.com .	Nominees must be quality professionals with an international reputation. www.asq.org/join/about/awards
National Association of Home Builders Research Center Quality Awards: National Association of Home Builders (NAHB) Research Center and Professional Builder magazine.	Open to all U.S. home builders; recognizes the role that customer-focused quality plays in construction, business management, sales, design, and warranty service.	Call Ed Caldeira at 800-638-8556, x6310; e-mail ecaldeira@nahbrc.org .	Two awards: the National Housing Quality Award and the National Remodeling Quality Award. www.nahbrc.org/awards
Nova Awards: The Construction Innovation Forum.	Honors innovations that improve construction quality and lower costs.	Call Brenda Romano at 248-409-1500; e-mail info@cif.org .	Nominations represent proven cost savings and quality improvement on actual projects.
Shewhart Medal: ASQ.	Based on a career of achievements, honors technical leadership in the field of modern quality control with emphasis on the development of theory, principles, and techniques.	Call Steve Bailey at 302-774-2375; e-mail steven.p.bailey@usa.dupont.com .	Named for the "father of statistical quality control" and ASQ's first Honorary Member, Walter Shewhart. www.asq.org/join/about/awards

continued

U.S. National Awards	Criteria	Contact Information	Notes
Shingo Prize for Excellence in Manufacturing: Utah State University, College of Business.	Established in 1988 to promote an awareness of lean manufacturing concepts and to recognize companies that achieve world-class manufacturing status.	Contact the Shingo Prize for Excellence in Manufacturing at 435-797-2279; fax 435-797-3440.	Applications are open to manufacturers in the United States, Mexico, and Canada and to researchers throughout the world. www.shingoprize.org
Simon Collier Quality Award: Los Angeles Section of ASQ.	To honor, encourage, and specifically identify outstanding individual or group leadership, accomplishment, and ingenuity in organizing, promoting, operating, or improving quality systems and programs in industry, government, education, business, healthcare, or service organizations, that fit the professional objectives of ASQ.	Call Imre A. Fischer at 562-491-9244; e-mail ImreFischer@aol.com .	Collier was a founding member of ASQ, the first Edward Medalist and the fourth Honorary Member of ASQ.
SME International Honor Awards: Society of Manufacturing Engineers (SME).	Recognizes accomplishments in advancing the concepts of orderly production, education related to manufacturing, research leading to improved productivity, and successful integration of infrastructure and manufacturing process.	Call Jean Mattivi at 313-271-1500, x1701; e-mail mattjea@sme.org .	Awards include the Eli Whitney Productivity Award, the SME Frederick W. Taylor Research Medal, and the Donald C. Burnham Manufacturing Management Award. www.sme.org
Society of Plastics Engineers Award Program: Society of Plastics Engineers.	Recognizes individuals who are making out-standing contributions to the plastics field.	Call Jim Toner at 203-740-5437; e-mail jptoner@4spe.org .	Includes categories such as engineering and technology, design, research, education, and business management. www.4spe.org/myspe/ awards/speawards.htm
Automotive Awards	**Criteria**	**Contact Information**	**Notes**
DaimlerChrysler Supplier Awards: DaimlerChrysler.	Uses a balanced scorecard concept to judge suppliers for the Commodity Award.	Interested suppliers should contact their DaimlerChrysler purchasing agent.	Program includes Gold Awards given to supplier sites that exceed DaimlerChrysler expectations.
Ford Motor Co. World Excellence Awards: Ford Motor Co.	Based on their performance regarding quality, delivery, and cost, Ford suppliers are honored with platinum, gold, and silver awards.	Call Brian Dunlavy at 313-390-5411.	Program also includes the Recognition of Achievement Award, honoring suppliers whose work supports Ford's consumer-driven strategy.

continued

Automotive Awards	Criteria	Contact Information	Notes
General Motors Supplier of the Year Award: General Motors.	Recognizes GM supplier companies worldwide that exceed specific performance standards in the areas of quality, service, and price.	Interested suppliers should contact their worldwide purchasing buyer for more information.	Selected by a team of quality, engineering, manufacturing, and purchasing experts from GM operations around the world.
JD Power and Associates Award Program: JD Power and Associates.	Awards presented to manufacturers in a variety of industries. The program is best known for its customer satisfaction awards in the automotive industry.	Call Michael Greywitt at 818-707-9526; e-mail michael.greywitt@jdpa.com .	Categories include everything from the assembly plant and best full-sized pickup in initial quality to highest quality original equipment seat supplier and highest quality AM/FM/cassette supplier. www.jdpa.com
Total Quality Awards: Strategic Vision.	Based on car buyers' satisfaction with buying, owning, and driving a vehicle.	Call Daniel Gorrell at 714-544-3466; e-mail danielgorrell@aol.com .	More than 15 categories such as compact car, luxury car, and medium sports utility vehicle. www.vision-inc.com

Government Awards	Criteria	Contact Information	Notes
Innovations in American Government Awards: Council for Excellence in Government and Institute for Government Innovation at Harvard University, John F. Kennedy School of Government.	Given annually to programs that serve as examples of creative and efficient government at its best.	Call Kelly Diffily at 202-530-3251 or Institute for Government Innovation at 800-722-0074.	Premier public service award in the nation. Award first presented in 1986. www.excelgov.org/ innovations or www.innovations. harvard.edu
George M. Low Trophy: NASA's Quality and Excellence Award.	Follows criteria similar to the Baldrige criteria.	E-mail Bill.Loewy@ hq.nasa.gov .	Award is in memory of George M. Low. www.hq.nasa.gov/ office/codeq/gml/ gmltroph.htm.
President's Quality Award Program: Office of Merit Systems Oversight and Effectiveness, U.S. Office of Personnel Management.	Recognizes organizations within the federal government for exemplary performance in support of the initiatives identified in the president's management agenda.	Call Glenda Haendschke at 202-606-1875; e-mail quality@opm.gov .	www.opm.gov/pqa
Public Service Excellence Awards: Public Employees Roundtable.	Recognizes groups involving two or more public employees.	Call Arneice Berry at 202-927-4923; email psea@ theroundtable.org .	Reward programs that reduce costs in government projects or services, that improve the quality of community life, or increase productivity. www.theroundtable.org/ psea.html

continued

International Awards	Criteria	Contact Information	Notes
Argentina National Quality Award Private Sector: Foundation for the National Quality Award.	There are three categories: large, medium, and small business, and two enterprises in each category are granted awards.	For information e-mail fpnc@mail.mya.com.ar .	www.premiocalidad. com.ar
Argentina National Quality Award Public Sector: Secretary of the State of Modernization.		For information e-mail pcalidad@sfp.gov.ar .	
International Asia Pacific Quality Award: Asia Pacific Quality Organization and the Walter L. Hurd Foundation.	Uses the Baldrige criteria. Candidates for the award must already have won their national quality award.	Call Jose Gonzalez Prado at 5-259-1099; e-mail imecca@ prodigy.net.mx .	Also sponsors the Walter L. Hurd Quality Executive Award and the Harrington-Ishikawa Quality Professional Award, both last awarded in 1999. www.qil.com/apqo/ iapqw.html
Australian Business Excellence Awards: Business Excellence Australia, a division of Standards Australia International.	Offers two recognition levels: the award level and the business improvement level.	Call Mary Anne Bakker at 61-2-82066568; e-mail awards@ businessexcellence australia.com.au .	Offering award- and category-level recognition in 2002–2003. www.business excellenceaustralia. com.au
The Gold Award for Quality: Joint Accreditation Scheme of Australia and New Zealand (JASANZ).	Award criteria focus on eight critical quality management elements outlined in ISO 9004:2000.	In Australia call 61-2-6282-5840. In New Zealand call 64-4-474-3348. E-mail admin@jas-anz.com.au	Established by the Australian Organization for Quality to recognize and encourage organizations in the pursuit of excellence and sound companywide quality management. Runners-up receive the Silver Award. www.jas-anz.com.au
Austrian Quality Award: Austrian Association for Quality (ÖVQ).	Based on the European Foundation for Quality Management (EFQM) excellence model.	Call the ÖVQ at 43-1-533-30-52; e-mail office@afqm.at .	www.oevq.at
Belgian Quality Award: Belgian Association for Total Quality Management and Mouvement Wallon de Qualité.	Based on the EFQM model and awarded twice a year.	Call Willy Vandenbrande at 32-0-50-37-06-68; e-mail willy.vandenbrande@ skynet.br .	A Quality Manager of the Year award is also offered. Cosponsored by Vlaams Centrum voor Kwaliteitszorg (VCK).
National Quality Award of Brazil: Foundation for the National Quality Award.	Recognizes the best management practices for performance excellence throughout Brazil.	E-mail Antonio Tadeu Pagliuso at fpnq@fpnq.org.br .	Applicants must meet Brazil Award Excellence criteria. www.fpnq.org.br

continued

International Awards	Criteria	Contact Information	Notes
Regional Quality Award Brazil: Sponsored by Associação Qualidade RS/PGQP.	Rewards Brazilian organizations who meet Programa Gaucho da Qualidade e Productividade assessment system criteria.	Call Luis Ildebrando Pierry at 55-51-3221-2663; e-mail pierry@ qualidade-rs.org.br .	
State of Rio de Janeiro Top Empresarial Quality Management Prize and Prêmio Qualidade Rio: State of Rio de Janeiro through the General Office of State Energy, the Naval Industry, and Petroleum of the State of Rio.	Both prizes follow the criteria of the Brazilian National Prize of Quality (similar to Baldrige criteria).	Contact Stella Regina Ruisde Costa through www.seinpe.rj.gov.br and www.premiotop.com.br .	Top Empresarial Prize is for small business. Each award has a bronze, silver, and gold category.
Canada Awards for Excellence: Administered by the National Quality Institute.	Recognizes Canadian organizations through two awards, the Quality Award and the Healthy Workplace Award. Quality Award candidates must demonstrate exceptional achievement in seven areas including leadership and process optimization.	Call Canada Awards for Excellence adjudicator at 800-263-9648 or 416-251-7600, x242.	The Healthy Workplace Award honors organizations that make employee well-being a strategic part of doing business. www.nqi.com
Bob Cardno Award: ASQ Toronto Section 0402.	Available to graduates of the quality certificate program of ASQ and offered at eligible institutions in the greater Toronto area.	Call R. O'Connor at 905-822-9981; e-mail ronoco.quintech@ sympatico.ca .	
Education Institution Awards: ASQ Toronto Section 0402.	Open to students who have successfully completed three of the component courses of the ASQ Toronto Section quality certificate program.	Call R. O'Connor at 905-822-9981; e-mail ronoco.quintech@ sympatico.ca .	
London Chamber of Commerce Business Achievement Awards: London, Ontario, Canada, Chamber of Commerce.	Honors area businesses using criteria focusing on business achievements; management/ employee relations; product, service, and technology innovation; training; contribution to employment; and commitment to community.	Call the London Chamber of Commerce at 519-432-7551, x29; e-mail Cheryl Chambers at cheryl@ londonchamber.com .	Categories include environment, innovation, and business incubator. www.chamber. london.on.ca

continued

International Awards	Criteria	Contact Information	Notes
Czech Republic National Quality Award: Czech Quality Award Association.	Has two categories: companies with up to 250 employees and companies with over 250 employees. Also awards the Czech Republic National Quality Prize.	Call Czech Quality Award Association at 420-2-661-0981; fax 420-2-684-8244.	www.czechmade.cz
Danish Quality Prize: Danske Kvalitets Pris (Danish Quality Prize Committee).	Based on the EFQM model.	Call the Danish Quality Prize Committee at 4586-720022; fax 4586-720066.	www.kvalitetspris.dk
Dubai International Award for Best Practices: Dubai Quality Group.	Best practices should demonstrate a positive and tangible impact on improving the quality of the living environment of people.	Call the Dubai Quality Group at 971-4-343-1950; e-mail dqg@dqg.org .	Groups are judged on their ability to bring about change in one of the various areas listed on the Web site. www.dqg.org
The European Quality Awards: The European Foundation for Quality Management (EFQM).	Presented to European organizations that demonstrate excellence in managing quality as a fundamental process for continuous improvement.	Call 32-2-775-35-11 or e-mail heyndrickx@efqm.org or info@efqm.org .	Special awards are given to companies that demonstrate exceptional use of the EFQM Excellence model. www.efqm.org
Finnish Quality Award: Finnish Society for Quality (Center for Excellence Finland).	Based on the EFQM criteria.	E-mail Helena Räihälä at helena.raihala@laatukeskus.fi .	
French Quality Award: French Quality Movement (MFQ).	Award criteria are based on the MFQ model, not the EFQM model.	Call the MFQ at 00-33-1-46-11-02-40 or fax 00-33-1-46-11-02-50.	www.mfq.asso.fr
German National Quality Award: Administered jointly by Deutsche Gesellschaft für Qualität (German Society for Quality) and Verein Deutscher Ingenieure (Association of German Engineers).	Based on the EFQM criteria.	Call the German Society for Quality at 069-954-24-0; fax 069-954-24-133. Call the Association of German Engineers at 49-0-211-6214-0; fax 49-0-211-6214-575.	The German National Quality Award aims to promote business excellence. www.dgq.de or www.vdi.de
Hellenic National Quality Award Greece: Ministry of Development.	Similar to Baldrige and EFQM criteria.	Call the Ministry of Development at 301-720-4600; fax 301-720-4500.	
Hong Kong Award for Industry: Quality Trade and Industry Department.	Open to companies based and operating in Hong Kong with products wholly or partly manufactured in Hong Kong in the 12 months prior to the closing date for entry.	Call Ephrem Shea at 2398-5146; e-mail ephremshea@tid.gov.hk .	www.hkpc.org/hkai

continued

International Awards	Criteria	Contact Information	Notes
Hungarian Quality Development Center Award.	Based on the EFQM criteria.	Call European Organization for Quality at 32-2-501-07-35 or fax 32-2-501-07-36.	www.eoq.org
Rajiv Gandhi National Quality Awards: Bureau of Indian Standards.	Honors Indian manu-facturing and service organizations and individuals considered leaders in India's quality movement.	E-mail bismd@vsnl.net or bis@vsnl.com .	Designed in line with the Baldrige Award, Deming Prize, and European Quality Award. www.bis.org.in/rgnqa.htm
Northern Ireland Quality Awards: Northern Ireland Center for Competitiveness.	Uses the EFQM model for its criteria.	Call 028-9046-8362 or e-mail george.wilson@cforc.org .	Premier business prize in Northern Ireland recognizing role model organizations in different sectors. www.cforc.org
The Q-Mark Irish National Quality Award and Irish Business Excellence Award: Excellence–Ireland.	The Q-Mark focuses on continuous improvement and customer satisfaction. The Irish Business Excellence Award is based on a nine-element model, similar to the Baldrige Award.	E-mail Tony Clarke about the Q-Mark Irish National Quality Award at t.clarke@excellence-ireland.ie . E-mail Derek Moffatt about the Irish Business Excellence Award at d.moffatt@excellence-ireland.ie .	The Q-Mark was started in 1982 and is seen as a symbol synonymous with Irish quality. www.excellence-ireland.ie
Israel Improvement Teams Association Award: Improvement Teams Association.	Given to the team winning the annual competition organized by the association. Criteria are based on real achievements.	Call Improvement Teams at 972-3-5752650; fax 972-3-5755265.	This award was first given in 1990.
National Award for Quality and Excellence in Industries: Israel Association of Electronic and Information Industries along with the Israeli government.	Allocated annually to small (fewer than 150 employees) and large companies. Its criteria were first based on the Baldrige award and have since been enlarged.	Call Uri Har at 972-3-5198862; fax 972-3-5161003.	This award was started in the early 1990s.
National Award for Quality and Excellence in Public Service Israel: Quality and Excellency Division of the Civil Service Commission of the Prime Minister's Office.	Based on the EFQM model.	Call Meir Aharonov at 972-2-6705110; e-mail qualex@civil.service.gov.il .	This award was started in 1996.
The Quality Award of the Electronic and Information Industries: Israel Association of Electronic and Information Industries.	Allocated annually to small (fewer than 150 employees) and large companies. Its criteria were first based on the Baldrige award and have since been enlarged.	Call Uri Har at 972-3-5198862; fax 972-3-5161003.	This was Israel's first quality award. It was initiated in the early 1980s.

continued

International Awards	Criteria	Contact Information	Notes
Italian Quality Award: Associazione Premio Qualità Italia.	Based on the EFQM model.	Call 39-50-541751; e-mail apqi@interbusiness.it .	
Japan Quality Award: Japanese Quality Award Committee.	A maximum of six companies (two manufacturing, two service sector, and two medium/small business) are eligible.	Call Naoyuki Yanagimoto at 81-3-3409-2641; e-mail yana@jqac.com .	Established in 1995. www.jqac.com
Japan Quality Medal: Union of Japanese Scientists and Engineers (JUSE).	Deming Application Prize–winning companies are invited to apply for this medal many times over.	Call International Relations Section of JUSE at 81-3-5378-9812; e-mail juse@juse.or.jp .	Established in 1970. www.juse.or.jp
Japan Quality Recognition Award: JUSE.	To contribute to the development of Japanese industry and the expansion and enhancement of quality improvement activities centering on total quality management.	Call International Relations Section of JUSE at 81-3-5378-9812; e-mail juse@juse.or.jp .	Established in 2000 to commemorate JUSE's 50th anniversary. Has two awards: recognition of TQM achievement and quality system innovation. www.juse.or.jp
The Nikkei Quality Control Literature Prize: Established by the Nippon Keizai Shimbun (Japan Economic Journal) and JUSE.	Recognizes literature that contributes to the progress and further development of total quality control.	Call Ichiro Kotsuka at 81-3-5378-9812; e-mail juse@juse.or.jp .	The work must be published in Japan.
Korea National Quality Management Award: Sponsored by the Ministry of Commerce, Industry, and Energy, and the Korean government.	Presented to the company scoring the highest in the following categories: leadership, strategic planning, customer focus, information and analysis, and process management.	Call Mary Kim at 82-2-369-8172; e-mail marykim@ksa.or.kr .	The award is administered by the Korean Standards Association.
Latino Magnifico Quality Awards: International Latino Magnifico Quality Awards Foundation Inc.	Recognizes U.S. and international Latino-owned, -managed or -operated businesses, institutions, organiza-tions and government entities that practice quality production and excellence in achievement.	Call International Latino Magnifico Quality Awards Foundation at 215-533-2629; fax 215-674-3314.	www.magnificos.org
Mexican Quality Award: Fideicomiso del Premio Nacional de Calidad.	Based on the National Quality Model.	Call Ana Aceves Ramírez at 52-55-5322-0767, x70 or e-mail aaceves@ economia.gob.mx .	Based on continuous improvement and customer satisfaction criteria.
Netherlands National Quality Award: Dutch Institute for Quality (INK).	Uses the EFQM model for its criteria. (National model differs from the EFQM model only on minor issues.)	Call the INK at 31-73-613-87-87.	www.nederlandse-kwaliteit.nl

continued

International Awards	Criteria	Contact Information	Notes
New Zealand Quality Award Program: New Zealand Business Excellence Foundation.	Includes the Progress, Commendation, Achievement, and National Quality Awards.	Call 64-9-270-5164 or e-mail info@ nzbef.org.nz .	Program evaluators are trained by Baldrige examiners. www.nzbef.org.nz
Polish Quality Award (PQA): Polish Chamber of Commerce, Polish Center for Testing and Certification and Club Polish Forum ISO 9000.	Any company can apply for the PQA provided it has been operating in Poland for the last four years. Categories include large organizations, small and medium-sized enterprises, and public sector, manu-facturing and service organizations.	Call Miroslaw Recha at 48-22-630-9702; e-mail pnj@kig.pl .	The award is based on the European Quality Award. www.pnj.pl
São Paulo Paulista Management Quality Award: Paulista Excellence Manage-ment Institute, São Paulo Industry Federation, and São Paulo Government Quality Institute.	Follows simplified criteria of the Brazilian National Quality Award and Baldrige Award.	Call or fax Dalton Oswaldo Buccelli at 55-11-5579-0199; e-mail ppqg@ppqg.org.br .	There are four award recognitions: bronze, silver, and gold medal, and one trophy (Governor Excellence Award) for the top applicant in each of the eight award categories.
Scottish Quality Award: Quality Scotland Foundation.	Uses the EFQM model for its criteria.	Call Quality Scotland Foundation at 44-131-5562333; e-mail info@ qualityscotland.co.uk .	www.qualityscotland. co.uk
The South African Performance Excellence Award: South African Excellence Foundation.	Recipients must have a system that ensures, through sound leader-ship, continuous improvement in the delivery of products or services and that provides a way of satisfying and respon-ding to customers.	Call the South African Excellence Foundation at 27-12-349-2765 or e-mail Hendrik Dieckmann at hdieckmann@ csir.co.za .	Open to companies, small and medium-sized enterprises, and public sector organizations in South Africa. www.saef.co.za
Premio Príncipe Felipe a la Calidad Industrial (Prince Felipe Industrial Quality Award): Asociación Española para la Calidad (Spanish Association for Quality).	Uses the EFQM model for its criteria.	Call the Spanish Association for Quality at 91-575-27-50 or e-mail aec@aec.es .	www.aec.es
Swedish Quality Award: The Swedish Institute for Quality (SIQ).	Applicants can choose to use SIQ's Model for Performance Excellence, the Baldrige criteria or the EQFM criteria.	Call SIQ at 46-31-723-1700; e-mail siq@siq.se .	The award is open to applications from all sectors (including business, education, healthcare, and government). More than 20 regional, local, and sectorial awards exist in Sweden. www.siq.se

International Awards	Criteria	Contact Information	Notes
Swiss Quality Award: Swiss Association for Promotion of Quality.	Uses the EFQM model for its criteria.	Call the Swiss Association for Promotion of Quality at 41-62-205-45-45; e-mail info@saq.ch .	www.saq.ch
IQA National Quality Award: The Institute of Quality Assurance (IQA).	Presented to the student or quality professional who submits the best synopsis from a dissertation, thesis, or project report on any aspect of quality.	Call IQA at 44-0-20-7245-6722 (London); e-mail iqa@iqa.org .	www.iqa.org
United Kingdom Quality Award for Business Excellence: The British Quality Foundation.	Uses the EFQM model for its criteria, with some adaptations.	Call the British Quality Foundation at 020-7654-5000; fax 020-7654-5001.	www.quality-foundation.co.uk
Vietnam Quality Award: Directorate for Standards and Quality.	Presented to Vietnamese manufacturing and service organizations that produce high-quality products and services in Vietnam and foreign markets.	Call the Directorate for Standards and Quality at 84-4-9439731; fax 84-4-8252733.	The program follows seven steps of criteria that are very close to the core values of the Baldrige Award. www.moste.gov.vn
The Wales Quality Award: Administered by the Wales Quality Center.	Based on the EFQM model, it aligns with the European Quality Awards.	Call Lawrence Hallett or Kathy Phillips at 44-1443-841192; e-mail info@wales qualitycentre.org.uk .	Award sponsors change each year. Application fee is £50. www.walesquality centre.org.uk

About the Authors

PRINCIPAL AUTHORS

G. Dennis Beecroft is president of G. Dennis Beecroft Inc., a management consulting company that specializes in cost of quality, problem solving, quality improvement, training effectiveness, and quality management systems. Dennis is a licensed electrical engineer with the Professional Engineers of Ontario, a certified lead auditor and senior member of the American Society of Quality.

Prior to starting his own business, Dennis was the managing director of the Institute for Improvement in Quality and Productivity at the University of Waterloo for 14 years, where he provided training and consulting for organizations in Canada, United States, Mexico, India, Israel, Singapore, New Zealand, and Korea. Before joining the University, Dennis spent 23 years with Westinghouse Canada in various management positions in manufacturing, engineering, maintenance, project management, and quality. Dennis also holds the position of special graduate faculty for the faculty of graduate studies at the University of Guelph and is an adjunct faculty member with management sciences at the University Of Waterloo.

Dennis can be contacted at Dennis@g-dennis-beecroft.ca

Grace L. Duffy is president of Management and Performance Systems, specializing in leadership, quality, communication, and customer service. She helps organizations design and implement effective systems for business success. Grace holds an MBA in management and information systems from Georgia State University and a bachelor's in anthropology and archaeology from Brigham Young University. She is an ASQ certified quality manager, quality improvement associate, and quality auditor.

During her 20 years with IBM, Grace held a series of positions in technical design, services, management, and process improvement. Grace was with Trident Technical College in Charleston, South Carolina for 10 years where she served as department head for business, curriculum owner and faculty for quality and corporate management programs and as a management consultant for private industry. Grace has been an active member of the American Society for Quality (ASQ) since 1993. She currently serves as chair of the 20,000-member ASQ Quality Management Division and chair of the ASQ Society Bylaws Committee.

Grace may be contacted at grace683@usa2net.net or through Quality Press.

John W. Moran is a Senior Vice-President of Information Systems, Administrative and Diagnostic Services at New England Baptist Hospital in Boston, MA. Mr. Moran holds BS, MBA, MS, and Ph.D. degrees. He can be reached at jcmoran@rcn.com .

GUEST AUTHORS

George Alukal is vice president of quality and process improvement at Chicago Manufacturing Center (CMC), where he manages projects in quality and lean manufacturing. With more than 20 years' experience in manufacturing, he has expertise in management, quality, process improvement, and lean. He is a certified quality manager, auditor, engineer, and has passed the ISO 9000 lead assessor examination.

Alukal is a member of the board of examiners for the Malcolm Baldrige National Quality Award and was a judge for the Illinois Manufacturing Association's Team Excellence Award. He is the chairman of ASQ's Advanced Manufacturing Interest and is a speaker on TQM and lean topics.

He earned a BS in engineering from the Indian Institute of Technology, Madras, an MS in engineering from Cornell University and an MBA in general management from the Kellogg School of Management of Northwestern University.

He can be reached at (312) 266-9602, or by e-mail at galukal@cmcusa.org .

Richard D. Collins has been director, Six Sigma Design and senior MBB, with American Express since 1997. Prior to his current role, Richard was the Master Blackbelt within the Fort Lauderdale Service Delivery Utility where he was instrumental in successfully deploying Six Sigma. Richard graduated from the University of Central Florida in 1989 with a BA in psychology, following which he earned a doctorate of chiropractic from Logan College of Chiropractic.

Richard has spent a number of years as a practicing physician and as a consultant working with a number of organizations and companies within the healthcare sector. He can be contacted at rdcwgc@aol.com .

Mike H. Ensby is currently an instructor with Clarkson University's School of Business in Potsdam, New York, where he was formerly the director of the Shipley Center for Leadership and Entrepreneurship. He retired from active duty with the U.S. Air Force as an officer in 1997. His final USAF assignment was as the management and leadership course instructor for the Air Force ROTC program at Clarkson. Since February 2000, he has been the director of the undergraduate interdisciplinary engineering and management office, a unique academic program for nearly 300 Clarkson undergraduates. He graduated with honors from the University of Maryland with bachelor of science degrees in production management and management science. He also holds a master of arts degree in procurement and acquisition management and a master of science in engineering and manufacturing management. He received quality manager certification from the American Society for Quality in 1997 and is active with the ASQ Quality Management Division. Mike can be reached at mhensby@clarkson.edu .

R. J. (Randy) Garrison, Jr. is a voting member of the United States Technical Advisory Group (U.S. TAG) to ISO/TC 207 on Environmental Management (ISO 14000) and is a voting member of ANSI/ASQ Z1 committee and QEDS—Quality/Environmental/Dependability/Statistics committee. He serves on five subcommittees: SC 2, Environmental Auditing, SC 4, Environmental Performance Evaluation, WG 3, Design for the Environment (DFE), WG 4, Environmental Communications, and the (JWG) Joint Work Group, ISO 9000 (ISO/TC 176) and ISO 14000 (ISO/TC 207) on Auditing—ISO 19011. Randy is a senior member of ASQ, and RAB QMS certified lead auditor, and is currently completing the requirements for EMS auditor.

Randy can be contacted at jefgroup@bellsouth.net .

Anthony Manos is senior business adviser at the Chicago Manufacturing Center (CMC), where he provides professional consulting services to small and mid-sized manufacturers, focusing on developing and refining quality and process improvement and implementing lean enterprise. Manos has extensive knowledge of lean manufacturing and quality in a wide range of work environments.

With more than 12 years' experience in quality management, Manos is an expert in all aspects of quality, including developing and implementing programs, using statistical process control (SPC) and design of experiment (DOE), training, and auditing. He has guided many companies through implementation and certification to quality management standards such as ISO 9000 and QS-9000.

He can be reached at (312) 922-9448, or by e-mail at tmanos@cmcusa.org .

Jeffry M. Mead is a leadership coach, trainer, and organizational consultant who has spent the last 17 years working with leaders in organizations to improve their effectiveness, efficiency, and the organization's results. Mr. Mead has an MEd in Psychology from Boston College and can be reached at coachjeffm@aol.com .

John W. Moran III currently works for a top asset management firm and previously was a consultant for a "big five" consultancy. Mr. Moran holds a BS in mathematics and economics and an MS in information resource management. He can be reached at wallymoran@hotmail.com .

Michael D. Nichols is director, Six Sigma Design and senior MBB for American Express. Prior to joining American Express in 1999, Mike worked for over 23 years in various performance-engineering related capacities within Federal Express where he twice received the prestigious Five Star award from the office of the CEO. He has a bachelors degree in finance and a masters of science in industrial systems engineering from the University of Memphis. He is a certified quality engineer, certified quality manager, and certified quality auditor by the American Society for Quality, and has served ASQ for seven years on their National board of directors. In late 2000, Mike was appointed as a fellow of the Society in recognition of his contributions to quality. Mike can be contacted at MDNQuality@aol.com .

Terry L. Regel is a quality management consultant with 25 years' experience in quality management planning, quality improvement, quality systems development, quality systems implementation, quality auditing, and quality training. He is a fellow of American Society for Quality, an ASQ certified quality auditor, an ASQ certified quality engineer, and an RAB quality management systems lead auditor. He holds a bachelor's degree in chemistry from the University of Mississippi.

Regel is the coauthor of the book *After the Quality Audit: Closing the Loop on the Audit Process* published by ASQ Quality Press. He is an instructor for ASQ, a member of the Quality Press Standing Review Board, a book reviewer for *Quality Progress,* and the ASQ Quality Audit Division chair. He has made numerous presentations on quality applications and quality auditing at ASQ meetings, ASQ's Annual Quality Congress, and ASQ division conferences.

If you have questions regarding the material in chapter 13, you may contact the author at tregel@att.net .

Kevin Sharlow is a senior manager in the healthcare consulting practice of PricewaterhouseCoopers, LLP (PwC). Kevin has over seventeen years of experience in the healthcare industry, specializing in revenue cycle operations, accounts receivable management, and business process assessment and redesign for both hospital systems and physician practice organizations. With over 150,000 people working in more than 150 countries worldwide, PwC is one of the "big five" professional services firms providing a broad range of audit, tax, and business consulting services across 24 industry-specialized practices. Mr. Sharlow can be contacted at: PricewaterhouseCoopers, 1100 Bausch & Lomb Place, Rochester, New York 14604-2705, (585) 231-6182, kevin.sharlow@us.pwcglobal.com .

Dr. Mary Thornley, president of Trident Technical College, holds a doctorate of education in curriculum and instruction from the University of South Carolina; a master of arts in teaching English from the University of North Carolina at Chapel Hill; and a bachelor of arts in English and French from Mars Hill College, North Carolina.

Her professional involvement includes serving on the Commission on Colleges of the Southern Association of Colleges and Schools (SACS). Also, she was selected to represent South Carolina on the SACS executive committee. This year, she was elected to serve on a national board, COMBASE (an organization devoted to high-quality community-based programming). Also this year, Dr. Thornley is president of the South Carolina Association of Colleges and Universities.

Her community involvement includes the following: 1999–2000 president of Trident United Way and 1999–2000 president of the Rotary Club of North Charleston. Other community affiliations include service on three local chamber boards, the Charleston Regional Development Alliance, The Education Foundation, Trident Area Consortium for the Technologies, and Trident Workforce Investment Board.

In 2000, Dr. Thornley received the prestigious Milliken Medal of Quality Award from the South Carolina Quality Forum. In 1996, she received the Barbara H. James Presidential Award for Outstanding Contributions to Tech Prep in South Carolina. In 1992, Dr. Thornley received the Martha Kime Piper Award from the South Carolina Women in Higher Education Administration for Outstanding Contributions to Advancing Women in Higher Education.

Dr. Thornley may be reached through the Trident Technical College Web site at www.tridenttech.edu .

Richard A. Waks is founder of RAW Development and Consulting, a group that specializes in the design of assessments, consulting interventions, and training curricula. His targeted workshops help clients achieve their most vital strategic objectives by focusing all levels of their organization on systems improvement, culture change, cross-functional integration, and leadership development. Rick is a graduate of Hampshire College in Amherst, Massachusetts, where he received a BA in creative writing, with a concentration in adult learning theory. He can be reached by e-mail at RAWaks@aics.net .

Index

A

academic consultant, 105
ACT (Analyze—Conclude—Test), 77
activity analysis grids, 77
activity-based costing (ABC), 78
adoption decision, 25
Adoption Model, 25
Advanced Manufacturing Interest Group
    (AMIG), 131
American Customer Satisfaction Index, 156
appraisal cost activities, 34
appraisal costs, 32
ASQ certifications, 164–66, 215–27
ASQ Certified Quality Auditor (CQA), 224–27
ASQ Certified Quality Engineer (CQE), 215–18
ASQ Certified Quality Manager (CQMgr),
    219–23
ASQ Quality Awards Listing 2002, 229–41
    Automotive, 233–34
    Government, 234
    International, 235–41
    U.S. National, 229–33
audit closure, 175
Audit Function Improvement Process, 173–75
audit function, performance monitoring, 175
audit management planning, 162–64
audit manager, 163–64, 166, 168–69, 175
audit performance, 168–69
audit-related certifications, 164–66, 215
audit report, 173, 175
audit results, 170–72

audit team, 169
auditor credentials, 164–67
auditor evaluations, 167
auditor training, 166–67, 168

B

bait and switch, 97
balanced scorecard (BSC), 180–93
    critical success factors, 192–93
    designing, 183–89
    developing internal goals and targets,
        188–89
    implementing, 191–92
    producing, 190
batch size reduction, 134
benchmark, 187–88
big five, 103
Blackbelt (BB), 201, 203–5
boilerplate consulting, 98
British Standards Institute (BSI), 113

C

Canada Awards for Business Excellence (CABE),
    58, 113
Canada Awards for Excellence (CAE)—
    Quality, 58–60
    award criteria, 62–63
    scoring, 64

Canadian Framework for Business Excellence, 58
capacity, 12–13
cellular/flow manufacturing, 135, 141–42
change,
    accelerating, 12–13
    implementation, 79
    individual, 5–6
    leaders and, 7–8
    organizational approach to, 7
    successful, 4–5, 11–12
    transition, 79
    triggers of, 4–5
    why, 3–4, 6
change commitment continuum, 10, 13
change effort, support for, 10–12
changeover, 132–33
client project review, 106–7
coaches, 104
comparative statistics, 187–88
conflict, 91–93
consequence analysis, 77
consulting firms, 96, 105–6
contact to cash supply chain model, 41, 42
control chart, 78, 156, 157
controlling costs, 34
core process redesign (CPR), 67–80
    laws of, 80
    methodology, 70–79
    redesign areas, 69–70
    when and why, 68
core process redesign pathway, 70–79
    assessment, 70, 73–74
    focus, 70–73
    implementation, 70, 78–79
    negotiation, 70, 74–75
    redesign, 70, 76–78
corporate planning models
    CAE Quality Model, 58–60
    EFQM Excellence Model, 60–61
    2002 Baldrige Award Model, 56–58
corrective action request (CAR), 170
corrective action team, 173, 175
cost of failures, 36–38
cost of poor quality (COPQ), 31, 200
cost of quality (COQ), 31–34
    data, 33–34
    definition, 32

model, 34
CPR team charter, 71–72
cross-functional flowcharts, 77
cross-functional team, 87
current state map, 136–37
customer expectations, 148–50
customer improvement system, 159
customer needs, 73–75
customer quality needs hierarchy, 114
customer relationship management (CRM), 48,
    152–56
customer requirements, 150, 155
customer response, 148
customer retention, 152, 160
customer satisfaction, 35, 114, 147–60
customer satisfaction data, 156
customer satisfaction surveys, 154–55
customers,
    external, 150–57, 159
    internal, 150, 158–59
    importance of, 147

D

decision making, 21–29
decision-making models, 22, 25–29
decisions, group versus individual, 24
decisions, types of, 23–24
defective product, 132
Deming Prize, 55, 113
Deming's 14 points, 208
Deming, W. Edwards, 209
departmental team, 87
deployment champion, 202, 203
design for Six Sigma (DFSS), 203, 205–6
DMAIC methodology, 199–201, 205

E

enterprise resource planning (ERP), 47–48
environmental management system, 111, 123–27
European Foundation for Quality Management
    (EFQM) Excellence Award, 60–65
    award criteria, 62–63
    scoring, 64–65

European Quality Award, 60–61
Evolutionary Model, 25–26
executive sponsor, 202, 203
external resources,
    compensating, 108–9
    consulting firms, 105–6
    danger signs, 97–101
    monitoring progress, 106–8
    reasons they fail, 95–96
    request for proposal (RFP) process, 101–3
    to use, or not to use, 109–10
    types of, 103–5
    work papers, 110

F

failure costs, 33, 34
feedback loop, 20
finding statement, 171
findings, 171–73
5S, 134, 142
flow, 135, 141–42
Ford Motor Company, 14
future state map, 136–37

G

Gallup Organization, The, 156
goals, performance improvement, 188–89
Greenbelt, 201–2, 203

H

handoff diagrams, 77
Hierarchy of Needs, Maslow's, 11–12
house of lean, 134
house of quality, 42, 150, 151

I

improvement model, 22
improvement planning, 35–36
improvement projects, 35–36, 38

improvement team, 87
independent generalist, 104
independent specialist, 104
information management, supply chain,
    43–44
information technologies (IT), 46–49
interim executive, 104
internal auditor credentials, 166–67
internal auditor requirements, 166
internal audits, 118–21
International Organization for Standardization
    (ISO), 111, 123
inventory, 44
inventory waste, 132
ISO 9000 quality management standards, 111–12,
    113–14, 117–18
ISO 9001, 114–15, 147–48
ISO 9002, 114
ISO 9004, 112, 114–15
ISO 14000 family of standards, 123, 124–26
ISO 14001, 124–25
ISO/TC 207, 124, 125, 127

J

Juran, Dr. Joseph, 149

K

kaizen, 143
kaizen blitz, 143
kanban, 135, 141
Kano model, 148
Kano, Noriaki, 148

L

leaders and change, 7–8
leadership,
    executive, 83–86
    techniques for effective team
        motivation, 86
lean,
    building blocks of, 133–35

core concepts of, 139–40
definition of, 129
history of, 130–31
how to sustain, 139
implementation of, 135–39
wastes of, 131–33
why, 130
lean enterprise, 129–44
logistics, 40

M

Malcolm Baldrige National Quality Award
    (MBNQA), 56–58, 113, 147–48
    award criteria, 62–63, 148
    scoring, 64
management audits, 161–76
"management by fact," 48
management training program, Ford Motor
    Company, 14
manufacturing, evolution of, 131
Maslow's Hierarchy of Needs, 11–12
Master Blackbelt (MBB), 201, 203–5
military standards, 111
motion waste, 132

N

National Quality Institute (NQI), 59
nonconformities, 172
non-value-added activities, 131

O

operational control, supply chain, 44
operational decisions, 23–24
operational planning, 162
organization, moving, 83
organization, stuck, 83
organizational improvement using teams, 81–93
organizational planning, 23
organizational redesign, 69–70
over-processing, 132
overproduction, 132

P

PAF Model, 32–33
partnership audits, 168
people waste, 132
performance improvement goals, 188–89
performance measurement, 179–81
    tools, 180
point of use storage, 135
Polaroid Corporation, 4
prevention costs, 32
price of conformance, 31
price of nonconformance, 31
problem solving, 17–21, 28–29
problem-solving barriers, 20–21
problem-solving model, 18
problems, defining, 18
process approach, 116
process capabilities, 73
process improvement team (PIT), 87, 208
process management model, 44
process management system, 44–45
process model, 32
process performance, 74
process redesign. *See* core process redesign
progress decisions, 25
Progress Model, 25
project champion, 202, 203
project charter, 200
project team, 87–88
proposal, request for, 101–3
proposals, comparing, 103
pull system, 135, 140–41
push system, 140

Q

QS 9000, 112
quality at the source, 135
quality awards, 55–66, 229–41
    award criteria, 62–63
    scoring for models, 64–65
quality control, 55
quality eras, 112
quality function deployment (QFD), 42,
    150–51

quality improvement, 35–36, 115–18
quality improvement planning, 65
quality improvement strategies, 115–16
quality management principles, 115–16, 148
quality management systems (QMS), 111–21
quality models, 55–66
quality principles, 211
quality program, successful, 210
quality systems, 41
quality techniques, process management–based, 42–45
quick changeover, 135

R

RAB certification, 164–66
RADAR logic, 64–65
redesign, 76–78
Registrar Accreditation Board (RAB), 164
report card. *See* balanced scorecard
request for proposal (RFP) process, 101–3
resources, external,
    compensating, 108–9
    consulting firms, 105–6
    danger signs, 97–101
    monitoring progress, 106–8
    reasons they fail, 95–96
    request for proposal (RFP) process, 101–3
    to use, or not to use, 109–10
    types of, 103–5
    work papers, 110
responding to RFP, 102–3
resultant costs, 34
Revolutionary Model, 25, 26–28
R's, six, 85–86

S

Sayle's 12 Golden Rules, 166–67
scored checklists, 170
self-managed team, 88
silver bullet external resources, 104–5
Six Sigma, 39, 195–205
    deployment, 202–5
    key roles and expectations, 201–2

management system, 197–98
    methodology, 197, 198–99
    phases, 199–201
    why do, 196–97
standard cost of failure, 36–38
standardized work, 134
"stat" analysis, 78
Strategic Advisory Group on the Environment (SAGE), 123
strategic planning, 35–36
streamlined layout, 134
stretch goals, 189
success metrics, 184–85
supply chain balancing, 42
supply chain communication management, 47–48
supply chain design and strategy, 44
supply chain management (SCM), 39–51
    history of, 40
    metrics, 48–50
    processes, 45–49
supply chain model, integrated, 50
supply chain operations reference (SCOR) model, 49
supply chain performance, 42–45
supply chain performance management, 48–49
supply chain processes, 43
supply chain tensions, 42

T

team charter, 71–73
team destroyers, 92–93
team development, 91
team motivators, 86
teams, 81–93, 134
    building, 81
    different forms of, 86–88
    elements of dynamic, 89–90
    essential characteristics of, 88–89
    executive's role, 83–86
    maximizing, during improvement and change, 90–91
    using conflict to strengthen, 91–93
Technical Committee on Environmental Management, 123
technology, impact on change, 5, 211

total productive maintenance (TPM), 135, 142
total quality management (TQM), 112, 113–16, 130, 210
Toyota Production System (TPS), 39
TQM charts, 78
training consultant, 104
transportation waste, 132
Trident Technical College, 82, 207–10
triggers of change, 4–5, 8–9
trust busters, 92–93

U

Union of Japanese Scientists and Engineers (JUSE), 55

V

value-added activities, 131
value chain, 46
value stream mapping (VSM), 135–37
virtual team, 88
visual controls, 134

W

waiting waste, 132
Wal-Mart, 40
waste, 131–33
"Way" consulting, the, 105
work papers, 110
work team, 87